A WONDERFUL STROKE OF LUCK

FROM OCCUPATIONAL THERAPIST TO PATIENT AND BEYOND

JANET R. DOUGLAS

This book is a work of non-fiction. Unless otherwise noted, the author and the publisher make no explicit guarantees as to the accuracy of the information contained in this book and in some cases, names of people and places have been altered to protect their privacy.

Library of Congress Control Number: 2024904006

ISBN: 979-8-89228-091-4 (Paperback)
ISBN: 979-8-89228-093-8 (eBook)

Printed in the United States of America

Janet Douglas is an inspiration to us all, reminding us that a holistic approach is always best. However, nothing is better than the sheer determination and motivation to improve her functional ability that Janet clearly possesses

Deborah Abelson
Rotational Occupational Therapist for Orthopaedic Team
Royal National Orthopaedic Hospital, Stanmore, United Kingdom

Though professionals can enjoy, as well as learn, from Janet's clear and concise sharing; lay people, who appreciate a good yarn, will find the telling of her tale, a remarkable and valuable exposition of what it feels like to experience and recover from a stroke. Informed by her past training as an occupational therapist, her personal reflections are uniquely poignant. The ways in which she has worked with her circumstances to create a new life are absolutely inspirational. She is truly a gifted writer. This book is both a treat and a gift to all who read it.

Rev. Michael J. McNulty, MPS
Senior Deacon
Divine Mercy Parish
Winnetka, IL

The book "A Wonderful Stroke of Luck" is a powerful memoir of the lived experience of stroke. It is both heart aching and heart warming. Jan recounts her experiences with humor and insight. This book offers a unique perspective that would be particularly valuable for those who have experienced a stroke, their clinicians and care-givers.

Jane E. Sullivan, PT, DHS, MS

In this inspirational personal account of the journey of recovery following her stroke, Janet Douglas shares thoughtful and evocative insights into the experience. Using her unique perspective as both a

Both the author and this book are miraculous. The fact that Jan Douglas survived a devastating stroke and went from being a person unable to read to the person who has written this book literally blows my mind. Jan never gave up and always thought "I want proof that I can't do that" rather than the other person's "I don't think you can do that". That is the attitude every stroke survivor needs to advance. There are so many opportunities to live a full life. It just depends on your attitude: is the glass half empty or half full? This is a story of hope and inspiration for all, and every stroke survivor (and his or her caregivers) should read this book, immediately. It is a very good read.

Harlan Ten Pas, CPA/Attorney

With a seasoned writer's both humorous and heart wrenching flare, Ms. Douglas writes of her recovery and discovery of cognition and function after a devastating stroke. With an uncommon,at the least,recall,her defiant strength is on display in this inspiring tale of a life, her life, recovered, indeed rescued, from within. This is a celebration of success in the face of devastating odds and one that the reader can understand, admire and internalize, tears and all!

Bruce L McClennan M.D. FACR, Professor Emeritus,
Diagnostic Radiology Yale University School of Medicine

Ms. Douglas captures the struggles, emotions, and triumphs of stroke recovery. An excellent book for anyone who has overcome a challenge. Truly, an inspirational read.

Denice DeAntonio, RN, BSN, M.Ed.

This is a compelling and insightful read. As a practicing occupational therapist I have learned a lot about possible symptoms when someone is experiencing a stroke aside from the "average" ones plus how the recovery period can be so much longer than the therapy time provided.

to remake your life to your satisfaction. I felt I was there with her as she navigated the ups and downs of a long road towards who she has now become – a person who accepts that she is a different version of her former self.

Gail Fisher, PhD, OTR/L, FAOTA

Clinical Associate Professor

University of Illinois at Chicago, Department of Occupational Therapy

"Struck, stricken, stroke…" In her own words, Janet takes us on a journey from confusion and denial to realization and acceptance with humor and unflinching accuracy. Her book recounts stroke recovery with engaging detail from devastation to reconstruction and a new life.

Janet's account of her stroke recovery is informative while also being a compelling story. Weaving personal biography with the narrative of her recovery, she gives us an insider's view of the slow, painful, but ultimately fulfilling, process of putting the pieces together after such a life altering event. Chasing the elusive "ninety percent" recovery, she illustrates that, in her words, "there is no expiration date on improvement." In the end, she shares that what matters most is not acceptance of limitations, but acceptance of oneself. I thoroughly enjoyed her story and found its honesty very gratifying and affirming. As a psychologist who has spent many hours helping stroke survivors, there is a clear ring of truth to her story that make this book essential reading for survivors of brain damage and those supporting them

Robert J. Hartke, Ph.D.

Rehabilitation Psychologist

It wrestles with the border between the physical, emotional and intellectual impact wrought by the stroke and her own reaction to the conditions that limit her independence. Is denial of paralysis due to the loss of the right parietal lobe of the brain or is it simply a stage of grief due to loss. Is the difficulty in reading an indication of a loss of intellectual function or is it due to the loss of a portion of the visual world- a visual field deficit- associated with damage to the visual pathways in the brain needed to see the left side of the page.

This shows the power of a spirit determined to find a life worth living after having so much taken away.... and being better for it.

Thomas J. Hoeppner, PhD

Associate Professor of Neurological Science

Rush University Medical Center,

Chicago, Illinois

What does it feel like to have a massive stroke? The first chapter of the book sets the stage by providing a clear and compelling description of the experience that that transformed the author and changed her life. I am an occupational therapist and used to work with stroke survivors, and I appreciate how Ms. Douglas adeptly paints an insightful picture of what she felt physically and mentally as the stroke altered her view of her body, relationships, and the world. As a former director of occupational therapy and business executive, Ms. Douglas experiences her role as a patient to be challenging and frustrating, especially when others did not view her as the expert of her own body and mind. She gains new insights into what therapy has to offer and wisely critiques where it falls short. Ms. Douglas skillfully articulates the social and environmental barriers she experiences in the workplace, in health care settings and while traveling; an exposé for readers who have not experienced a life-changing disability.

The author recounts her journey with a dry wit and an ability to laugh at herself and keep things in perspective. Her lessons learned will help brain injury survivors and caregivers understand the implications of having a severe stroke and the importance in stubbornly persisting stroke survivor and a stroke rehabilitation professional, she provides us with rich and powerful prose to help us to gain a deep understanding of the triumph, frustration, joy, and sadness that accompany the transformation that occurs as a consequence of stroke. With humor, irony, many detailed descriptions, and brutal honesty, this book will likely make health professionals more sensitive and empathic, family members more comforted and reassured, and stroke survivors more confident and empowered.

Elliot J. Roth, MD

Chairman, Physical Medicine and Rehabilitation

Northwestern University Feinberg School of Medicine

Shirley Ryan AbilityLab, formerly Rehabilitation Institute of Chicago

This is an amazing story. An occupational therapist skilled in the art of helping others overcome the loss of function in one part of the body is suddenly struck by a devastating stroke that takes out half of her body. You can almost feel the stroke spreading over her brain like a flash flood over the most treasured faculties- moving an arm, walking, reading,— and these were only the most obvious losses. The others came more subtly, insidiously… the loss of a sense of time, of memory and of dreams ... all wrapped up in emotional turmoil. Are these intellectual and emotional reactions to the loss of her mechanical skills or a direct effect of loss of a critical part of the brain? A clinician finds herself on the other side of the white coat with as much bewilderment as understanding.

It reads like an Oliver Sacks case richly told from the perspective of the patient as well as the clinician. It is witty, cutting and informed with interwoven layers of English and American medical practice and culture, work life, family and literature in the determined search for understanding and overcoming her loss.

It is at once a clinician/patient's story of experiencing, surviving and coming to terms with a devastating stroke, a memoir, and a primer on neuroscience.

CONTENTS

Remember sometimes not getting what you want is a wonderful stroke of luck.
—His Holiness, the Dalai Lama

FOREWORD

> "And just as the Phoenix rose from the ashes, she too will rise. Returning from the flames, clothed in nothing but her strength; more beautiful than ever before."[1]

It is not often that after thirty-three years in practice one can remember details of someone one looked after more than a decade ago. For some reason, however, I clearly remember Jan Douglas's case.

I was the consultant neurosurgeon on call at the Radcliffe Infirmary in the center of Oxford. It was a very old hospital dating back three hundred years, and until it closed in 2007, it was home to neurosurgery at Oxford. It was a lovely place to work, and being in the center of town, it was convenient for everyone.

I remember my resident taking an urgent referral from the John Radcliffe Hospital, the major hospital in Oxford, somewhat removed from the city center but the hub for emergency services.

The emergency care physician had a woman from America, previously well, who had been admitted with a stroke, secondary to a large intracerebral (in the brain) hemorrhage. The clot was causing considerable pressure. Both she and her husband were medical professionals.

I requested that she be transferred urgently for removal of the clot. It turned out that her husband was a surgeon himself so making the case for surgery was straightforward, and I took Jan to the theater and removed the clot.

Subsequently, after a few days stabilizing her, she was flown back to the United States. I had the good fortune to meet up with them some time later when they were passing through Oxford, and it was wonderful to see how much she had recovered.

What Jan's account so eloquently portrays is the struggle she so heroically faced to achieve that recovery. As a neurosurgeon dealing with acute situations, one does not see that side.

I find this book uplifting and encouraging to anyone who has suffered a stroke or is involved in the care of such a person.

Tipu Aziz, F. Med. Sci.
Professor of Neurosurgery
John Radcliffe Hospital
Oxford, England

CHAPTER 1

I Don't Want to Ruin the Party

LYING ON THE GRASS WITH MY HEAD ON AN UNKNOWN PERSON'S jacket, I hear the *hee-haw-hee-haw* braying of an ambulance siren getting closer. My head hurts, my mind is thrumming with random, disjointed pieces of information, and my left arm and leg are gone. All I feel is a cold, empty space where a short time ago warm skin wrapped bone, blood, muscles, and nerves. I am conscious of the incongruity between my attire and my position. People don't lie on grass wearing fancy yellow suits—and why is there a black straw hat lying beside me? I know the siren belongs to an ambulance that is coming for me. I am at my nephew Jonny's wedding reception at a country hotel on the outskirts of Oxford, England. People are crowding around me. I feel embarrassed, exposed, and, above all, guilty. This was supposed to be the happy occasion, a gathering of family and friends for something other than a funeral, and here I am creating a scene, a distraction, diverting attention from where it belongs—on the bride and groom. The thought makes me shudder.

Just an hour earlier, at the ceremony in the chapel of Jonny's college at Oxford University, I had read from Khalil Gibran's *The Prophet*, and afterward, along with my husband, Bruce, and our daughters, Sarah and Sandy, boarded one of several buses provided to transport guests to the reception at a country hotel. Within minutes of boarding the bus, I began to feel sick. As sour, black-coffee–flavored bubbles erupted in my mouth, my throat, and the back of my nose, I wondered fleetingly if the cup of coffee I had drunk hurriedly while changing into my wedding outfit might be the culprit. I tried to stifle dry heaves and longed for a cracker—something, anything—to calm the gastric turmoil. Once the bus arrived at the hotel, I got off as quickly as I could and went in search of a carbonated drink, thinking that might help.

My chest started to feel tight. I was struggling to breathe. I began running through checklists in my mind of symptoms from my occupational therapy training, I quickly eliminated stroke as a possibility because I had none of the typical warning signs: *Sudden numbness or weakness—negative; confusion— negative; blurring of vision—negative; dizziness or loss of balance— negative; sudden, severe headache—negative.* There was no mention of nausea; it could not be a stroke, then, despite my family and personal history. This is not how stroke starts. I sent my younger daughter, Sandy, to find my husband. He arrived, concern etched deeply into his brow.

"Bruce, I don't feel well," I told him. "I think I might be having a heart attack."

My symptoms appeared to match what I had heard about heart attacks in women. I was "past fifty; in a high-stress occupation; closet type-A personality—all calm and collected on the outside; seething torment within." In short, I was a prime candidate for a heart attack. I briefly considered asking for aspirin but remembered that I could not take it because of some kind of sensitivity. In my youth, I had developed beet-red blotches all over and vomited in my hospital bed after taking aspirin following knee surgery. Bruce helped me to sit down on the grass and dispatched someone to get water. I fretted about getting grass stains on my new yellow suit and then someone suggested that I lie down. Someone else wanted to take off my black straw hat, but I protested. My hair would be a disaster underneath. What self-respecting English woman would be at a wedding hatless? Various family members came to see how I was. Feeling embarrassed and exposed, I repeated the same words: "I'm fine. I don't want to ruin the party." We had attended four family funerals in the last two years—my mother, two of my brothers, and my surviving brother's wife were all gone. This was supposed to be a day of celebration.

The day had started out with so much promise—enough blue in the sky to make a pair of trousers for a sailor, an indication that it would be a dry and sunny day, perfect for a garden wedding. I had driven two hours from the home of friends in the village of Newton Blossomville, every bit as beautiful and bucolic as it sounds, early that morning. Driving a rented Mercedes, the world was my oyster; I was queen of the road. I was pleased with the complimentary upgrade, but Bruce, who is not a fan of ostentation, was mildly embarrassed.

As I lay down with my head on that man's jacket, I became acutely aware of the smell of freshly mown grass—shades of Mr. Foster, the school groundskeeper mowing the tennis courts outside the classroom window. I pictured Dad and the boys pulling on their cricket kneepads to play for the village team. I conjured visions of cream tea laid out, cucumber sandwiches and scones piled on trestle tables in the shade of fragrant lime trees, waiting to be set upon by players and spectators alike. Lost in reverie, I was unconcerned for what awaited me, anxious only for the focus of attention to be on the bride and groom and not on me, the aunt lying on the grass. I tried to blend in with the scenery to avoid the curious glances of people moving past me. I recognized some of the faces, relatives and friends, but others were not familiar. Phrases started popping into my head from all over the place—a line from a book, a snatch of a song: *"It is a fact universally acknowledged that a single man in possession of a good fortune must be in want of a wife."*[2] Was Mr. Bennett at Jonny's wedding?

"I don't want to ruin this party …" It seemed someone else spoke those words, but they fit what I was feeling. Harvest hymns started to play in my head, loud and disjointed.

I tried to sing along, but my mouth was mealy. There was a strong smell of gas. I traced it to the cupboard under the stairs, where the meter was in the house where I grew up. The vegetables were in neat rows, visible from the kitchen window. A bicycle was parked outside the window for Tony to escape his share of the chores. Mum had gone to take care of Grandma Rimington, who was struggling with the aftereffects of a stroke. The air was redolent with late-summer flowers and drying, musty, crackling leaves. *"We plough the fields and scatter the good seed on the land, but it is fed and watered by God's almighty hand."*[3]

Harvest festival hymns and blended voices accompanied by a roaring organ filled the space between my ears.

A physician among the guests came over to confer with Bruce. They decided to call an ambulance to take me to the hospital. It seemed like a good idea. I didn't want to be a spectacle anymore—no more sympathetic clucks; no more offers of medicine, cups of tea, cold towels, or ice.

"I don't want to ruin this party," someone said, in my voice this time. "Please let me slip away unnoticed. At the hospital, they can give me something to make my stomach feel better and then bring me back in time for the cutting of the cake," I mumbled into the air around me.

As we waited for the ambulance, the desire to be somewhere—anywhere— else was overwhelming. I wanted to melt into the grass like an ice cream dropped by a passing child.

A crowd gathered around me. I tried to identify them. There were a few of my former patients and a gaggle of coworkers, even someone from school. Past and present were starting to blur, and I was not thinking clearly. Struggling to remain coherent, I repeated, "Please just leave me here. I don't want to ruin the party."

"He sends the snow in winter, the warmth to swell the grain, The breezes and the sunshine And soft refreshing rain."[4]

Suddenly, my entire left side was buzzing, throbbing, and tingling with giant pins and needles. I looked to see if something was biting me, stinging me—a nest of ants? A swarm of bees? A snake? Had I unwittingly disturbed some malefactor in the grass?

The buzzing in my arm swelled to a deafening roar. Could anyone else hear it? Then I felt an electric current jolting through me, lighting up nerve pathways like a subway station map. Sharp, burning, jerking, I felt the cranial nerves.

"On Old Olympus Towering Top, A Finn and German Viewed Some Hops."[5]

A mnemonic for the cranial nerves, learned in college, took on a painful identity. I could feel them all. The side of my face was illuminated, then my eye, neck, and upper arm. The buzz spread down my arm like an electrical current through water, sizzling radial, median, and ulnar nerves until they stood out, as if drawn in pen on my arm. They *were* drawn in pen on my arm a long time ago by a professor, a mentor, in my early career.

My leg twitched as if in response to a hard tap from a patella hammer tap on my kneecap. The stinging stream coursed down my leg, past my ankle, and stabbed my foot.

I wanted to cry out at the discomfort. It was not pain but a distinct sense of having been struck by lightning or having grasped an exposed high-voltage wire. It went on long enough for me to picture myself in the electric chair, facing execution for some unspeakable crime. No movement was perceptible to me or others, but on the inside, half of my body was convulsing with the feeling of an elbow banged on a hard surface. Then a buzz saw ripped through and cut me in two, top to bottom, left and right cleaved from each other forever.

Abruptly, it stopped. Then there was nothing. With no feeling at all on my left side, I tried to move my fingers, my arm, and my leg. There was nothing at all, nothing but an empty space. A tincture of dread spread from bottom to top of what I could still feel of my body. With sudden, unwanted clarity, I knew what it was! Struck, stricken, a stroke! It was my inescapable destiny, my genetic inevitability. I pulled Bruce closer with my remaining arm and whispered, "I am having a stroke. Tell the paramedics that."

Stroke is a hateful word with an even more hateful definition. It is the thief of independence, of career, of relationships, of dignity, of quality of life. I had been on the outside looking in so many times as daughter, sister, granddaughter, niece, and occupational therapist. This was the start of a different view, from the inside looking out. At that moment, I had no comprehension of what lay ahead of me.

As I shared my revelation with Bruce, I simultaneously began another mental checklist. I had given up the profession of occupational therapy but not the knowledge. I could not move my left arm or leg, but I could speak. The right side of my brain must be involved. The pathways cross over in a freak of evolution; the right side of the brain controls the left side of the body, and vice versa. I was on my way to becoming a left hemiplegic.

Oh, God! No! I was becoming an old hemi! "Old hemi" was the mildly pejorative title we had assigned to stroke patients as student occupational therapists. That was when patients were still patients, embodiments of diagnoses, not real people. They had to be kept at arm's length, never allowed to cross the Rubicon into our personal lives. It was before we had the maturity and experience to develop real empathy. They were "old hemis" because when you are twenty-one, everyone over the age of thirty is old. Still mentally alert enough to recall my dislike of working with those patients but not the reasons why, I realized with a flash of horrifying insight that I was becoming that patient that I had least liked to work with. I ran a brief orientation check. *Where am I? Oxford. What is the date? August 31, 2002. Who is the president? George Bush. Oh, this is England, so who is the prime minister? Tony Blair. I met him once.*

My mind shot off at a tangent, more at ease thinking of something else and anxious to be out of the moment. Mr. Blair had carried my suitcase off a train once. I had no idea who he was. My brother, Don, was at the train station to meet me to take me to visit Mum in the hospital. He stood, gobsmacked, as I descended the steps of the train with a group of men into a barrage of waiting TV cameras and elaborately dressed dignitaries in military uniforms, dark suits and red ties, or robes. The sheriff of Nottingham was there in splendid regalia, and the sight of him and the remembrance that I had read that he was a former bus driver, an immigrant from the West Indies, a very far cry from the days of Robin Hood, gave me an instant of amusement. A flock of obsequious flunkies pushed forward to help. I became entangled in a tussle with one as he tried to remove my suitcase from the hand of my knight, who, it appeared, was the focus of the grand reception.

"I'll take that, sir," he said.

"No, you won't," I huffed, pulling on the handle. "That's mine!"

"Do you know who that is?" asked Don, his face registering amusement as the crowd started to disperse.

"No!" I replied testily. "All I know is that I was up all night and right when I found my seat on the train, this annoying guy asked me to change seats so he and his colleagues could sit together. I moved across the aisle. Then someone else came with one of those microphones that looks like a ferret on a stick and then another one with a large camera, and they proceeded to gab the whole way here. All I wanted to do was sleep! Then that man tried to grab my bag."

Don threw back his head and guffawed. "Your bag was just carried by the next prime minister. That's Tony Blair!"

I heard an approaching siren and slammed back into the present. My mental functioning was deteriorating quickly. Thoughts were becoming disjointed, random, past and present all jumbled together, a movie reel unraveling.

As the paramedics examined me, I told them I used to be an occupational therapist so I knew I was having a stroke—not surprising, given my family history. My mouth took off at a gallop. "If there is such a thing as a 'cancer family,' there must surely be a 'stroke family' too. My father died from a stroke; my maternal grandmother, paternal grandfather, and two uncles did too. All three of my brothers had strokes in middle age."

Barely pausing to take a breath, I spat out my own medical and life history. "I was diagnosed with essential hypertension in my mid-twenties, despite having none of the obvious risk factors, other than my genes. My one pregnancy was disastrous due to preeclampsia. After I was on bed rest for two months, Sarah was delivered naturally but in the operating room instead of the delivery room, in case an emergency C-section was required. I was told, emphatically, to be grateful that I had one healthy baby and under no circumstances to do it again."

Shock affects people in different ways; some tremble, some faint, some cry, and others talk. I talked and talked and talked, my words spilling out faster with every turn of the ambulance wheels.

They were not asking me any questions about my history, but I felt duty- bound to tell them everything I could think of that might be relevant. After a brief pause to round up some thoughts that were starting to slip away, I was off again.

"This stroke cannot be happening. There must be a mistake. I take my medication faithfully every day, including today. My blood pressure is maintained at 150/90, considered within normal limits." (A year later, the American Heart Association would lower the recommended level to 120/70, closing that stable door well after my horse had bolted.)

Talking incessantly to the paramedics, I felt calm and resigned. Bruce tried periodically to hijack the conversation by interjecting rational information, but this was my story to tell, and I was not about to yield the floor. The paramedics went quietly about the business of attaching me to monitors, taking my blood pressure, and talking on a squeaking, squawking, radio between patches of ear-numbing static.

"I want to let you guys know as much as possible from my own lips while I can still use them," I babbled. "I was an occupational therapist, you know. I realize it is only a matter of time before I lose consciousness. I will not become, even for a moment, one of those patients about whom people talk as if she isn't there. I have been a crusader against the 'Does she take sugar?' routine all my professional life."

As a young therapist, I was involved in a campaign aimed at getting medical professionals and others to stop talking across sick and disabled people and to address them directly. I was also a volunteer ambulance driver and once drove wheelchair-bound patients to take part in a blockade of the House of Lords parking lot to protest Parliament's inaccessibility to handicapped people. "See how you like it!" we yelled as the dukes, baronets, and life peers and their drivers honked, hooted, and blustered at us to get out of the way.

"You should have seen the patients' faces! They hadn't had that much fun in years." My mouth was starting to get very dry and stiff, and talking was getting harder. I could still find and form the words, but it was an effort to articulate them. I was slurring my words like an inebriate, and I had not had a drop to drink. My words were coming out wrapped in thick blankets, but the paramedics seemed to understand me so I kept going. Whether the words were spoken audibly or only in the confines of my head, I don't know. I just knew I had to keep talking. If I stopped, I might never start again.

As they loaded me into the ambulance, Sarah and Sandy were there, watching. I saw the fear and pain in their eyes and again felt a surge of guilt for spoiling a day that had held so much promise for them. Sandy could not come with me. There was only room for two. In a second, she was enveloped by aunts and cousins, all promising to take care of her. They would drive her to the hospital later. I told them all not to worry. I would be back soon.

The ambulance took off with me attached to all kinds of tubes and wires, Bruce rubbing my head and neck, and Sarah holding my hand.

In the ambulance, the nausea got much worse. The urge to vomit was powerful, but I could only retch. My left side felt icy cold, and my head felt as if a giant metal claw had entrapped it. It was like one of those games at a carnival where you put in a penny and grab a prize. The prize appeared to be my head. On the journey to the hospital, there were shades of consciousness from bright dawn awareness to gray twilight to black night. There were enough dawns and dusks to account for several days, but I knew that could not be right. Of course, it was not right; it was just my slipping in and out of consciousness as the pressure on my brain built. We arrived at a hospital emergency department, where a big awning and stark red neon sign trumpeted "Casualty." Of course, in England they call it that. I was unloaded without much ceremony, just the squeaking and clanking of a stretcher and a hydraulic lift. It was warm outside, and the fresh air and sun felt good on my face. Someone said I was at the John Radcliffe Hospital.

There was a hushed consultation; they pulled back my eyelids and shone a light into my eyes. An x-ray machine hovered over my head and glided back and forth, clicking and snapping. I imagined the familiar smell of developing solution nearby. I felt the clamp and sting of the blood-pressure cuff again, and the next thing I knew I was outside, being lifted back into the ambulance again. By now the journey seemed to have been going on for days; it was, in fact, about two hours from the time I left the wedding until I was taken into surgery.

I was bound for the Radcliffe infirmary this time, according to one of the paramedics. There was mumbling about a neurosurgeon on call and special facilities. My case was too serious for this hospital. Perhaps I should have been scared, but it never occurred to me that I was in danger. I was annoyed and frustrated but never scared.

Bloody, silly buggers! Dark thoughts to which I could not give voice filled my mouth as I was wheezed, whooshed, and clanked back into the ambulance. I could not have coped with a soap sandwich that day. (In my childhood, eating a slice of bread passed lightly across a bar of carbolic soap to cleanse the mouth was a commonplace punishment for children wicked enough to utter a "bad" word.)

"Why did you bring me here? I have neither the time nor the inclination to be dragged around the countryside in an ambulance with half my body gone. I have people waiting for me at a wedding."

Bruce kept reassuring me that I was going to be fine. I knew I would be fine, but why could not they get me to the other hospital quickly and do whatever it was they were going to do? I had to get back to the wedding. It was rude to walk out in the middle of something as important as a family wedding. The siren was blaring full blast, warning everybody to get out of my way! *Oh, so now you are in a hurry! Am I getting worse?*

"I know what they will do to me. They will make a hole in my head and relieve the pressure so my head won't buzz. My arm and leg will come back, and I will be fine. You have wasted so much time, so many hours, that I will miss the cutting of the cake. It's infuriating! If they had taken me to the right hospital in the first place, I could have been on my way back by now. There is to be a brunch tomorrow. For sure I'll be back by then! But what about my hair?" I asked. "They will probably shave my head. My hat will cover it. It won't matter. Where is my hat?" Bruce didn't respond at first so I shrieked into his hearing aid as loudly as I could. "Where is my bloody hat?"

"Sheila has it; it's in good hands," he reassured me.

I was hauled noisily from the ambulance and wheeled under another brightly lit Casualty canopy. This time it was dusk, and moths were fluttering around the lights.

I used to be terrified of moths touching me on hot summer nights when they would fly in though my open bedroom window. I would hide under the perspiration-soaked sheets and yell until Dad or one of my brothers came to catch the offending creature and remove it from my view. One landed on my sticky face as I was being wheeled toward the hospital entrance, got stuck, and couldn't get off. I felt the flutter of its wings on my cheek but had neither the will nor the wherewithal to brush it away. There was no point in making a fuss. Who would come anyway? No one knew me here. An unfamiliar man was waiting inside the lobby, past the automatic doors that swung open to admit us. He advanced toward me with a smile and introduced himself as

Professor Aziz, the neurosurgeon on call. He was a slender man with straight black hair and a mustache, wearing scrubs under a white coat. I perseverated on the professor's name. It rang a bell. Somewhere in literature there was a character by that name. Was it Agatha Christie? *Death on the Nile?* The professor's accent was hard-to-place, polished, upper-class English with a dash of something else. Feeling obliged to make polite conversation, I asked him if he was from India or Pakistan.

"Neither," he replied softly. "I am from Bangladesh."

After sending me for various scans, the professor met me in the hallway again and asked the technician pushing the cart I was lying on to push me into a small room. Bruce and Sarah were gone; it was just Professor Aziz and me in a space not much larger than the cart. He confirmed that an artery in my brain had ruptured, and there was a pool of blood already measuring eighty cubic centimeters—roughly a third of a cup or a salad plateful of soft clot—that had to be drained. It was still bleeding, so he would have to make it stop first and then remove the clot. He explained the nausea. It was the result of pressure on my brain. While I was minding my own business on the bus, blood had been gushing into my brain like water from a fire hydrant on a city street in summer.

With a serious but kind expression, he explained clearly, pausing after every sentence to see if I was following him, that he would cut a small piece of bone out of my skull that would allow him to move aside layers of brain tissue until he found the source of the bleeding. He would tie off the offending vessel, suction out the soft, clotting blood, and put everything back, including the bone flap that he would attach with staples and—

"I know, I know. Can you just get on with it, then, so I can get back to the wedding?" I mumbled.

He responded gravely, rationally, "We can't predict the outcome precisely, but we will do our best."

These words, spoken by a neurosurgeon, carried the awesome weight of the responsibility he bore and the knowledge that my survival and where I would land on the spectrum between death, full recovery, and the shades of existence between those poles lay in his hands.

"I have a rendezvous with death at some disputed barricade." Alan Seeger's words flowed across my fading consciousness. *If I am going to pop my clogs tonight, so be it.* There was no fear, no panic, just quiet, calm resignation. Thus, I embarked on my journey through tunnels, bright lights, and bone-chilling cold, fully cognizant that all, none, or only part of me would return.

BIBLIOGRAPHY: CHAPTER 1

American Heart Association. "Answers by Heart Fact Sheet." Accessed July 11, 2018. https://www.heart.org/idc/groups/heartpublic/@wcm/@hcm/documents/dow Austen, Jane. *Pride and Prejudice.* London: T. Egerton, 1944.

Dreamer, Percy and Williams, Ralph Vaughan, eds. *The English Hymnal.* Oxford: Oxford University Press, 1906.

Herlevich, N.E. "Reflecting on old Olympus' Towering Tops." Nov-Dec 1990, *Journal of Ophthalmic Nursing Technology* 9(6) 245–6. Abstract accessible online July 11, 2018. https://www.ncbi.nlm.nih.gov/pubmed/?term=Herlevich+NE%5BAuthor%5D

Seeger, Alan, "I Have a Rendezvous with Death." Accessed July 11, 2018. https://www.poets.org/poetsorg/poem/i-have-rendezvous-death

Wikipedia. *Godspell.* Music and lyrics for play by Stephen Schwartz. Accessed July 11, 2018. https://en.wikipedia.org/wiki/Godspell

Wikipedia, "Tipu Aziz" biography. Accessed July 11, 2018. https://en.wikipedia.org/wiki/_Aziz

CHAPTER 2

Lost and Found

I HAVE NO DOUBT THAT I CAME VERY CLOSE TO DEATH THAT NIGHT BUT have no captivating near-death experiences to recount, no white light, no friendly ancestor guide, just a blank, empty space where several hours should have been. While I was shrouded in anesthesia, unaware of anything, the three people closest to me who made up my unlikely but extremely precious nuclear family sat and waited. We are an unlikely family only because we are such a diverse little group. I am English, born in a small village, raised in strict Church of England tradition, educated in all-girls schools without benefit of separation of church and state from kindergarten through college. Bruce is American, born in Brooklyn, New York, raised as an Orthodox Jew until he rebelled in adulthood and became an ethical humanist, and educated at Ivy League schools. Sarah is our only natural child. After my traumatic pregnancy, the doctors advised me not to get pregnant again. I did not want her to grow up as an only child. I was acutely aware of the fact that by the time she was turning five, most of her playmates had a younger sibling. One day I asked her if she would like to have a baby brother or sister.

"Lord no!" she answered with a vehemence that belied her tender age. "Babies don't do anything. They just lie in their cribs and cry. If you want to know what I really want, I want a kid to play with."

That interchange set us off on a quest to find a kid for Sarah to play with via international adoption. Friends made us aware of a little girl, abandoned as a baby, who was now living in an orphanage in

Medellin, Colombia. We all fell in love with her photograph and set out on the long road to bring her home. It took about a year to work our way through the formalities of evaluation, home visits, and psychological counseling for all three of us before Sandra Milena, a pint-sized Colombian powerhouse, erupted into our lives. At first she was a foster child, but long before the ink was dry on the adoption papers, she had become a full-fledged member of our family. Sarah became a caring and sharing big sister, and Sandy never failed in her duty to fill the vacancy for a playmate. That night in Oxford, family members delivered Sandy to the surgical waiting room to join her father and sister for the long vigil.

Later, Bruce and the girls described that night as the worst of their lives. They sat in the surgical waiting room, each wanting to be strong for the other, wanting news yet dreading what that news might be. They had seen me wheeled past them en route to surgery, uncommunicative and pale as a ghost. One of the doctors told Bruce that the prognosis, as he already suspected, was poor. Bruce's scientific training pushed him to ask for the odds. The response? Probability that I would survive: 10 percent; probability that I would not: 90 percent. I imagine Bruce was fighting to keep his own emotions in check, desperately wanting someone to comfort him but knowing he had to keep himself together for the girls. Bruce is a take-charge person; he wanted to be in the operating room, assisting, observing, doing something. Sitting outside with no knowledge of what was unfolding in the chamber where I was hermetically sealed, beyond his reach, was torture for him. Bothered by the lack of communication and hours of being isolated in cramped, airless quarters, I could see him jumping to his feet any time he heard footsteps in the hallway, telling whoever was going by that he was *Doctor* Douglas and would they please tell him what was going on? Making endless trips to the nurse's station to press for information, he would become increasingly agitated and frustrated as the hours went by, wishing desperately that we were at a hospital where he knew people and they knew him; where he had some influence. Here, he was nobody, just some random spouse asking too many questions.

Bruce would blame himself for not taking my blood pressure issue more seriously and for letting me go to the reception on the bus. He swatted helplessly at a million and one random, irrelevant bugs of guilt swarming in his head, none of which had anything to do with the current situation. Sarah, pale and grim-faced, sat quietly, deathly afraid but trying to be positive and calm for her father. I believe she could hear my voice in her head, telling her to keep her chin up and look on the bright side. Sandy, either because she was in denial (her default location when the going is tough) or because of her own indomitable optimism born of surviving an extraordinarily rough start in life, resolutely chanted to herself, her father, and her sister that Mom was going to be fine, no question.

Professor Aziz emerged briefly after five hours and gave them his cautiously optimistic opinion that I had come through the surgery better than he had dared to hope. The prognosis was still uncertain. He described the bleed as "massive," saying the brain would swell, and there might be seizures. Only if and when I regained consciousness could they begin to assess the level of permanent brain damage. There would be damage from the pressure of the clot, captured between the soft tissue of the brain and the hard, bony wall of the skull. Certain areas of the brain would have the blood supply cut off permanently, and there could be some damage from the surgical intervention itself. I was on life support, but they hoped to be able to wean me off shortly,

The professor was certain I would survive, barring complications, but where on the spectrum of wasteland between real life, death, and mere existence I would emerge could not yet be predicted. Bruce and I had both signed living wills, stating that if either of us was in a situation in which decisions had to be made about turning off machines, each would do it for the other. We had facetiously referred to giving each other "PPP"—plug-pulling privileges. That night, knowing he possibly might have to make that decision, Bruce and the girls wanted me alive and were not about to consider alternatives to getting back the wife and mother they loved. There would be no thought of pulling any plugs.

Eventually, around two o'clock in the morning, as Bruce recalled, the anesthesiologist slipped into the room, removed his mask, and reached out to shake Bruce's hand. The doctor's face was tired and lined from where the strings of the mask had dug into his skin. Bruce was not sure that he wanted to hear what the doctor was going to say; he grabbed the girls' hands and hung on tight to comfort them and to steady himself. Images of our life together, our family, our adventures, and, above all, our love for each other raced through his mind, and he blotted out the rising dread that it might all be past tense now. The doctor's face betrayed little, no doubt a result of years of practice in talking to families in such circumstances. He touched Bruce's arm gently and told him I was stable, though still not breathing on my own, and barring any further catastrophe, I would live.

Bruce told him he was an oral surgeon, trained in anesthesiology. The doctor's demeanor changed immediately as he adopted a more collegial tone and switched from lay to medical terminology. Bruce relaxed a little as the doctor politely guided him into the recovery room, gave him a mask and gown, and brought him to my bedside. When he first saw me as the patient, hooked up to equipment with which he was very familiar, the gravity of my situation hit him with full force, causing his knees to buckle. As he stumbled, the anesthesiologist caught his arm, gave it a squeeze, and told him to look on the bright side: The worst was over, and I was alive.

Bruce paused briefly to look at the monitors registering my vital functions and saw elevated blood pressure but a steady and regular heartbeat. He kissed my cheek and then, having seen me with his own eyes, left to give the girls an update. Sarah burst into tears as they hugged each other, saying in unison, "Thank God she's alive!" Sandy, beaming, took Sarah by the hand to join close family members, who had been sitting tensely, drinking endless cups of what passed as tea from a vending machine in the general waiting room, waiting for word of my condition. "She's alive!" Sandy announced, skipping over any nuances for the time being. "I told you she wouldn't leave me!"

For the next five days, as I remained comatose, Bruce struggled to deal not only with his own feelings about my uncertain future but to keep his upper lip stiff; that is not something that comes naturally to a

Jewish boy from Brooklyn. He had to be positive for the girls and the overwhelming stream of family and friends who arrived at the hospital, desperate for news and wanting to do whatever they could to be helpful. He wanted to rant, rave, kvetch, and kick, but there was no place for that. He had to keep calm and carry on.

First thing Monday morning, thirty-six hours after the surgery, with my future still in limbo, a middle-aged female hospital administrator showed up at my bedside and, in a very officious manner, demanded that Bruce give her a fifteen-thousand-dollar down payment toward the cost of my treatment right away. At first, exhausted and stressed as he was and being seventy- seven years old and hard of hearing, he could not understand what she was saying. Showing absolutely no sensitivity to his or my circumstances, this hard-faced woman raised her voice several decibels and repeated that this, being the British National Health Service, no questions were asked about payment throughout the process of rendering superb emergency medical care. Now, with my survival assured and a long, costly period of medical care ahead of me, the fact that I was not a contributor to the NHS assumed great importance.

She wanted to make it clear that the cash deposit was necessary to ensure that I wouldn't leave the hospital without paying. The thought of someone in a coma skipping out on paying a bill might have been comical, had it not been so offensive. For Bruce, it provided a cathartic release as he unleashed a torrent of pent-up emotion against a convenient human target. She had thrown a lighted match into a keg of emotional gunpowder. His invective— pointed, polite, clean, and more heavily Brooklyn-accented with every passing phrase—acknowledged that it wasn't the administrator's fault that his wife had had a stroke and was in a coma, but he skewered her for every other imperfection. He cited the lack of information, the cramped facilities for people waiting, the tasteless cold coffee, the lack of respect, the antiquated phone system that did not accommodate international calls, and every other slight, real or imagined, that he had endured during the longest night of his life.

"Who do you know who walks around with fifteen thousand dollars in his pocket? What are you going to do with my wife if I don't produce the money? Put her out in the street? My wife is

English; is this the way you treat your own sick people? Today is a public holiday in the United States. All the offices and banks are closed. Do you have any suggestions as to how I should get the money? Can I speak to your boss?" Questions sprayed her like bullets. With her starchy professional demeanor quavering, she backed toward the door and was gone.

Agitated, unshaven, out of his element, and badly in need of a hug, Bruce went looking for Sarah and Sandy and our two sisters-in-law, both named Sheila, who took him under their wings until he was able to make phone calls to the US the following morning. Bruce reached my assistant, Bill, at home in what was the middle of the night for him—in the heat of the moment, the six- hour time difference had been overlooked—and gave him the news. After a tearful exchange of information, Bill looped in my boss, who reassured them that the company travel insurance policy would cover the full cost of medical care and transportation back to Chicago when the time was right. The National Health Service would be relieved of the burden of my care, sparing Bruce any more encounters with his officious nemesis.

Now free to focus on my care and updating the growing number of visitors who were showing up at the hospital to offer help and support, he was grateful for the arrival from Michigan of his son, Cliff. The sole lingering recollection I have of Cliff from the hospital is that he had the ability to locate and massage sore spots on my neck and shoulders. I have no recollection at all of a physician colleague who flew from Chicago to be with me and escort me home. One of our sisters-in-law had a ticket to fly to Chicago shortly after the wedding for a holiday with us. She and I had planned to go to Cabo San Lucas the third week in September. She decided to go ahead to Chicago with Sandy and Sarah as soon as I regained consciousness.

As I started to emerge from the coma, collecting my thoughts was like trying to put cottonwood seeds back in a burst pod or the dandelion clock back on its stem. Thoughts were light, flimsy, and slippery. Some tickled; I tried to grab them, but they flittered past my grasp. They were all the parts of who I was or who I had been. I chased them for a while, but it was tiring. I lost interest and fell back to sleep.

When I awoke with a start, someone was looking over me but too close to my face, inside my privacy shield. The face was vaguely familiar, but it was distorted, one-eyed, and menacing. I did not know who it was. I made an effort to focus, to reach out, to say something, but I could neither move nor make a sound. I was looking through a kaleidoscope, fragments of shape and color, prisms of light, early Picasso paintings sprayed on an undulating canvas. I was icy cold, and my back hurt. Much later, someone said that I was sore from lying on a hard operating table for several hours but all I knew was that I was in pain and it was too bright, too noisy, too cold, and impossible to do anything.

I closed my eyes again. *Okay, lucky, successful, induced coma, intubate, intensive care, catheter*—hard, pebble-shaped words skimmed across a murky pool of grayness. I wanted to go back where I'd been before. It was quiet, light, and peaceful there. Then, abruptly, intrusively, someone poked me and told me sharply to wake up. They were touching my face and rubbing my cheek with rough-grade sandpaper. I was incapable of rousing myself. I knew they were there but much too far away for me to reach them. I reached toward them with hands outstretched. I wanted to push them away. They appeared not to see me trying to reach them. I was not moving, trapped in a confined space as cold as a tomb. I was as lifeless as a corpse. I felt a surge of panic.

Do they think I am dead? Am I dead?

"I need a blanket," I said, but they ignored me. Something bright assaulted my eyes, piercing, stabbing, stinging like saltwater. They were shining flashlights in my eyes. What had I done? Why were they doing that to me? They were mumbling and chattering too close to my face. I could not comprehend what they were saying or even what language they were speaking, yet I knew it was about me.

"I need a blanket," I said again. There was still no response, so I repeated, "I need a blanket"—louder this time. Their faces were weird, crazy-mirror images. I yelled at them to go away and leave me alone. I tried to get up and run, but every part of me was nailed to the bed. Nothing would move. I was trapped—panicking, thrashing, and trying to escape. Someone was sitting on me, holding me down. "Get off me! Get off me! Let me out!"

People were talking at me again: "Wake up," commanded an unfamiliar voice. Something was stuck in my nose, and my arms were tethered. I could not wake up; I did not want to. More voices and a lot of metallic crashing and banging sounds crowded my head, and I shivered uncontrollably.

"Get me a blanket." I tried pleading. Maybe that would work.

"Keep her still," said an authoritative voice. "We don't want her fully awake, we just want to know that she's coming out of the anesthesia."

Arms and hands grabbed and moved me periodically. Each time they touched me, I felt hooks pulling barbed wire inside me, doing their best to yank out my insides. There was an intermittent crushing of my arm as the blood pressure cuff inflated and deflated by remote control. It pinched a nerve. Pins and needles again.

"You are hurting me! Stop it at once! Go away! I need a blanket." I was screaming for someone to save me, to get me out of there. I was bound hand and foot, mummified, swaddled in thick gray-brown smog that dimmed the light and muted the sound. Briefly, everything was white peace again until—*smack*—something metallic hit the bed, shooting arrows into every part of my body. Is this what Saint Sebastian felt? I pictured the stained-glass window in the church of my childhood that bore his image with arrows piercing every part of his body. The clatter pierced the stillness, assailed my ears, and dragged me back into the chaos around me. When I opened my eyes again, it was to see Bruce's face—at least part of it, enough for me to know it was him. I saw him trying to smile, a tear glistening in the one eye I could see. He was leaning in close and whispering. "It's over. Your surgery is over. You are in the recovery room. You are going to be fine. You can't talk because you have a tube in your throat. If you can hear me, squeeze my hand."

I squeezed his familiar warm hand, felt the wedding band hard against my fingers, and started to cry, croaking painful sobs, and then sank gratefully back into oblivion.

My time in the Oxford hospital, twelve days in all, was nothing more than one long day to me, a blank space where several days and nights should have been. I hovered above the calendar like a day-old helium balloon. I had no markers for when one day ended and another began.

There was nothing but artificial light—no window, no real darkness, just the relief of closing my eyes. I had no freedom. I could not move in the bed, sit up by myself, or turn over. I shivered, my teeth chattered, and above all, my head hurt. It was an ache full of paradoxes: dull and sharp, localized and dispersed, empty and full, heavy and light. Even the slightest movement of the bed produced acute pain.

People talked at me; it is what you do with coma patients. I have done it myself. As a young occupational therapist in a white starched dress with a green belt, I sat in the Accident Unit at the Royal National Orthopaedic Hospital in Stanmore, talking for hours at patients with brain injuries. It was part of their treatment. The hope, sometimes vain, was that spoken words would hook some slender filament of recognition, enough to reel the patient back from the depths of disconnection.

Family members would provide names of siblings, pets, interests, sports teams—anything that might strike a chord. A twitch, a rapid blink, a tear slowly rolling from the corner of a tightly closed eye might indicate a response, a movement in the direction of waking up. Sometimes I would read from a patient's favorite book, trying to be as animated as possible in my delivery, fearing, irrationally, that a monotonous drone might lead to deeper coma. Most of the patients I talked at in the unit were there because of an automobile or motorcycle accident but occasionally because of a fight or sports injury. They were usually young and strong at the time of their injuries, and most gradually emerged into consciousness. Sometimes they fixated on the person who had talked at them, and on one notable occasion, when I was in another hospital having minor surgery myself, a young man at whom I had talked extensively for several weeks as he recovered from a motorcycle accident, showed up at my bedside to return the favor. He had noticed my absence, made some inquiries, absconded from the hospital, and navigated central London by himself while still listed on his chart as semi-comatose.

Other, older patients, like my father, did not emerge from coma. I sat at Dad's bedside, talking at him for an agonizing week after he suffered a hemorrhagic stroke, prattling about football scores, giving him updates on a snooker match that blared from the television set in his room, as he slid deeper and deeper into unconsciousness and, finally, beyond reach.

His doctor had told me that he could linger in the state he was in—blood leaking slowly but treacherously from arteries that were worn tissue-thin by years of poorly controlled blood pressure—for an indefinite period. The bleeding might stop of its own volition, and he could recover a bit but it was unlikely. He could linger in his current state for weeks. He knew that I had a four-year-old, so he suggested that I go home for a bit and come back if there was any change. Knowing there was nothing I could do for him, I kissed my dear, sweet, kind father goodbye, with a lump in my throat the size of Mount Everest, fairly sure that I would never see him alive again. Bruce met me at O'Hare Airport, as many hours later as it took to travel from Nottingham to Chicago, with the saddest face and the news that Dad had *slipped his surly bonds and gone to grasp the hand of God* while I was crossing the Atlantic.

People continued to talk at me, and gradually I recognized the words, if not the voices. Faces started to emerge, one-eyed, out-of-focus. They scared me. I shut my eyes tight, hoping they would go away.

As the mist started to lift, I saw Bruce sitting beside the bed, talking to people and finally responding to my constant refrain of "I need a blanket." I must have been speaking aloud, as he produced one and leaned over to cover me. As he did so, I got a whiff of overpoweringly bad breath and snarled, "Brush your teeth!"

Sarah and Sandy were there, and then they were gone. I asked for them repeatedly, but they never came. I was both sad and annoyed that they were gone. I needed them.

"Who made them leave?" I asked Bruce querulously. "What have you done with them?"

"We thought it would be best if they went home to wait for you there. There wasn't much they could do here."

"They could have been with me," I snapped, "and they didn't even say goodbye."

"They did," he said, "but you were sleeping."

"I don't know what you are talking about. I haven't slept at all since I got here."

The wedding was on August 31. I did not become fully conscious until around September 18.

At some point I was moved out of the Intensive Care Unit and into a room that I shared with three other patients. During my time there, one of my roommates died. I shared a woman's last hours on earth. She was someone's daughter, wife, mother, and friend, and in my inchoate consciousness, it made no impression on me. When I learned of this event, months later I felt sad and disrespectful. I would have liked to make amends, but there was no way that I could. We had been casualties on the same battlefield, but I was the lucky one.

When I was allowed to have visitors, more half faces appeared—my brother, sisters-in-law, cousins, nieces, nephews, dear friends. I knew I knew them, though I could not put a name to any of them. Their images were like old, blurry slides projected on a crinkled screen, but they were not aware that there was a wall between them and me. Some commented that that my English accent returned, as fresh as the day I'd left twenty-eight years ago. But I was not aware that I had been away for twenty-eight years or where I had been. I was having rote conversations with people, smiling, laughing, thanking them for coming, but nothing was registering. It was as if I were under a spell and being controlled remotely. My past life and much of my identity were consigned to the Lost and Found, and I had lost the claim ticket; I was incapable of recognizing much less articulating what had happened.

When I was well enough to leave the acute care setting, they appeared not to know what to do with me. Conversations took place in front of me about where I should go for the lengthy rehabilitation that lay ahead. I recognized an attempt to involve me in the conversation but struggled to maintain a coherent strain of thought. I did not care what they did with me if only they would be quiet about it.

Professor Aziz said I could go home to Chicago if the proper arrangements were made. For an instant, I wondered why in the world they would send me to Chicago. Mum would have a fit. She cried for days when I told her I was going the first time. "Everyone will think you are going to be a gangster's moll," she had sobbed, clenching and unclenching her fists as she paced the kitchen floor.

Bruce told me I had three choices: the Rehabilitation Institute of Chicago (RIC), Grant Hospital, or Schwab Rehabilitation Center. The insurance company insisted that they would only pay for an accredited facility. I chewed on this information for a bit and made my pronouncement.

"I'm not bad enough for RIC," I said, having no idea how bad I was. "I used to work there. It is more for spinal cord injury, closed brain injury—the hardcore stuff. I can't go to Schwab; it's on the wrong side of town, and no one will visit me." The third option, Grant, now known as Lincoln Park Hospital, had a rehabilitation unit on the fourth floor. I knew it well. I had worked there too. I would go there for a few days if it meant they would let me go home. I saw no need for rehabilitation. Just a few nights in my own bed, and I would be fine. I thought I had made the decision myself but in reality, there had been many conversations between Bruce, my employer, the insurance company, and my own doctor back in Chicago. That decision was made, along with travel arrangements, with my saying many of the right words but having no real understanding of what was happening.

Once before I had sustained a contre-coup concussion after falling off a horse. I went to the hospital, had intelligent conversations with the medical and nursing staff, had a CT scan, and was sent home with instructions for the family to wake me every two hours during the night. I have no recollection of that incident whatsoever. I only know about it because other people told me. The brain, like a computer, has many windows. Some can remain open and operational while others shut down, and there are no permeable walls between them.

On September 11, 2002 (the irony of the date was not lost on me, though remembered details were scant), I was loaded into an ambulance and traveled from Oxford to Heathrow Airport. I was sedated but able to hear the mournful howl of the siren and periodic horns and hoots of other traffic on the road. I was not alone in the ambulance. Besides the driver, there was a doctor, a nurse, a paramedic, and Bruce; all of them would travel with me to Chicago. At Heathrow Airport, I was taken from the ambulance and loaded onto a British Airways plane, a so-called air ambulance. It looked a lot like a Boeing 777, and it was, specially adapted to evacuate sick or wounded victims of major disasters.

Is that what I am—a major disaster? Once on the plane, they took me to the very back. I was not too sick to be offended. "But I always get upgraded," I protested, referring to my elite status on United Airlines.

"Not today, dearie," came the response from a cheery Englishman in a flight attendant uniform. "We have something much better for you."

"Much better" turned out to be an entire row of seats, over which I hung suspended on a stretcher. I would spend the next months in a hospital bed, but to this day, when I try to recall that period, I always have the distinct impression that I was hanging from the ceiling.

Once installed in my hanging crib, wires and tubes intact, a friendly flight attendant started to close curtains around me to give me privacy.

"Wait," I said. "Don't do that. I'm claustrophobic." They let me have a crack to peer out and explained that they didn't want to upset the other passengers. *Do I look that bad?* I wondered.

The inside of a plane was so familiar to me—the cold, dry, slightly musty air; the smell of burned coffee grounds; cold, hard, unripe pineapple on fruit plates; dust motes dancing in the beams of reading lights. The reading light is important. I have a deal with myself. I work on the outbound journey, to prepare for whatever project I am engaged in, and the return trip is reading for pleasure. My briefcase is stuffed with a magazine, usually *Vanity Fair*, books, a mystery, a saga, the Dalai Lama's *Art of Happiness*, or a new business text to be devoured at lightning speed. Layovers, weather, mechanical delays, or cancellations were divided between business and pleasure reading.

Over the past several years, I had flown at least a hundred thousand miles a year. On my frequent routes—New York, San Francisco, Detroit, and London—I was on first-name terms with many of the cabin crew. We joked that I could do their job in a pinch; they said they were glad they didn't have to do mine. Some weeks I spent more hours in the air than they did, and I worked at least eight hours a day between flights. There were no leisurely layovers for me. Work might involve going down a coal mine or to a meat-packing plant, a nuclear-powered submarine base, or an automobile factory. Several recent transatlantic flights had involved a mad dash to get to the bedside of loved ones who were sick and dying before it was too late.

This transatlantic journey was a patchwork of lapses into unconsciousness, semi-consciousness, feeling high, having hilarious conversations with fellow travelers who stopped by my perch to wish me well, and brief, un-sustained periods of lucidity. There was no need for the reading light, and if I never had a cup of coffee again, it would be too soon. My medical team checked my vital signs periodically, emptied some plastic bags, filled others, fiddled with wires, and asked how I was feeling.

Bruce, who to my chagrin, had been upgraded to first class, despite not having nearly as many miles as I had, was sleeping when a flight attendant asked him for his credit card.

"What do you need it for?" he asked, surprised.

"Your wife has been shopping, sir. She asked for the duty-free catalog and said you wouldn't mind."

In my drug and stroke-induced stupor, I had managed to circle enough items to give presents to everyone I could think of. There were Swatch watches for the girls -one pink, one blue (neither ever saw the light of day); a Wedgwood ashtray for the cleaning lady (who had never smoked in her life); Wedgwood cufflinks for two or three men who had been kind to me; Union Jack pens and a Wedgwood clock for Bruce, as a gesture of appreciation for all that he had done for me. I had spent nine hundred dollars. Poor Bruce was so relieved that I was alive and going home that he paid up without question. It was much later when he gave me a hard time and finally asked for the money back! Our family motto became "When the going gets tough, the tough go shopping."

Being the first anniversary of 9/11, security was extremely tight at O'Hare Airport. After all the other passengers disembarked and their suitcases were unloaded, the plane taxied to a remote part of the airport. I was the last remaining piece of baggage to be unloaded. Strapped to a stretcher with all my tubes and wires intact, I was loaded onto a waiting ambulance, bound for Grant Hospital. Once at the hospital, feeling more like an empty suitcase than myself, I was placed on a gurney and wheeled into an elevator. Bells dinged at several floors before I emerged at the acute medical floor. Bruce had arranged a reception committee for me. Sarah and

Sandy were there with Sheila, who was going to make the trip to Mexico by herself, despite my protestations that I would be fine by the end of next week and ready to go with her. The faces of other people gathered in the room were somewhat familiar, but everyone looked strange, and I could not name anyone.

As fatigue and drugs overtook me, I slid back into the dark, losing my grip on what little consciousness I had held on to in making the trans-Atlantic journey.

BIBLIOGRAPHY: CHAPTER 2

American Heart Association. "Answers by Heart Fact Sheet." Accessed July 11, 2018. https://www.heart.org/idc/groups/heartpublic/@wcm/@hcm/documents/dow

Wikipedia. John Gillespie Magee, Jr.'s poem, "High Flight." Accessed July 11, 2018. https://en.wikipedia.org/wiki/John_Gillespie_Magee_Jr.

CHAPTER 3

Scrambled Eggs

I WAS STARTLED OUT OF A RARE, DEEP SLEEP BY A KERFUFFLE AROUND my bed. Several people all appeared to be talking at once. There was a wheelchair parked next to the bed with a large, stuffed, white plastic bag hanging from the back. From the stalks of back-and-forth dialogue between the participants in the conversation, I gleaned that I was going to the fourth floor, the Rehabilitation Department. Arriving by wheelchair as the patient, rather than on foot as the director of occupational therapy, as I had from 1979 to 1986, felt like a blow to the stomach. I was confused, as if the wind had been knocked out of me, and it was hard to breathe.

What tilt of the world accounted for this change of circumstances? Incapable of grasping anything beyond vague familiarity with the environment and myriad swirling images, I was trapped in the present. With enough insight to know that I knew something about rehabilitation and enough brain damage to render me unable to recognize that I needed it, I found myself uniquely qualified to be the patient from hell. I assumed a supercilious air, caviled constantly, perseverated on unimportant issues and dismissed the serious ones, and totally rejected or missed the point of much of the therapy that came my way.

One topic that occupied a great deal of my mental capacity was food; in particular, scrambled eggs. I dislike eggs intensely. This is an aversion born of surfeit. Growing up as I did, during a time of food rationing in the aftermath of the Second World War, our diet had to be supplemented by anything that could be produced at home.

We had chickens, kept in a coop made of wood, corrugated iron, and chicken wire at the top of our garden. Their clucking, squawking, and scratching, along with their unmistakable grainy odor, provided a backdrop for outside activities all year long. Every spring, twelve-day-old chicks—yellow, fluffy, and no bigger than a sparrow—traveled by train and truck to our house, defying all odds, to enter a cycle of eating, laying, and being eaten.

These chickens produced enough eggs to feed not only our family of six but several neighboring families as well. In consequence of our good fortune, we had eggs just about every day. We had soft-boiled eggs with toast soldiers, fried eggs, egg sandwiches, hard-boiled eggs, poached eggs, pickled eggs, coddled eggs, scrambled eggs, omelets, and for dessert, egg custard. When the hens stopped laying eggs, had an accident, or got into a fight, we ate them. I am not overly fond of chicken either. Chicken, though, was preferable to pigeon, which occasionally showed up in a pie, thanks to Dad's trapping enterprise in the church belfry. One of the many services he provided to his church was to keep the pigeon population under control.

At first, breakfast was served in the rehab patient's room. On my first evening, an aide brought the menu for me to select breakfast, lunch, and dinner for the following day. The menu was attached to a clipboard and hard to maneuver with one hand. It was also hard to read when my brain could not decipher what my eye was seeing, and a large chunk of the page was missing. After a struggle, I managed to circle what I thought was toast for my breakfast. Next day, breakfast arrived on a tray, a plate covered by one of those stainless steel warmers with a hole in the middle. The food service attendant lifted the lid with a great flourish and revealed scrambled eggs!

"That's not what I ordered," I said.

"It is," she replied.

I ate the toast, but put the cover back on the eggs and pushed them away. The transporter came to get me for physical therapy, and the incident was forgotten. At lunchtime, once again what was on my tray was not what I had ordered. The next day the same thing happened at breakfast—scrambled eggs again! I was angry!

"This is not what I ordered!" I barked.

"Yes, it is!" came the stern reply.

I hated this place! The food was bad enough to begin with, but they could not even get a simple order right. I began to keep count of the number of wrong breakfasts, making a mark on the edge of my bed table with the pen that was conveniently lying there. On the twelfth day of scrambled eggs, I demanded to see the food service supervisor. She arrived as I returned from my third or fourth therapy session of the day. Her name was Ella, and I knew her from my days of working at the hospital. A capacious, comforting, yet commanding African American woman, she was the one who would solve my problem.

"What's wrong, honey?" she asked.

"Ella," I whined, "I've been here for months, and my order has been messed up every single day. They keep bringing me scrambled eggs, and I hate scrambled eggs. I would never order them." I heard the childish petulance in my own slurred words but was too mad about the eggs to be embarrassed. Ella was reassuring and told me it would not happen again. I should just fill out my menu, and they would bring me whatever I ordered.

Later, my rehab nurse came to tell me that I was fit enough to join the other patients in the day room and eat breakfast there. Linda, the occupational therapist came, as usual, to help me through what is euphemistically labeled "activities of daily living." A better term would be "atrocities of daily living." It involved going to the bathroom first. I was still wearing a catheter, so this exercise seemed a bit futile. Confronting the hideous, lopsided face in the mirror, I tried to scrape a thick coat of mold off the tongue with a toothbrush, dragged a brush through half a head of somebody's hair; finished by swiping at the face with a wet wash cloth as Linda asked if I was ready to be helped back to bed.

Yes, I was definitely ready to be helped back to bed and to stay there for the rest of the day. No such luck! Linda helped me transfer from the wheelchair to the bed. This involved a hop, a skip, and a lunge; sometimes I made it to the bed but other times fell short and landed back in the wheelchair. A couple of times I missed altogether and landed on the floor. Once on the bed, the struggle to get into my clothes began.

The first few days in rehab, I declined to get dressed in my own clothes, choosing instead to go to PT wearing two hospital gowns, one on forward and the other backward. I was alert enough to realize that indecent exposure could result from wearing just one. I was freezing cold and caught sight of heating pads being removed from a machine and applied to various parts of the bodies of other patients.

"May I have one of those?" I plaintively inquired.

"No, you may not," came the decisive reply from Chris, my physical therapist. "If you are so cold, why don't you get dressed in the morning instead of coming down here in your nightgown?"

Chris was a very large, muscular, young black man. He was built like a football player so I was not about to argue with him. I thought that as the former director of occupational therapy in *this very hospital*, I might expect a little more respect. Chris told me that he had spent quite a lot of time in Germany, so I dubbed him the Exercise Nazi. He and I conversed mostly in German, a fact worthy of mention only because while I had studied German in school, I had dropped it at sixteen and, other than with a German land-lady and a couple of brief layovers at airports or train stations in Germany, had no cause to speak or read it since.

From that point on, I did not get breakfast in bed, and I had to get dressed to go to PT. Linda came the next morning and asked what clothes I would like to wear. My choice was limited to one of two sweat suits brought from home. I chose the purple one.

After the torturous visit to the bathroom and having completed the herculean task of getting myself back on the bed, I lay on my back, hanging from the ceiling, and struggled to wind a leg that was not there into pants that had something seriously wrong with them. By something wrong, I mean there was no opening for a second leg, even if I had one. To make matters worse, my catheter kept getting caught and yanked, producing an agonizing pain. This exercise could be classified as torture. People have been prosecuted for less severe crimes against humanity.

Finally, after much grunting, groaning, and gyrating, my lower half was clad, except for the brace, known as an ankle foot orthosis (AFO) that I would try to put on later. Linda showed me how to fasten my bra and put it over my head. I knew the drill—affected side in first; affected side out last. That assumes one has an affected side.

I had no side at all. I battled to get the unruly, uncooperative appendage through the aperture that Linda had created above my head. It wouldn't go. After about twenty tries, I was exhausted, slick from perspiration and completely stuck. Not knowing whether to laugh or cry, I was on the edge of hysteria. Linda gave me a look, and in an instant we opted for laughter. She took pity on me and helped me finish getting my clothes on. I was resplendent, upholstered rather than clad in the sweat suit that the girls had brought from home. It was very rumpled and had a few stray cat hairs clinging to it. Chloe and Eloise, the cats, had been sleeping in my closet again, but who cared?

Next, it was time for the brace and shoes. Linda handed me the brace and patiently showed me how to lift up my affected leg with my unaffected hand. We were very careful not to say *bad leg* or *good arm.* We were scrupulously nonjudgmental about deadbeat appendages. After a half a dozen tries at snaking the foot into the brace, I felt my blood pressure increasing along with my frustration level. At the point at which my AFO was about to become a UFO, Linda once again intervened

"You've done enough for one day. Good work! Tomorrow is another day."

I felt like a six-year-old learning to tie my shoelaces, except that even that task would be way beyond me. I was starting to feel the same way about platitudes and euphemisms that I felt about scrambled eggs.

Muttering " Whoopee! Good old me! Way to go!" I sat back and waited for someone to take me to the dayroom for breakfast. I was starving from all the exertion.

My assumption that someone would push me turned out to be erroneous. Part of my promotion involved getting myself there. I was in a private room, right by the nurse's station, so the nurses were always there to help me—in theory, at least! I had to figure out a means of locomotion that would get me where I needed to go. If I pushed the big wheel with my right hand and scooted along the floor with my right foot, I could move forward a few inches.

I hit the wall. Ouch! I felt pain somewhere in my arm. I took a deep breath and aimed for the door again. A few more inches and whack—I hit the wall again. There was something wrong with the wheelchair.

It would not go in a straight line but kept turning toward the wall. I was close to tears again but was determined to make it to breakfast. I pushed harder with my hand and foot and this time executed a complete circle! Try as I might, I could not reach the string to call the nurse. It was on the other side of the bed.

After another try at moving forward, I became entangled in the curtain around the bed. I started to shout for help, but my voice was strangled in my throat. Eventually, an aide heard me and came into the room. She saw the tangled mess of curtain, wheelchair, and humanity and started to extricate me. I complained bitterly about the defective wheelchair and begged her to push me to the dayroom. She took pity on me, informed me that she could get into trouble for doing this, and pushed me down the long hallway to the dayroom.

"You are very late," said the person in charge.

"Don't get me started," I wanted to say, but again no words came out.

Around the large table were several patients in varying states of disrepair. Some were dressed, albeit in a haphazard fashion; some were in hospital gowns. A couple of my tablemates didn't seem to be aware of their surroundings, and quite a few were wearing at least part of their breakfast on their faces or down their fronts. I was acutely aware of the state of other people in the room but painfully unaware of myself as I pushed up to the table. There was a place setting and a plate with the inevitable stainless steel lid. Someone asked if I would like coffee. The thought of it set my stomach churning.

"I don't drink coffee," I responded. I lifted the lid from my plate, and there they were again—scrambled eggs! A wave of intense anger surged through me as I slammed the cover back over the eggs.

"I did not order eggs!" I spat through clenched teeth.

"You must have; food service only brings what is on your menu."

I looked at what else was on the tray. There was an English muffin.

"They aren't English, by the way." I mumbled. "They are as American as French toast!"

I ate the muffin. I could not wrestle the tin foil off the top of the butter or jelly, so I ate it dry. There was a carton of milk and one of orange juice. I cannot drink milk because I am lactose intolerant.

Nobody used that word, but as a child at school, I was provided with one small bottle of milk every day, courtesy of the government. It was to help strengthen the young generation as the country struggled to recover from six years of war and to supplement the meager rations available to families at home. It was mandatory that we drank it. I vomited so many times after drinking the milk that finally I was granted an exemption by means of a note from the family doctor. In place of the milk, I was to have a bottle of National Health Service orange juice. The only thing about the drink that was even remotely connected to an orange was its color. Even the color was not natural, more likely a chemical forbear of Agent Orange. It was a concoction of which a medieval witch could have been proud. Containing vitamins and minerals, it came in a blue glass medicine bottle with raised writing on it and a screw top. It tasted vile but since it failed to produce the dramatic effect of the milk, I was stuck with it!

I grabbed the carton of orange juice, stabbed the foil top with my fork, and slurped it down through the holes. No one offered to help with anything, and I vaguely recalled that independence is a virtue in rehabilitation.

I had been in this room many times, but I had never eaten breakfast there. As the director of occupational therapy, wearing a starched white lab coat over street clothes, I had bounced into this room once a week to face a roomful of stroke patients. In a forty-five-minute exercise program, I had instructed patients how to lift the affected arm with the unaffected arm, to stretch it above their heads, to swing to one side and then to the other, and to march with their legs while seated in a chair. We had pointed our toes, or at least the toes on one foot, made circles with the ankle that moved, and shrugged a shoulder or two to loud music emanating from an elderly radio in the corner of the room. I had hated every minute of it and had strained not to show that I thought it was an exercise in futility. I wanted it to be over so I could get on with the rest of my day. Every time I led that class, I remembered that one of my fellow OT students had complained that working with stroke patients was like watching trees grow or paint dry. I had wholeheartedly agreed.

That class, along with a Thursday evening social activity, was my cursory nod to the work of the Stroke Rehabilitation Unit. The rest of my workdays were spent in the operating room, observing or assisting in complicated hand cases with Dr. Sarrafian; in the cast room; or in the OT Department, fashioning elaborate dynamic splints and developing exercise routines to encourage the return of useful function to the postsurgical hand.

When I first met Dr. Sarrafian, an Assyrian American educated in Paris, he was chief of orthopedic surgery. I knew that he had a special interest in hand surgery. In response to my telling him I was a hand therapist and shamelessly dropping the names of the lions of the field under whom I had trained, he quoted a famous hand surgeon who once said that the only therapist he would allow near his patients would be one whose arms had been amputated at the elbow . He or she would be unable to do any harm to his patients. This, said in a charming French/Middle Eastern accent and with a definite twinkle in kindly eyes behind horn-rimmed glasses, had not dampened my enthusiasm, and in the face of my persistence, he finally consented to give me a trial.

At first, he referred only the most difficult and resistant-to-recovery patients until he could be sure that I would do no harm. Over time, we built a solid working relationship, and soon he insisted that I spent my Tuesdays in the OR, so I would know *exactly* what he had done and thus be less likely to undo good surgical results.

I was jarred back into the present by a cacophony of metallic noise assaulting the one of my senses that was more acute than ever, my hearing. Patients had started scraping, tapping, shuffling, and squeaking away from the table and out of the room, some with canes, some with walkers, and others in wheelchairs. Some of the wheelchair-bound folks had one leg stuck out in front on a leg rest. They moved faster than everyone else because they had two good—sorry, "unaffected"—arms.

Miraculously, someone came for me so I did not have to push myself. My destination was speech therapy. I had profound respect for what speech and language pathologists do, but I, in my own considered and informed opinion, had no need of their services.

"Broca's area, the part of the brain that controls speech, is on the non- dominant side—in my case, the left—and the hole in my head is on the right, as made evident by this clearly visible bald spot," I smugly informed the therapist. "If my speech is slurred, it is because I am extremely tired and am being stuffed full of drugs."

Upon arrival in the speech room, I was situated in front of a large mirror that sat on the table in front of me. Looking in the mirror in and of itself was a thoroughly offensive exercise and enough to tip the balance of my teeter- totter mood into the negative column. The face in this mirror could not belong to me. I have never had a clear picture of what I look like in my mind. I have wondered, in the abstract, if I met myself in the street if I would know it was I. I neither like having my photograph taken nor looking at pictures of myself. I did not recognize the face in front of me at all. In my youth, the adjective used to describe me was pretty. Not beautiful, but I heard "pretty" a lot.

Dad took me aside right before I left for college to have a little talk. Sitting across from him at the checked-tablecloth-covered kitchen table, I had seen tiny beads of perspiration forming on his bald, freckled head. Almost forty when I was born, the only hair he had ever had in my lifetime was a tonsure of copper-faded-to-salt-and-pepper tamed curls. Sitting in a straight-backed chair in front of the window, he fiddled nervously with his starched collar and loosened his tie, the copper hairs on the backs of his gnarled hands glinting in late afternoon sunshine.

"All kinds of men are going to tell you that you are pretty," he said, shifting uncomfortably and trying to avoid direct eye contact, "but you are not. You are *all right* but not pretty, and you must not believe what they say. Men will say anything to take advantage of you. Do not believe them, and never let their fancy words flatter you."

I could tell by the look on his face that he would rather have been anywhere in the universe than having that talk with me. One of six brothers and father of three sons, I was the first young female he had encountered in a close, personal way. My fragile teenage self-esteem could have taken a huge hit from his words, but it didn't. I was on to him and immediately recognized his awkwardly expressed but heartfelt desire to protect me from evils lurking in a world that he barely understood.

His world had been small. Too young to serve in one war and too old to serve in the next, he had missed out on the only real opportunity country-born men of his generation had to travel. A surge of gratitude and tenderness propelled me to plant a kiss on top of his salty pate as I thanked him for his concern, assured him that I would not fall for idle flattery, and watched him beat a hasty retreat to his vegetable garden, leaving a trail of fragrant, blue pipe-tobacco smoke behind him.

This face in front of me could never be described as pretty. It was grotesque. The skin was ghostly pale with brown blotches on it, rusty nail heads hammered randomly on the nose and forehead. The eyes were sunken and red-rimmed with dark circles underneath. One eye looked bigger than the other; both looked as if they were squinting at the sun. The nose was red, as if its owner had a cold. The mouth was the worst. It drooped at one corner, and the lips were cracked and peeling, as if they had been on a polar expedition or badly burned by molten lava.

I recoiled at the ugliness of the face and then stuck my tongue out at it. To my disgust, the face stuck its tongue out back at me too but not straight out, the way I had done. The ugly face's tongue lolled out to the side in all its furry, spittle- dripping glory. I looked away in hopes that it would be gone when I looked back, but it wasn't. I turned away, muttering to the face to stop following me. One more glance at the hair above the face made me think that it might be mine. Another of Dad's comments after I had a particularly bad haircut was that he had seen better stuff on a coconut. The hair framing one side of the ugliness looked exactly like a coconut.

"Move your tongue from side to side, up and down," the therapist ordered. My mouth was full of saliva. He told me to swallow. A speck of saliva went the wrong way, and I started coughing uncontrollably, choking, wheezing, and gasping for breath. My face burned, and tears streamed down my cheeks as I spluttered and fought to stifle the paroxysms and get my breathing under control. He looked concerned. I tried to speak, to tell him this happened to me all the time, but that event triggered a fresh bout of loud hacking and snorting, punctuated by explosive snotty sneezes. My haughty demeanor was hard to maintain while in the throes of choking to death.

I was handed a cup of ice chips to soothe my ravaged throat, but that hurt my teeth. It trickled out of the side of my mouth until, mingling with the river flowing from my eyes, created a pool in the salt cellar between my collarbone and my neck.

As if to add insult to injury, the therapist produced flash cards from the toy box on his desk. He held the cards up in front of me and asked me to read the words written on them. What kind of a trick was this? The cards were old, and parts of the words were missing. There was nothing intelligible written on them. Everything in this place was falling apart! These cards were in the same condition as my pathetic wheelchair! Still, I humored him, and to prove I was not as dumb as he thought, I made a supreme effort and read from his stupid cards—CAT, DOG, RAT. *Really! Does he think I am a kindergartener?*

Becoming more frustrated and angry with every passing second, I resolved to get out of this room as quickly as possible. I started to push away from the table, announcing as imperiously as I could that the session was at an end.

"I can speak and read perfectly well, thank you. As a matter of fact, there is very little wrong with me at all, and as soon as they remove this damn catheter, I'll be out of here!" I started to huff out of the room but only traveled a few inches before being attacked by a door frame that stubbornly refused to get out of my way. I wished this cursed wheelchair could feel pain the way I did as it smashed and slammed my elbow and knee, first against metal door frame and then against the wooden door.

I did not like the speech pathologist. I hated that he treated me like a patient. I cannot recall his name; I blocked it in my subconscious. I have no doubt that he blocked mine too, not wanting to remember—any more than I did—the contentious, insurance-company–mandated hours we spent together. I was saved from further torture by the arrival of John, the transporter from PT. John was Puerto Rican, always upbeat, and funny, and he had me smiling by the time we reached the gym. I knew John from when he used to bring patients to the department when I worked there. He remembered me and treated me with respect.

John wheeled me up to a raised mat. Chris said I was ready to stand by myself.

"It's about time!" Even though I was fully dressed, I was still cold. Once I was lying on the mat, I asked again for a heating pad.

"Bitte?" I pleaded

"Nein!" Chris responded emphatically. I seethed at the injustice of it.

An impressive list of German curse words crept under my breath, just loud enough for Chris to suspect what he was hearing but not loud enough for him to be sure.

"We're going to work on straight leg raises today," said Chris.

My right leg flew off the mat before Chris could give the order, up, up and away, to a perfect ninety degrees. "That was easy," I bragged. *"Wie viel?"*

"That's enough for that side, Dusseldorf." In keeping with our German theme, this was the nickname he'd given me. "It's the other one I want you to move."

"What other one? This is the only one I have."

Chris produced something he called a gait belt and fastened it around my waist. It was a piece of striped webbing with a large chrome buckle. Chris and John lifted me to my feet, and immediately my head started to swim, and everything in the gym seemed to be revolving.

"You think *Das betreten is not verboten*." I had quoted Rupert Brooke. "But it is. I can't stand on it." I lost my balance and collapsed back into the chair. We tried a few more times, and then it was time for lunch. I was not hungry, and the prospect of having to the trek to the dayroom again was overwhelming, so I asked to be taken to my room. Once there, I cornered a nurse's aide and convinced her that I needed to be put back to bed. Back in the still, comforting hardness of my bed, I fell into a deep sleep. I had no idea how long I slept. In fact, I had no concept of time at all!

Bruce and I had a few words about this. I told him that I did not appreciate that he kept me waiting all the time. He was still on the staff of the hospital, despite having retired a few years before. Doctor colleagues saw him around and started asking if he would mind taking a look at a patient.

"Of course you wouldn't mind taking a look at a patient; anything rather than sit by my bedside," I chided.

Reluctantly, he gave in. After staying with me for about two minutes, he then was gone again for hours. I stared at the clock on the wall in my room, and the hands did not move. I looked for what I estimated to be ten minutes and then looked back, and they still had not moved.

"Still stands the church clock at ten to three and is there honey still for tea?" Rupert Brooke sprang to mind again.

Shards of memory penetrated my fog from time to time. They might be in English, French, Spanish, or most often, German. They might be lines from a poem or song, a passage from a book, a scene from a movie, or some long-ago conversation. It was as if an earthquake had hit my brain, causing seismic shifts between tectonic plates that controlled time, memory, place, and identity. I would learn later that this was an accurate assessment of what had happened. At that time, the memories, while random and intrusive, were welcome and somewhat reassuring, like old friends seen after a long absence. Talking of old friends, where was my husband? Bruce had not been to see me for days. I had no idea where he was. Why was he not at my bedside night and day? I called him from the telephone on my nightstand to complain that he never came to see me; he never answered the phone. Sometimes someone I had never heard of answered the phone belligerently, said it was a wrong number, and didn't I know it was the middle of the night? No, I didn't know it was the middle of the night. It was all the same to me, night or day, and the numbers I dialed were most definitely my own home phone number. Did this idiot on the other end not know that I had had the same number for years, and why was he answering my phone anyway?

When Bruce finally showed up, I confronted him, crying, "Why haven't you been to see me all week? I know you were in the hospital because I heard them page you. Why can you find time to see your patients-strangers-and not your sick wife?"

Patiently, resignedly, he responded, "I have been to see you. I was here this morning and spent at least an hour with you before you went to PT."

"You did not!" I growled. "That was yesterday!"

My issues with time and place were not reserved for Bruce. A friend came and stayed by my bedside for an entire week. (That is what I thought, but it turned out that she came every evening after work but went about her life in between visits.) When they announced that grand rounds would take place on Saturday morning, I told everyone that Professor Aziz was coming to visit me.

When Dr. Odland next came to see me, I asked if I could go out at the weekend, after Dr. Aziz's visit, to see my brother. He looked at me quizzically, pondered for a moment and then said, "As long as you are back by dinnertime, you can go out for a few hours on Sunday. Where does your brother live?"

"Chesterfield."

Looking even more perplexed, he backed toward the door, mumbling, "I'll be back. I'm going to have a word with Bruce."

Elated, I began to make plans. I figured it would take about an hour to get from Oxford to Chesterfield and an hour to get back. That would give me two whole hours to visit with Keith. I would not even have to get out of the car to go to the bathroom. Thank God for catheters!

When Bruce deigned to visit several days later, I told him excitedly about my plans. He looked doubtful. "I'm not sure that I can do what you are asking."

"Bruce, what could you possibly have to do on Sunday that is more important than driving me to Chesterfield? I am not asking for much. It is just a few hours with my brother. Dr. Odland said it is fine with him as long as I am back for dinner. It will be my first trip out of this place, so why are you being so difficult? If you are too busy to drive me, I'll ask Sarah. She'll take me. We can use my car, and dammit, if she's busy, I'll just call a limo."

Bruce was unyielding. I was not going to Chesterfield. My pass was canceled I was not going anywhere! I was devastated and furious.

"It's a conspiracy," I railed. "How can you be so cruel? Bruce, why did you turn them all against me? How can you keep me from seeing Keith? You like him. Why won't you take me?"

The key to this conundrum was that Oxford, Chesterfield, Professor Aziz, and Keith were in England, and I was in Chicago. I had crossed the Atlantic by plane, hanging from the roof, and I still felt as if

I was hanging from the ceiling of my room when I was allowed to get into my bed. I had no idea that I was almost four thousand miles from Chesterfield.

The memory of my triumphant crossing of the Atlantic had blown away, along with all other fragments of recent history. I was alone on the ice of now, with no past and no future, and now was a nasty, frosty place to be.

The daily grind continued. Every evening I filled out my menu card or asked someone else to do it for me. I noticed that when I did it, I got eggs. When someone else did it, I got toast or oatmeal. Clearly, this vendetta was personal! They did not like me. Well, that was okay because I didn't like them either!

In the mornings I labored diligently for hours, only to find that I had stuffed two human legs into the same pant leg and resembled a gigantic fleece-clad mermaid. Guilty images of people I had tortured in a similar fashion emerged from the deep. Liam Coyle, an Irish housepainter, father of eight, and paraplegic from a car accident had vowed that he would come back and haunt me if I made him catch his catheter in his pant leg one more time. Beryl Francis, who had bilateral hip replacements, had told me she would see me in hell before she would use that ridiculous stocking aid I had brought for her. I had stood smug and superior in my pristine uniform at the foot of patients' beds and told them authoritatively that they could do whatever it was I thought they should be doing.

Once dressed, I bumped and scraped my way to the dayroom. Some days, if possible, I conned an unsuspecting staff member into pushing me; other days I had to do it all by myself. On a good day, it took me about an hour to get there; other days, two or three hours.

By about day eighteen—an arbitrary number because I lost count when some aide cleaned the crude pencil notches off my table—I was in a state of permanent rage but no one knew. I was in my "bunker" most of the time. The bunker was the garden in my mind, my secret hideaway. It was peaceful, quiet, with tulips of every color, a stream, and a maze in which to hide. Surrounded by an old stone wall, it was the place I went when the real world got too tough, scary, or painful to handle. I'd had it since I was a small child.

My mother was bipolar with an associated narcissistic personality disorder. She was never officially diagnosed as such and never received the treatment that could have transformed her life and the lives of her long-suffering spouse and wounded children. Only my experience in the psychiatric part of my training and hours of discussion with mental health professionals allowed me to put a name to what terrorized us all. In my bunker, people and events were just as I wanted them to be. There was no anger, no pain, and no shouting, just quiet, calm peace.

The great thing about the bunker was that nobody knew whether I was in it or not. I had perfected a repertoire of facial masks that ranged from interest to amusement, from acquiescence to questioning, from concern to outrage, and I could transition seamlessly between absence and presence. The thing about my expressions in bunker mode was that they weren't connected to anything. There was no feeling behind them; they were just masks.

I needed a place to go when Mum's moods swung from gregarious, smart, and funny to angry, dark, and vindictive. The wall provided a carapace to protect me when the verbal blows rained, hitting their target with uncanny precision. I could go there when words uttered in jest came back to bite me, sometimes months after an interchange, during which she had laughed loudest.

When I was in my bunker, I could communicate with the outside world as if I was in it. I could smile, carry on humorous conversations, and betray nothing of the fear, anger, sadness, or confusion that might lurk beneath. I never needed that bunker more than in those dark, disjointed days when I was not in possession of the facts of my own life, and the present was such a hard and painful place to be.

Day after day, I arrived at the dayroom, having been stuck in the doorway of my room, stuck in the hallway, and stuck—again—in the doorway of the dayroom. *The wheelchair really should be replaced. I worked here for seven years. I should not be stuck with this worthless piece of junk that's incapable of going in a straight line.* Those were among the more charitable statements that emanated from my mouth. Less politically correct ones were swallowed whole.

After one particularly trying journey, instead of easing into my place at the table and following my established protocol of ignoring the eggs if they were there and eating whatever else there was, I issued a proclamation. "If there are scrambled eggs on my plate today, I am throwing them at the wall!" Absolute silence followed, and I soon found myself being wheeled very quickly back to my room.

John never came to take me to PT.

"Yay!" The more appropriate response might have been "Uh-oh!" The psychiatrist arrived before lunch. I had been exhibiting signs of hostility and making threats that could be considered acts of aggression. I had shown signs of not being in touch with reality and seemed to be a little "depressed." He wondered if medication would help.

I wondered aloud why the light at the end of the tunnel always had to be powered by a pharmaceutical company.

"It's the stupid medication they are already giving me that is making me act the way I am, and if I had a plate of scrambled eggs at hand right now, I'd throw them at you!"

No new medication was ordered, and my routine continued except for one minor adjustment: I no longer went to breakfast. In fact, I no longer ate hospital food at all. It was a full-on boycott! My food was now brought in by family and friends. Dinner was still served, but either a visitor ate it, or it was returned, untouched, to Chez Cuisine Terrible from whence it came. The quality of the food was not good, and I learned one evening that I was not alone in that opinion. After much commotion, crashing, and clanking, a loud voice trumpeted, "Dinner trays have arrived!"

In the comparative quiet following the proclamation, I heard a male voice say, "Be still, my beating heart!"

Absolved of all concerns about sustenance, I was now free to concentrate on the delights of my day. First; the atrocities of daily living, then the Exercise Nazi, then lunch brought in by one of my surrogate family members. Nonny and Poppy might bring a tuna sandwich from the White Hen Pantry or Grandpa Ken might drive a cheese sandwich, freshly made by Grandma Jo, all the way from the western suburbs of Chicago.

I had arrived in the United States in my twenties to find myself in a country of over 350 million people, not a single one of whom was related to me. I had a relationship with just one person, and he was away from home much of the time. He was not only a busy oral and maxillofacial surgeon but also an elected member of the Illinois House of Representatives. Missing my own close if complicated family, I had set about the business of creating a surrogate one. Charter members of my American family were Stanley and Shirlee Winter, our first neighbors; and Ken and Jo Means, parents of Rich, a friend of Bruce's who had served as best man at our wedding.

After lunch, it was time for my nap, then occupational therapy, and then PT again. The situation around my nap started to get ugly. The nap was never officially approved. I just needed it. I was always tired, fatigued in a way that actually had little to do with how much sleep I had. The only reason that I got any sleep at all, apart from a sleeping pill, was that Bruce heated up a small down quilt in the dryer every night so that I had a brief period of comfort, snuggling in its soft, luxurious warmth. During the night, I was awakened frequently by noise, discomfort, or the nurse taking my blood pressure or offering medication. On one terrifying occasion, I lost my arm in the bed. I apparently rolled over on it and could not locate it. The arm was not part of me but the shoulder was, and it hurt most of the time. On top of lack of sleep, I was always dizzy. When I stood up, the world spun. At first, I could always find a nurse or aide to help me get out of the chair and on to the bed. Sometimes Bruce stopped by around lunchtime, and he would give me a hand. As it became harder to find staff who would cooperate, and I found myself leaning on food service, flower delivery people, or other people's visitors for a helping hand.

Chris was not happy. He gave Bruce a dressing down for enabling me to be noncompliant with my therapeutic regimen. That's PT speak for not making me stay up and work all day. A large sign appeared above my bed that read "UNDER NO CIRCUMSTANCES PUT THIS PATIENT BACK TO BED."

I was busted! Angry and resentful, I accused Bruce of joining forces with the enemy.

"My heart aches and a drowsy numbness pains my senses as though of hemlock I had drunk or emptied some dull opiate to the drains one-minute past and Lethe-wards had sunk."[6] Quoting Keats was clearly not going to get me off the

hook or win me any sympathy, judging from the stern expressions on the faces that surrounded me.

Around day twenty-one, another doctor stopped by to visit. I recognized him as a neurosurgeon with whom I had worked quite a lot. It was a semiprofessional visit so he asked a few questions about my surgery, looked at my head wound, and asked how I was doing in general. I told him about the dizziness and the world turning. He went out and returned holding what I assumed was my chart,

"I see they put you on Dilantin in Oxford. That is a drug that's used to prevent seizures, and a side effect can be vertigo," he said. "Let me talk to your primary doctor and see if we can discontinue, given that you are most likely past the threat of seizure by now."

The following day Dilantin was removed from my diet, and within twenty- four hours the vertigo was gone. Vindication! I was not a slacker. I was not a lazy good-for-nothing! I was not noncompliant; I was Dilantin-doped! A small smugness at confirmation that the medicine was at fault elevated my mood, if only temporarily. I had been fed a steady diet of humble pie with a side of crow ever since this thing happened to my head, and it felt good to have scored a point.

Now, with that the barrier to my progress removed, I was almost euphoric. I was ready to fling myself wholeheartedly into my routine. "Wholeheartedly" did not mean too much because although I was no longer dizzy and the world had stopped spinning, I was still incredibly fatigued. It was as if my body was running on a lower octane gas than it needed. A foot on the gas pedal produced only a sluggish response. The way I felt wasn't related to how much sleep I had. It was not physical tiredness but "brain fag", a term I found later in an old English text.

Although I was starting to feel better and would have liked to get around a bit more by myself, I was hindered by the fact that the replacement wheelchair provided failed to work any better than the original one. I complained to anyone who would listen that it would not go straight. There was something wrong with the wheels; they kept turning to the right. I offered a solution. Perhaps the air pressure in the tires was uneven. Dad had told me when he taught me to change a wheel on my first car that if I felt the car pulling in one direction or the other, the first thing I should do was check the pressure in the tires.

It seemed reasonable, but like most of my other suggestions, it fell on deaf ears. I asked for a tire pressure gauge but none came. Eventually, I received another pass to go home on Sunday afternoon. This time I knew I was in Chicago, and the distance from hospital to home was about twenty miles.

BIBLIOGRAPHY: CHAPTER 3

Bartleby. Entry for John Keats's,"Ode to a Nightingale." Accessed July 16, 2018. https://www.bartleby.com/101/624.html

Brooke, Rupert. *The Complete Poems of Rupert Brooke.* London: Sidwick & Jackson, Ltd., 1934.

Pfizer, Inc."About Dilantin." Accessed July 11, 2018. https://www.dilantin.com/about-dilantin

U.S. News and World Report. "CV Shahan Sarrafian, MD." Accessed July 11, 2018. http://health.usnews.com/doctors/shahan-sarrafian-826985

Wikipedia. John Keats's poem, "Ode to a Nightingale." Accessed July 11, 2018. https://en.wikipedia.org/wiki/Ode_to_a_Nightingale

CHAPTER 4

An Impatient Patient

THIS WAS A RED-LETTER DAY! FIVE WEEKS BEFORE, I HAD LEFT HOME for a week. On this day, what was left of me was going home for the first time but only for half a day. I was pushed to the car in the wheelchair, with my arm in a sling, my leg in a brace, and my pee bag discreetly positioned beside me. I had learned to stand, pivot, and ease myself into the car but could not yet walk independently.

The journey from the hospital took about forty minutes, and looking out of the window made me drowsy. We finally arrived at the house, and I felt tears prickling behind my eyelids. Our driveway is long and flanked by tall trees. I was conscious of the sun dappling through the leaves. It was early October, and some leaves were already looking dry and ready to fall. I had found the house, originally, after weeks of trawling the neighborhood with a couple of realtors. The first time we turned into the driveway, it had been like rounding a corner and finding myself back in England. I had felt completely at home— the house, the garden, the pond instantly familiar, although I had never seen them before. I developed a relationship with the house that reminded me of the first Mrs. Wilcox in E. M. Forster's *Howard's End.* More than bricks and mortar, it became a place of refuge and a hobby, as I spent years renovating it to meet the ever-changing needs of our family.

Bruce stopped the car right next to the pond in front of the house. He opened the windows so I could feel the warmth of the sun.

"Season of mists and mellow fruitfulness, close-bosom friend of the maturing sun." Keats' "Autumn" says it best. What a welcome change it was from frigid air conditioning and the smell of Lysol—and worse—that I had left behind.

I saw Sarah, Sandy, Nonny, Poppy, and a few of our friends waiting outside the house. I looked at the pond and saw not only our two stately rented swans but five gangly, stubbly adolescent cygnets as well. Over to the right in the paddock, our two elderly horses were grazing sedately, and I felt overcome by gratitude to be back in my own space, even if the powers that be would only let me stay here for a very short time.

Bruce waited for a while and then asked if I noticed anything different. I looked around and then saw a newly installed waterfall at the far side of the pond. He had it put in to welcome me home. Knowing how much I love the wildlife that comes to the pond in winter, he had done this so that the pond would not freeze. Tears trickled as I reached for his hand, no words necessary.

I was hesitant to go into the house, eyeing the robust step up to the front door. I was ready to settle for staying outside when José, who helps us take care of the horses and the garden, appeared from the path to the old barn with a wooden ramp he had built so he could push me up the front step in my wheelchair. His kindness pushed me over the precipice to sobs of appreciation and sadness, feelings I did not recognize and could not begin to manage. Bruce brought the wheelchair to my side of the car, and I pushed myself out with my legs pointing toward the ground, thanking God that it was an SUV, and I could slide out with a reasonable amount of decorum. "Screw decorum," I mumbled to myself, confronting the reality that I had a bag of pee slung over my arm.

Once inside the house, I was greeted enthusiastically by our dogs. Much sniffing, licking, petting, and patting ensued. They did not seem to notice anything different about me. I must have smelled the same to them. Chloe and Eloise, the Siamese kittens, hovered, arching their backs and circling until they mustered the courage to approach and rub themselves against my pant leg.

I had only a few hours of freedom and was soon loaded back into the car. By the time we passed the trees at the entrance to the driveway, I think I was already asleep, like a kid going home from a birthday party.

Soon after my home visit, a nurse came into my room one morning and told me that it was time for the catheter to go. I foolishly thought that I would immediately be able to go to the bathroom by myself.

There were many times when I felt an urgent need to pee and used the tiny amount of power afforded me to summon a nurse to take me to the bathroom. The nurse arrived eventually, after about six pulls of the bell cord, and huffily informed me that I never go to the bathroom; I use a catheter. I did not care for this particular nurse because she got right up in my face and had very potent bad breath. I nicknamed her Hallie Tosis All the nurses had bad breath, and Bruce's was the worst of all. Because he was an oral surgeon, one would think he would be able to do something about it. I raised the subject of mouthwash with him a few times, but he never took the hint.

As the nurse removed the catheter, I felt one barbed wire being eased slowly but excruciatingly through a tunnel of nerve endings. Once it was out, I found that contrary to my expectation that all would be well, I could not pee at all. The nurses brought in a commode, seated me on this makeshift throne, and turned on the faucets in the sink full blast. Toilet training! *How old am I? Will I get a sticker if I oblige?* After the desired result was reached, I was allowed back to bed or to perform whatever chore was expected of me at the time. Three or more times each day, we repeated the routine with me on the throne and the water running full blast. I was Pavlov's dog. It worked! Every time the nurse turned on the water, I peed. The problem was that I was not always on the throne when someone turned on water. Accidents occurred. I wet the bed. I wet the chair. I was humiliated! People were not always nice about it. Hallie Tosis said pointedly that she had better things to do than keep cleaning up after me. She ordered me to try harder to control my bladder. This was the situation: I did not know I needed to go and then someone turned on water, and I had to go immediately. It took at least an hour for anyone to respond to the buzzer, and then it was too late.

I had enough of depending upon unreliable people and decided to take matters into my own hands. I did not have time to sit around and wait for a nurse to deign to respond to my call. The next time someone turned on water and I had to go, I made the momentous decision to get off the bed and onto the commode by myself. I got two legs off the bed and planted on the floor. I got my one hand on the throne. *So far, so good!* The next thing I knew, I hit the floor with a thump. I had no idea how that happened. Since I was close to the nurse's station, the thump was loud enough to attract attention. A nurse rushed in and yelled, "I need an assist in here!" Another person arrived, and the two of them manhandled me back in the bed, chastising me for getting out of bed by myself and for being wet. I got another demerit! There was a lot of rumbling about incident reports, and I knew that was not a good thing. Nobody likes to drop a patient. The hospital could get into a lot of trouble. The Joint Commission on the Accreditation of Healthcare Organizations disapproves of patients being dropped. *Good! I hope they get what's coming to them!* I felt no sense of responsibility for falling. It was their fault. They should have come when I called.

A few nights later, while tucked up in bed, I felt the call again. I tried to summon help but the bell cord had fallen off the bed and was dangling by the side. No problem! I could reach it if I just got a little closer to the edge of the bed. It took a herculean effort to move in the bed. I could not pull in the direction I was going because I had nothing to pull with. I had to push with my unaffected arm—damn the political correctness; it is my good arm—my leg and my back. I wondered when they started making sheets out of Velcro.

I half sat and leaned over to see how far away from the cord I was and—*splat*—I hit the deck! I was scared. I had fallen from a great height, from what I perceived as my bed hanging from the ceiling, and hit my head on something really hard. The door to my room was open, and once more two people appeared by my side. This time they did not attempt to pick me up. They had a conversation about me as if I were not there. I wished fervently that I were not.

"She hit her head on the drip stand," said one.

"She'll need x-rays," opined the other. "Better call the resident on call."

I had heard this particular doctor paged many times, always at night. His name was Dr. Badlani. The first time I heard his name, I thought it was Bin Laden and wondered how I knew him. I had hoped I would never need his services. This night as I heard him paged for my room number, I thought, *Ask not for whom the bell tolls; it tolls for thee.*

Dr. Badlani arrived quickly. Of medium height and build, wearing blue scrubs, he gave me a cursory examination and asked if I hurt anywhere. Before I got a chance to answer, he ordered x-rays of my head, shoulder, and hip. I was puzzled but compliant. I was actually in no position to be anything but compliant, crumpled up in a heap on the floor. Two men, also wearing scrubs, banged through the door pushing a cart. They put a big puffy collar around my neck, covered me with a sheet, and lifted me onto a gurney. I got the distinct feeling that I was in trouble again. There was grumbling about the lateness of the hour and having to wait for the technician on call to come in. I had better things to do with my time too, though I would have been hard- pressed to name any.

After what seemed like about twelve hours, I was taken back to my room, there having been no evidence of bony injury. That would not be confirmed until the x-rays were read by the radiologist the following day, so I was to remain on bed rest until further notice. Yes! I love Dr. Badlani! My joy was short-lived because there was the matter of the incident report. This was my second, third, or maybe even fourth fall in as many days.

The physiatrist, the physician in charge of the Rehabilitation Unit, came to see me while I was confined to bed, pending the radiologist's report. He asked a lot of questions about my therapies and how I was doing. I really did not want to discuss any of that stuff, so I deftly steered the conversation toward the fact that his dog has just had puppies. He had mentioned that earlier. He wondered if I would like to talk to the psychologist or the social worker.

"About what?" I asked, surprised by the suggestion.

"Well," he said, "after an experience such as yours it is not uncommon for a patient to be anxious or depressed."

"Well, I'm not. I am just fine."

He looked at me kindly and said, "We are going to have to start thinking about you going home, and adjustments will have to be made."

"My bedroom and bathroom are on the ground floor," I snapped. "No adjustments will be necessary."

"That's not what I meant," he said. "I meant you might need help adjusting to the reality of your new life in a wheelchair."

Bruce, who was becoming used to having his head bitten off for any minor infraction, chiefly his abandonment of me, ventured a suggestion. I had seen a grief counselor before, Dr. Michael McNulty, and liked him, and maybe Dr. McNulty would come to see me in the hospital. I injected that there was no need for Dr. McNulty to get involved because nobody had died. I returned my attention to the physiatrist, again changing the subject as quickly as possible.

"I can't think about going home yet because I can't walk," I explained. "Once my leg comes back, I'll be out of here immediately. I don't need my arm, as I'm already doing almost everything with one." My asking him if he had any new pictures of his puppies signaled that the conversation about my future plans was at an end.

Once the radiologist confirmed that I had no broken bones or concussion from the fall, therapy started again in earnest.

I was much better at getting dressed but found the process tedious and annoying. When confronted with any unpleasant task, I tried to get it over with as quickly as possible. The result was that mistakes were made. One morning I could not stand up in PT. After a brief generalized panic that my paralysis had spread, it became apparent that my immobilization had something to do with the way my pants were arranged. Francine, the PT assistant, heaved me to my feet with my newest permanent accessory, the gait belt. Once I was up, she gave a gigantic yank to the waistband of my pants and admonished me, "Don't you be coming down here with your pants on twisted!"

There were days when one of the sleeves of my jacket was empty, days when I had one shoe, and days when I passed my own cursory inspection but clearly did not meet the sartorial expectations of others. They lost no time in letting me know if I was not up to their high standards.

PT consisted of standing in the parallel bars, supported by Chris and John or Francine, and trying to maintain my balance while one or the other tried to push me over. When they pushed to the right, I had no trouble at all. I stood my ground. When they pushed to the left, it was a different story. I started to fall until a brisk pull on the gait belt snapped me back to attention. They always stood me up facing the mirror. I hated that! It was supposed to provide visual cues, but for me it was very unpleasant. The crazy woman with the

Mohawk hairstyle bothered me. She looked a bit like an evil twin of my auntie Mary. She kept watching me, glaring at me as if I were the enemy. It was the same in speech therapy, except I was not going there anymore. Speech had been discontinued because the patient was not cooperating. As if! After I stood for a while, we went to the raised mat, where I lay and stared at the leg in front of me and tried to make it move. It resolutely refused. After PT, John occasionally pushed me back to my room. On a number of occasions, I heard blood-curdling screams emanating from within the curtained shrine of a patient's room. I turned to look at John, questioningly.

"Knee replacement," he said.

"Remind me never to have one of those," I quipped. I understood that these were the patients from the dayroom who had their legs sticking out in front of them. John explained that the screaming was because the patients' legs were attached to a machine that was forcibly bending the new knee.

When I first became aware of my surroundings, my room was filled with flowers. It reminded me of a funeral parlor. Flower arrangements came every day, sometimes two or three at a time. I couldn't cope with the cards, so they were deposited in a drawer in the table next to the bed. It would be months before I was capable of reading the cards and counting them. There were over a hundred. It was in the midst of my botanical garden in vases that my social life was conducted. I had visitors every day. Many brought food.

The news had been widely broadcast that I could not (or would not) eat what was served in the hospital because they never brought what I ordered. There were certain foods that I really craved; rice pudding was one of them. My friend Gail, a former speech and language pathologist herself—but I did not hold that against her—brought gourmet rice pudding a few times a week. Always immaculate in business attire, she produced the rice pudding from her briefcase. Pina, a talented chef with a mass of dark curls framing her Italian face, brought whole meals. Sometimes there was enough for several days. Nancy and Shehryah brought food from my favorite Indian restaurant. Amina brought dal. One night, in a particularly daring escapade, Sarah smuggled me out of the hospital in a wheelchair, and we went to a Middle Eastern restaurant down the street. We had no pass, and nobody knew we were gone. It was a thrill to be outside, if only for a brief time. Sarah reminded me, periodically, to wipe the food off the side of my mouth.

One day there was a big buzz because Bruce's nephew, Kenneth, a famous clothing and shoe designer, was coming to visit me. He had a huge fan base among the staff, and my stock rose as everyone crowded around me in the gym to pay their respects to him. Bruce's sister and her husband flew in with him, and I was pleased to have their moral support as I showed off my sitting, standing, and ball-kicking skills.

Saturdays were very long days. They used to be the shortest day of the week when I had to cram in the week's shopping, riding lessons for the girls and myself, haircuts, and all the motherly and wifely duties that had fallen off my priority list during the week. Now they dragged with just one session of PT in the morning and then nothing for the rest of the day. It was supposed to be time for rest and recuperation.

Bruce and the girls came, usually in staggered shifts. Bill, my long-time friend and administrative assistant, visited most Saturdays. A retired air force master sergeant, he had shown up years before in answer to a request for administrative assistance from a temporary placement agency. Expecting the customary young female candidate, I was taken aback by the arrival of a middle-aged man with military bearing and a firm handshake, who addressed me crisply as "ma'am." We hired him, and he stayed.

Nonny and Poppy, otherwise known as Stanley and Shirlee Winter, also came on Saturdays. They had been integral to our lives since shortly after our wedding. We moved into an apartment, across the hall from theirs right after we were married. One evening, we opened our doors at the same time, and our black cat, Grantham, named for my hometown, decided to explore their apartment. He shot across the hallway and disappeared in an instant. Four adult humans, as of then unacquainted, were united in amused astonishment. Introductions were made, and an instantaneous bond forged that would last until both passed away many years later. We were in need of them, and, as it turned out, they were in need of us too.

A Saturday evening tradition evolved. Nonny and Poppy brought in dinner. It might be a chicken roasted in Nonny's large stainless steel Dutch oven. It was in that same container that they brought a ham to our house every Christmas. This simple Christmas gesture was rendered remarkable by the fact that Nonny and Poppy were Jewish. An alternative meal was Chinese food delivery, pizza, or some other imported delight, and it was always accompanied by a homemade cake. Cakes were Nonny's specialty. Whether lemon with white frosting, chocolate with chocolate frosting and sprinkles, banana with chocolate frosting, or carrot with cream cheese frosting, they came in the same brown and cream cake carrier that I came to know for twenty-five years and were always delicious.

Whoever came to visit on Saturdays shared in the feast, and the nursing staff eagerly awaited the remains of the cake. The evening always started with me in high spirits, laughing and talking, regaling everyone with progress made. It often was truncated by my falling asleep or becoming so mentally spent that I could no longer participate.

Monday nights were "dog therapy." Early in my stay I was invited to participate. My response: "Of course I will!"

I adore animals and missed my own pets desperately. I asked if Chloe and Eloise, the Siamese kittens we had rescued, could visit. They were so tiny when they were dropped off, neither tipping the scale at one pound, that we had fed them special formula from bottles no bigger than our fingers. Their minute paws had clung to us, and both had grown up assuming that they were human in everything but scale. No, they could not come, nor could my own dogs.

Anyhow, when Monday night came, Bruce wheeled me to the gym, along with Sarah and Sandy. Within seconds of arriving, I was being slobbered over by Duncan, an English bulldog. He bore a remarkable resemblance to Winston Churchill. Duncan's trainer issued a few simple commands, and then it was my turn. I told him to come, sit, lie down, and roll over. He dutifully obeyed my every command. Duncan was the first being to do as I asked in a very long time.

As another diversion from the boredom of the evenings, I was invited to play Bingo. I almost blew a gasket at the very idea. Bingo was for patients and old ladies in church halls, not me. *I will not go to Bingo!* I thought.

I ran those Bingo sessions on Thursday nights, with Sarah and Sandy thrilled to help the patients cover numbers with cardboard tokens. As small girls, they had delighted in riding on the laps of patients in wheelchairs, going to the doctors' lounge with Bruce for doughnuts, and eating dinner in the cafeteria. The same food I declined to eat had been a treat for them, mainly because they loaded the large, pink plastic trays with anything they chose.

One morning the head nurse informed me that I was to be the subject of a case conference. Everyone who had anything to do with my treatment would be there. The purpose of the conference was for the clinical team to review my progress and set comprehensive, achievable goals for the remainder of my stay with the ultimate objective of preparing me to return home as independent as possible. Could the head nurse possibly think I did not know that? How many of those conferences had I attended over the years? The venue was the conference room, the same as always. Dr. Khalili would not preside, as he had in my time. He had passed away, with the help of Dr. Kevorkian, after being felled so unjustly by some hideous form of cancer. I missed Dr. Khalili. His funeral had been beautiful, a Taizė filled with musical and poetical tributes to his life and work.

A doctor I didn't really know would be in charge of my conference, the one who only talked to me about his dog having puppies. I was given a choice to attend or not. I chose to go. I was not terribly interested in what they had to say, and it would not be like the old days, but I didn't want a bunch of people I didn't trust talking about me behind my back.

Once in the conference room, I saw Linda; Chris; Hallie Tosis; the nameless speech and language pathologist; the internist, Dr. Odland; and the head inquisitor, the physiatrist.

The proceedings started with someone giving my name, rank, and serial number. "Female, fifty-seven [like in the newspapers], suffered a massive bleed in the right parietal lobe; craniotomy performed in England; transferred to this hospital on 9/11/03." So far, so good; they were getting it right. It went downhill from there. They went around the table and, one after another, smeared my character, criticized me, and, in some instances, uttered outright falsehoods. Chris said I had started out poorly and had been unwilling to put in the necessary effort to maximize my recovery. Ambulation did not appear to be likely, given that there had been no recovery in my left leg. He added that I was also resistant to propelling my own wheelchair from my room to the gym.

"The nerve of him!" I muttered under my breath, stifling German curse words. I was starting to get annoyed, hot, red-faced, and agitated. "Who wouldn't be resistant to careening along in a chair that only goes in circles and launches off, of its own volition, down a bloody great hill that ends at a concrete wall?"

Linda said I was doing "somewhat" better but had a tendency to be impulsive. My desire to complete the atrocities of daily living in a hurry frequently led to mistakes and poor outcomes. *Damn twisted pants*, I thought. Linda went on to say I was doing better in OT but still was exhibiting signs of denial and neglect. (I had *not* done anything wrong that I needed to deny, and exactly who or what was I neglecting?) I had not done well on the "House, Clock, Flower" test, in which I had been required to complete an infantile drawing of a house, a flower and a clock, Linda said. That was an outright lie. I had aced that test. Linda had said so herself. That the scrawl that resembled a spider crawling through ink appeared only on the right side of the page had escaped my notice.

There was a concern that my shoulder was subluxed, meaning the ball of bone on top of my arm was slipping out of the socket of the shoulder joint. That was not true either! That happened ages ago when I fell off Socks, my unpredictable quarter horse. I had not exactly fallen off; he had dumped me in a puddle. That was his way. He would be all nice and cooperative one minute, and then the next he would stop and dump his rider over the fence.

They said the sling I was wearing was to keep my arm from falling further out of the socket. I was to keep wearing it except while exercising in OT. I did not think it was necessary, and it was really uncomfortable. It had been years since I'd fallen off Socks. Why did I still need a sling?

Nobody ever asked for my opinion.

Just as I started to tire of it and thought of going back to my room, things really went downhill.

Hallie Tosis talked about my falling as if it were my fault. Foul-smelling lies skunked out of her mouth as she concurred with Linda that I was impulsive—"reckless," even. I was outraged! Was anyone going to take this nonsense seriously?

Who did not come when I pushed the bell? Who propped me on the side of the bed and left me there when she went to answer another patient's bell? Who let go of me as I was executing my perfect pivot between the bed and the wheelchair? Who did she think she was? Let she who was without blame cast the first stone.

Next, there was a report from the social worker that I had exhibited aggression and hostility toward food service employees. This was followed by a statement that I was not cooperating with or benefitting from speech therapy and had therefore been discontinued. Good! I never had a speech problem to begin with, and I was only there because the insurance company required that a patient attend all three therapies to justify hospitalization. I knew that game. They just wanted to be paid for having me there.

Dr. Odland, the internist, said my blood pressure was not yet where he wanted it, and he would continue to experiment with different combinations of drugs.

"Who can wonder that my blood pressure isn't where you want it to be? You try living in this place. You try listening to people telling lies about you," I snorted under my breath. "And you can throw any drug you want at me, as long as it has nothing to do with Dilantin, depression, or pain."

Dr. Odland expressed concern about any stress I might be under because that could affect my blood pressure. He went on to say he believed that stress was a major contributing factor to my spiking blood pressure and, consequently, the stroke.

"Don't take my blood pressure now please," I begged.

My response to being giving an opportunity to ask questions was to launch into a damning condemnation of the wheelchair I was using. I listed its defects—it went in circles, never straight lines; it banged into things and constantly smashed my elbow into the wall. I suggested that the manufacturer should be sued. It was an Everest & Jennings; they were supposed to be the best, but mine was the

Ford Pinto of wheelchairs! If I got it going fast enough, it would burst into flames. Might I please have a new one? In my closing argument, I informed the group, as forcefully as I could, that there was no reason that they should continue to imprison me against my will.

The conference concluded with the doctor recommending additional in-patient treatment, the goal of which would be to prepare me to go home in a wheelchair. They would order a new one, as requested. The doctor also suggested that I should receive counseling to deal with the transition. My ears perked up at this. No matter what they said, I would not go to counseling. I had no desire to pick at the scabs of life's wounds or rake painful memories from under the fallen leaves of time, while someone doled out tissues and asked me how I felt. How I felt was nobody's business but my own.

There was but one spark of humor in the whole proceeding. When they were going on and on about my wanting to do everything quickly to get it over with, Dr. Odland interjected, "That is not pathology; she is always like that." Yes! Somebody knew the real me!

A colleague from work visited later that evening and told me that everyone was praying for my recovery.

"Could you ask them to be specific?" I asked. "Could you ask them to focus on my left leg?"

"I'll pass on the message," she said, gliding effortlessly out of the door.

Later that night I was in my flower-filled room, watching a video of *Pride and Prejudice*—the one with the divine Colin Firth—for the umpteenth time. Sandy had smuggled in a small television and a bunch of videos from home. I love Jane Austen and can never get enough of her. Listening to her familiar dialogue relaxed me more than any drug. I was having my nightly dose before the medicine cart arrived with its cargo of pills.

Books and magazines lay piled up on my bed table, but they were too heavy to hold and too difficult to maneuver with one hand so I pushed them away for another day. I made every excuse possible for why I was not reading. I, who read a couple of books a week, was pushing books away. Why? That did not make sense. The truth would not emerge for several months. I could not read. I could recognize words and say them aloud, but I did not know what they meant.

I was drifting into a state of well-being, with Mrs. Bennett's familiar whining words lulling me to sleep, when I noticed a figure in my doorway with a cane pointed in my direction. It was Señora Lopez, my next-door neighbor. She was a slight woman of about seventy-five, who, from what I knew, spoke no English. She advanced on me, cane outstretched and pointing menacingly at my head.

"Mis flores," she said. *"Tu tienes mis flores!"*

Oh my God, she thought I had stolen her flowers.

"Mis flores, son mis flores, regalos de mi familia y de mis amigos."

I grasped for the right Spanish words. She was undeterred. Mercifully, the bell cord was within my reach this time, and I summoned help. With Señora Lopez's cane poised to delete whatever remained of my pride, prejudice, sense, and sensibility, a nurse burst through the door and removed the threat. She explained that Señora Lopez had not only had a stroke but also was in an advanced state of dementia. She meant me no harm. What kind of a place was this?

Whether it was the prayers of my colleagues, the surge of adrenaline resulting from Señora Lopez's aborted assassination attempt, or merely the natural progression of events, the following morning when Chris told me to tighten my quads and lift my leg, I did. It was cause for great celebration.

Bruce was paged. He did not always hear the overhead paging system, but that time he did. He arrived, looking somewhat alarmed, to be given a demonstration of me lifting the leg about two inches off the mat. I gave repeat performances throughout the day to anyone who was willing to watch.

It was shaky at first, but it changed my life. Just those few degrees of movement meant that I would not be going home wheelchair-bound. Independent ambulation was my new goal.

"Tighten, tighten, tighten, and shift the weight," bellowed Chris. I tried to tighten my newfound muscles, but somewhere along the way, the leg beneath me had turned into a prosthesis. It was not just that I was wearing an AFO; it was as if the whole leg was made of cast bronze, a Rodin leg. It didn't bend where the knee should be; it just flung to the side. I recited, "Tighten, tighten, tighten, shift the weight," and the leg executed a perfect arc. Next, I tightened, tightened, tightened and shifted the weight to the other leg and took my first real step.

Chris explained the components of gait: "Stance, strike, and swing, Dusseldorf. Stance, strike, and swing. Tighten, tighten, tighten, shift, and swing."

"Easy for you to say, Cologne." This German name for him was more polite than others I considered, and he always smelled good.

"Ja! Ja! Du kannst. You can do it; you can do it," he persisted.

"I have said that to more patients than you have had hot dinners," said I. *"Ich kann nicht!"* In this combative manner, I covered the length of the parallel bars, puffing and swearing. "Once this is over, I'll be doing the swinging and striking with my fists, not with my leg." I was careful to laugh when I said this because I was acutely mindful of the charges brought against me at the parole hearing; I mean, case conference. I did not want to give the impression that I was angry and "hostile" again. That still smarted. In truth, Chris and I had a good relationship. He was an excellent therapist, and the banter between us was always good-natured.

The therapy sessions continued, and I started to make real progress. I was promoted to using a straight cane—no walker for me! That was because there was fear that I would go in circles with the walker, much as I did with the wheelchair. I took it as a compliment that I had a plain cane and was not to become one of those people who shuffle along bent almost double. I would stand erect, at least as long as someone had a tight hold on the gait belt. Instead of raised mat and parallel bars, I now stood in the middle of the gym and took wild kicks at a large ball. The theory, according to Chris, was that if I could stand on my affected leg and kick the ball, one day in the distant future, I would walk without a cane. I thought that was about as likely as my playing soccer for England, but I humored him anyway.

Afternoons in occupational therapy always seemed to involve testing, followed by exercises using springs, slings, and things. I lifted weights and sanded a piece of wood with an implement that required two hands. My right hand held one handle, and the other one was enclosed in a strange-looking mitt. A T-shaped Velcro strap held my fingers curved around the dowel rod handle. My unaffected arm pushed the sander up a piece of wood clamped at angle on the table in front of me. The other one dragged along with it. The reluctant claw tried to escape the mitt but the Velcro was too tight. It gave up and went along for the ride. Next, after the arm was placed in a sling, and with gravity eliminated, I was tasked with making "gross movements."

Stacking cones on top of one another or putting pegs in holes on a table, I made some truly gross movements, flinging my back and neck around, wildly trying to achieve the desired effect. I was discouraged and bothered. Sweat trickled annoyingly between my shoulder blades, soaking my aptly named sweatshirt. I could not control the hand; it had no idea whether it was holding something or not. This seemed like a monumental waste of time. Had I really done this for a living? I was reminded by one of the OTs that I was or had been a hand therapist. I was a charter member of that elite group called the American Society of Hand Therapists. There were none of the telltale black, blue, and yellow skin or jagged scars of an industrial injury on the hand in front of me; no neat rows of sutures compatible with a tendon transfer; no hairy big toe masquerading as a thumb; no hooks Super Glued onto fingernails; no dynamic splints. I could not work my magic on this hand. Whose hand was it anyway? Trapped in a maze of pulleys, with the Velcro glove once again holding the intransigent fingers in place, I yanked with the unaffected hand, and the other one ground slowly upward. I used the verb "to grind" advisedly because my shoulder, which I now knew most definitely did belong to me, hurt with every millimeter of movement.

"The pain starts in the scapular region and extends through the shoulder girdle, radiating down to the elbow," I explained to the doctor when he made rounds. He looked suitably impressed but somewhat surprised that I used clinical terminology. He ordered iontophoresis—I'd never heard of this treatment, but I got my first taste of passive therapy, where something was done to and for me, instead of my having to do all of the work. All I had to do was sit in a chair while the therapist smeared gel around my shoulder blade and attached electrodes that emitted a slow, pulsing heat. What a treat!

John no longer transported me to and from therapy, so I had to make my own way. At first I went by wheelchair. I pushed, scooted, and bumped to the top of the slope and then let go and rolled down into the gym. Sometimes I went down faster than intended and almost collided with equipment or other patients, earning a rebuke or two as

I screeched to a halt, my shoe sole leaving skid marks on the polished floor. Going back was more of a chore, but the heel of my sneaker became proficient at digging in to the floor and allowing me to pull with my calf muscles. I did not use the big wheels at all—too treacherous.

Visitors often stopped by while I was in therapy. They were welcome as long as they encouraged me and stayed out of the therapist's way.

I never really thought of rehabilitation as a spectator sport, but my family and friends seemed to enjoy it. Sandy often came to PT and made me laugh as we focused on the antics of other patients. We observed one tiny woman, dressed only in a hospital gown and a diaper, speeding along on her walker while her diaper slowly slid down to her ankles, causing her to screech to a halt. We dared not make eye contact, but Sandy was holding my gait belt, and I could feel her shaking with silent laughter beside me.

Eventually, I was steady enough to walk to and from the gym with one of the PT staff hanging on to my gait belt. The walks got longer, and on one momentous day, Chris announced that we were going to walk outside. It was a beautiful, warm, early October day—perfect weather for my maiden voyage. Our itinerary called for walking from my room to the elevator and then taking the elevator down four floors to the lobby.

From the lobby, we passed through the automatic doors, made a right turn, and walked about thirty yards down Webster Avenue. We rested for a bit, with me leaning on Chris's muscular arm, and then we turned around and made our way back. Tighten, tighten, tighten, shift, and swing became more erratic on each repetition. By the time we arrived back, I was completely exhausted.

Chris gave me a bear hug and said, *"Wünderbar, Düsseldorf, Sehr gut!"* *"Danke schoen, Cologne."* I sighed.

The next afternoon, I returned from occupational therapy to find a visitor. I positioned my wheelchair beside the bed, leaving the large pleather chair available for my visitor. A youngish man, medium height, bald, wearing a tweed jacket and a smile of infinite gentleness walked toward me, hand outstretched. He looked familiar but I was not sure who he was. As he grasped my hand and said his name—Mike McNulty—I started to laugh. Great pealing guffaws burst forth, my shoulders heaved, and tears of mirth coursed down my cheeks.

I couldn't remember why or how I knew Dr. McNulty, beyond the vague recollection that it had something to do with a run of bad luck but I couldn't stop laughing. Choking through the gales of laughter, I managed to spit out a question or two.

"How did you find me? Can you believe this? Am I not the most potent magnet for misfortune you have ever come across? What shall I do for an encore?" No matter how I tried, I could not pull myself together and be serious. I knew Dr. McNulty had come to try to help me, but there was not a single thing I needed to talk to him about. Whatever the bad things that had caused me to talk to him in the past had been, they were not troubling me now. I currently had no problems whatsoever, beyond a need to get out of this place and get on with my life. Such was my degree of denial at this stage.

Sundays afternoons at home were helping me to put things back together. It was only a few hours, but it was a glimpse into my old world. It helped me to anchor my floating thoughts and start building bridges back to what used to be my life—days when life was getting up in the morning, going to work, making dinner for the family, going to the barn to feed the horses. Days when I would get up very early and drive to or be picked up by limousine and taken to O'Hare Airport to fly to somewhere I was needed, not as an OT but as a consultant in human capital risk management, no longer working with sick individuals but sick organizations. Days that had ended with my falling into what our family calls the "Big Bed," with Bruce and a cat or dog or two—except when I was on the road, in which case it would be a hotel, alone. Days when I knew exactly who I was and where I was going. Days when I was in charge, "the boss," made my own decisions and told others what to do. All that was a long way from the confused, dependent, drooling person with food on her face that was my new reality.

I was still having a lot of difficulty keeping my head together. Visits from colleagues helped create a framework of familiarity. They brought me news of people and events and used vocabulary that anchored me in a world away from being a patient and my recent experiences.

Most of them talked about when I would come back. One or two did not— they were the ones with clinical backgrounds. They talked to Bruce and turned up the volume so he could hear them. The one of my faculties that escaped unscathed was my hearing, so I heard them too. One talked about the severity of the stroke, how devastating it was, and how I would never be the same. Another told Bruce that the stress of the job would to be too much for me.

This may be over-dramatization, but the thought of whether I would or would not go back to work had not occurred to me. I had not thought much about anything beyond getting through each day. Early on, one of the doctors had asked me to state what percentage of recovery I would settle for.

"Ninety percent." I had answered, having no clue what that meant or how to measure. From the moment I overheard that my job would be too much for me, I knew I was going back. I did not know how or when, but I would be back. I asked to join the next staff meeting by phone and cheerfully thanked everyone for their good wishes and support. I told them I would see them soon.

After nine weeks, four Sunday afternoons at home, and a house visit with "the team" to determine what adaptive equipment I would need, I was going home for good! I would receive therapy at home three times a week. The next leg of my journey began …

BIBLIOGRAPHY: CHAPTER 4

American Society of Hand Therapists. Website. Accessed July 12, 2018. https://www.asht.org/

Chicago Relationship Center. "About Michael McNulty." Accessed July 10, 2018. http://www.chicagorelationshipcenter.com/about-michael

Forster, E. M. *Howard's End.* London: Edward Arnold, 1910.

Kiernan, Louise and Gottesman, Andrew. *Chicago Tribune.* "Doctor Turns to Kevorkian," 11/23/93. Accessed July 10, 2018. https://doctors.advocatehealth.com/i/paul-odland-chicago-internal-medicine

Thorek "CV for Ravi Badlani, MD." Accessed July 11, 2018. http://www.thorek.org/ravi-badlani/

U.S. News and World Report. "CV Shahan Sarrafian, MD." Accessed July 11, 2018. http://health.usnews.com/doctors/shahan-sarrafian-826985.

Wikipedia. John Keats's poem,"To Autumn." Accessed July 11, 2018. https://en.wikipedia.org/wiki/To_Autumn

Wikisource. John Donne's "Meditation XVII," from *Devotions upon Emergent Occasions.* Accessed July 10, 2018. https://en.wikisource.org/wiki/Meditation_XVII

CHAPTER 5

The Same but Different

IT CAME AS SOMETHING OF A SHOCK TO BE HOME AND ACTUALLY STAY there. It was the same dear place I had left all those weeks before, my little bit of England in America. There were the same occupants, same routine, and same schedule for everyone else. To me, it was profoundly different. There were now traps and obstacles where none had existed before. The steps to the front door and steps between rooms, scarcely noticed before, became almost insurmountable hurdles to independence.

Doors through which I had flown before—always in as hurry, perpetually late—were too narrow to accommodate my scooting through in a wheelchair. I used the chair on days when I was too weak, tired, or banged up from falling to attempt ambulation. There were many of those days, so I was often stuck somewhere in the house.

There was also a new pecking order. I had ruled this roost before, but now others were in charge. I had cooked the meals, but now they arrived in Pyrex dishes, courtesy of those same people who had fed me in the hospital. Ken, still tall and erect in his eighties, immaculately turned out, never a steel-gray hair out of place, drove all the way from the western suburbs to deliver Jo's legendary comfort food, with a proud beam warming his gentle countenance.

Jo, elegant and beautiful without benefit of a plastic surgery or hair dye, was a true Renaissance woman: wife, mother, and grandmother, she was a beacon for enlightened feminism, teaching, mentoring, leading young women, and running for political office when in her sixties, long before it was fashionable to do so.

Nonny and Poppy steered their elderly Cadillac northward as often as they could, bearing culinary gifts, always accompanied by the much-loved cake. Nonny was inspirational in the way she lived her life. Petite, hair now blonde and stylish, her skin was so white you could see the blue blood running through her veins. She was a perpetual cheerleader for our family, despite weathering her share of tragedy. She'd lost first a nephew and then her beloved son, but she bore her losses with courage and grace. Only the slightest shadow in her bright blue eyes hinted at the sadness beneath.

As a young woman, Nonny had formed a musical act known as the Marin Sisters. They toured the country singing with the big bands of the time, a remarkable feat for well-bred, young Jewish women in the 1940s. In later life, when she lost her only son to cancer, she worked tirelessly to raise funds for medical research.

Poppy was the perfect foil for Nonny. Small in stature but a giant in kindness and good humor, he never tired of telling the story of how they met. Now a little stooped and fanning what remained of his silver hair into an elaborate comb-over, he described himself as an erstwhile stage-door Johnny. Besotted from first sight, he had followed Nonny around, one among a line of admirers, until she agreed to become his wife.

"She could have had anybody she wanted," he was fond of saying. He then would add with a shy, slightly smug smile, "But she chose me!"

Other friends joined in to make sure we were well fed. Sarah and Sandy were both at home, their lives interrupted by their mother's drama. There were role reversals as they assumed responsibility for chores that had belonged to me. I did not take kindly to Sarah's telling me I had too many credit cards. She sat behind me at the kitchen table, paying a pile of bills that had grown to epic proportions during my absence.

"None of your business," I snapped.

Sandy had taken to sleeping at a friend's house while I was in the hospital and was still reluctant to sleep at home, saying it was not the same as it used to be.

When I was not in bed, I spent most of my time seated in the kitchen in the red leather reclining chair; that chair became my headquarters in the new order.

I mostly sat because walking by myself was not an option. I was too scared of falling. It was different in the hospital. There was always someone beside me, and the gait belt was a fixture. I had a perpetual ferocious headache and very little tolerance for noise. Conversations took place around me and occasionally involved me, but I felt much worse than when I was in the hospital. I wanted to go back to the hospital and stay there because that was who I had become. I was now a person who lived in a hospital room, went to therapy, and had visitors. Being at home had nothing to do with this new me. I no longer belonged there. People suggested I might be depressed, but I never got depressed; it was not allowed. I was back in my bunker. Even there, there was very little warmth or solace. I desperately missed the hospital and longed to be back in its sanctuary. I longed for the order and predictability of the routine and the certain knowledge that someone would come if I pulled the bell cord, even if not as quickly as I might have wished.

I fell asleep at night with Bruce and a cat or two, but it took a pill and a few hours of soothing (some might say, boring) television to get me there. I had a powerful thirst for words—spoken words, not written words. Written words made me either angry or sad, not because of what they said but because they didn't say anything at all. I could only read with my ears, not with my eyes. Spoken words, especially if they were from familiar stories, released a powerful cocktail of endorphins that made me feel relaxed, comforted, and safe.

It was about then that I became addicted to television—not watching it but listening to it. Bruce would sometimes turn it off, assuming I was asleep. I resentfully would ask why he did that, and he would respond, "Because you weren't watching."

"I was listening."

He did not understand. He could not hear the television at the best of times and had to depend on closed captions to know what was going on. Very few programs had captions, so it was frustrating for him.

"Please turn it off," he asked a couple of times.

Involved in a mindless plot, I was slow to respond.

"For God's sake, turn the damn thing off! I need to go to sleep," he barked impatiently.

I acquiesced, waited until he fell asleep, and then defiantly turned it back on. Something was wrong with my eyes, so the picture was never clear, but the spoken words were balm to a bee sting.

When I summoned the energy required to get out of my chair and eat at the table with everyone else, it was an ordeal. Being English, I have always eaten with a knife and fork—knife in the right hand, fork in the left—cutting and eating as you go, not cutting first, putting the knife down, and putting the fork in the right hand; I never did that. Now I had to. Now I had to eat American- style, with the fork in my right hand, sawing at my food, stabbing, dropping. I didn't know exactly where my mouth was, so I missed quite often. Bruce pointed surreptitiously at the side of my face to let me know, without saying that food was there. It was meant kindly, but I was always annoyed when he did it. I have no doubt that had I found out there was food on my face and he had not told me, I would have been even more annoyed. *Si laeseritus damnato, damnentur si non.* "Damned if you do and damned if you don't" would make an excellent motto for a Stroke Survivor Spouses Society, if one existed.

I was not aware of anything on the left side of my face and soon developed a compulsive tic that had me swatting the side of my face with my napkin, after every bite. Chew, swallow, swat; chew, swallow, swat; chew, swallow, swat. I found a rhythm that got me through the meal. Nothing tasted good, and most things smelled disgusting, but never mind.

Every few bites, I added *grimace* to my litany—chew, swallow, swat, grimace. I bit the inside of my cheek because it was numb. I did not know it was there, and it got in the way of my teeth. It felt like the first hours after a visit to the dentist, except the feeling didn't return very fast. I had a permanent, red, raw, sore cheek, resulting from several attempts at self- cannibalism. I couldn't come up with a Latin word for it, but there is a syndrome, Lesch-Nyhan disease.

LND is a psychiatric disorder characterized by people biting compulsively at the inside of their cheek. I probably caught it in the hospital.

Sometimes it was not food on the side of my mouth but drool. Saliva built up in the side of my cheek, but I didn't swallow it because I didn't know it was there. Sometimes, hours after a meal, I'd find a bite of something in my mouth. I wondered where it came from and realized it must have been left behind in my cheek. Was I saving it for later?

I was in a twilight zone most of the time, conscious but not connected. I felt utterly useless, like a hair dryer that hadn't been plugged in or a car without gasoline. I had a purpose, I supposed, but there was no source of energy to help me achieve it. I looked like I ought to be useful but I was not.

I leaped to mental attention when there was a phone call from one of my colleagues at work and to physical attention when the home physical and occupational therapists came. Therapy seemed nothing more than a balancing act between increased independence and safety, mostly achieved at the expense of my overused right arm and leg. If it were as entertaining as watching paint dry for the therapist, watching trees grow would have been wildly exhilarating compared with what it felt like to be the patient.

I mastered the art of making a grilled cheese sandwich with one hand. I made tea, put a load of laundry in, took it out, and folded it in a haphazard fashion. Since when did I do laundry? I was a working mother, an executive. If I never did laundry before, why was it so important to do it now? The cleaning-lady always did the laundry!

I was intrigued by the question of whether I could open a bottle of wine with one hand. Not that I was allowed to drink any with all the medicine I was taking. There was nothing mind-altering, nothing that produced the slightest buzz, but my blood pressure had to be brought so low—according to the new guidelines, no higher than 120/70—that it took four separate prescriptions to keep it there.

I figured out a way to open a bottle of wine with one hand! I put the bottom of the bottle in the opening of the garbage disposal unit, put the corkscrew into the cork, pushed and twisted, and voila—out popped the cork. Once an OT, always an OT. "Adopt, adapt, improve" is our motto. Self-sufficiency trumps battling with a nonexistent limb every time.

Within a couple of weeks, I was able to function independently within somewhat narrow parameters. If I couldn't do something with one hand, I didn't do it. It was as simple as that—unless, of course, I could do it with my teeth. My brain received no messages from my left arm except for the occasional sharp pain if I hit it on something, rolled over on it, or tried to get out of the car while it was still in the seatbelt. If my brain was sending messages to my arm, they were falling on deaf ears.

Home therapy was short-lived, as they soon ran out of things for me to do. I quickly met all the insurance criteria for home therapy. I could dress myself and put on my shoes and the dreaded ankle foot orthosis. I wore only baggy sweatpants with elastic waistbands and tops that went over my head; I declined anything that had buttons or zippers. Anything that could not be donned with one hand was avoided. Fashion was on the back burner; vanity was consigned to thrift stores. I felt scruffy and grubby most of the time. Even after being away from the hospital for a few weeks, the smell of it was still in my nostrils, oozing from my pores.

The only cure, I decided on a particularly bleak morning, would be to soak myself in my beloved Jacuzzi. I had been taking showers, another American custom to which I never quite adjusted. People like me, who grew up paddling in the freezing North Sea, never quite get over their distrust of water, and do not like it beating on their heads. That day I just knew I needed a real bath. It was good for the body and especially for the soul. I sat on the edge of the tub and gently lowered myself in. Bliss! I soaked in the warm water and enjoyed the jets that, miraculously, seem to be aimed at all the spots on my body that hurt, and there were quite a lot of them.

Everything went swimmingly until it was time to get out. I drained the water, reached for a towel, and then started to stand up. My right leg cooperated and started to straighten, to push me up, as it was supposed to do. The other one shot out in front of me, ramrod straight. It would not take any weight. When I put my heel down, it slid away from me. My right arm took all of my weight as I flailed around and eventually slipped and slid back down to the hard, cold, soapy bottom of my porcelain prison. I was beached whale! There was no sand on my beach, no sunshine to warm my bones, just hard, cold porcelain.

I repeated the exercise at least a dozen times with the same result. A couple of times, someone tapped on the door to ask if I was all right, if I needed help.

"Fine! Never better," I lied. "Enjoying myself." I was far too humiliated to admit I was stuck. I didn't even want to admit to myself that I was beached.

I was freezing cold and fatigued when, necessity being the mother of invention, I hatched a plot that would free me, once and for all. Thank God there were no cameras present, but in a move worthy of Cirque du Soleil, I hooked my right leg and arm over the side of the tub and flung myself up and out. I made brief hard contact with the side of the tub and then landed in a heap of mangled flesh and bone on the unforgiving tile floor. No time for counting bruises; I was out! I had been shown how to get up from a fall—and had shown countless patients how to do so. Training kicked in, and on my knees, holding on to the side of the sink, I pulled myself up. Once upright and clothed in my bathrobe, with enough adrenaline in my system to launch a rocket, I exited the bathroom. Smiling faces greeted me. "Wow," said Bruce, "you must have really had a good time in there."

"Yep, I had a blast!"

I did not use the tub again and when the bruises emerged, there were a lot of them. It was impossible to count them because they flowed together and gave my left side its own personal rainbow shades of blue, indigo, violet, yellow, pink and green for weeks.

On my last day of home therapy, we went to the mall and got involved in an incident that had me banned from escalators for life. People who are unaware of a certain body part -in this case, me, and specifically my left foot—do not belong on escalators. I enthusiastically stepped onto the moving staircase and sailed up the steep incline. At the top, I stepped off with my right foot and totally lost track of where the left one was. My next move was a long, sliding nose-dive on the gleaming hardwood floor. I was stunned to find myself spread-eagled at the feet of a gaggle of afternoon shoppers, some of whom were probably equally stunned to see me there. Lying stretched out on my stomach, struggling for breath, I briefly considered closing my eyes and pretending to be unconscious.

The idea of being transported out on a stretcher in feigned oblivion was, for an instant, infinitely more appealing than having to face the curious gazes of the bystanders as I was hauled to my feet. Fortunately, there was no major damage, except to my pride, and a little excitement was added to the lives of the shoppers as the therapists struggled to pick me up and free my shoe from the end of the escalator, right where it had flattened out and had begun to recycle itself.

Although I was restricted to taking the elevator from one floor to the other after the incident, visits to the mall became part of my therapeutic regime. Sarah and Sandy took me several times, and we walked from one end to the other with me mentally reciting, *Tighten, shift, swing.*

I assiduously avoided mirrors in the stores, but once in a while, I caught sight of a woman with a leg swinging wildly, like a semicircular pendulum, reflected in a store window. The woman's arm was always bent to a right angle, her hand hanging from the wrist like a dog's begging paw.

I never bought anything on my shopping expeditions. I had no money and couldn't carry anything anyway. The bent arm looked as if it should carry a shopping bag but dropped anything that was hooked on it. There was a disease called dropsy in Dickens's time, I recalled. Now I knew why I dropped things all the time; I must have dropsy. I must have contracted that in the hospital too!

I was prompted to use my left hand and tried but with very little success. If I tried to carry something from one room to another in the house, I either dropped it and stepped on it or found it clutched in my hand hours later.

I was extremely irritable. Quiet annoyed me. Noise annoyed me. One afternoon I was almost driven insane by the whining of a dog that had accompanied its owner on a visit to the house. I felt as if my head was an empty cave. Noises ricocheted from rock to rock, reverberating, crashing, echoing, and magnifying to the point of physical pain.

I was spending too much time alone, as Bruce and the girls were out all the time. I believed they left me for hours, and by the time they showed up, I was too tired for conversation. In reality, they never left me for more than an hour and usually after I had requested peace and quiet.

But I still couldn't tell the difference between an hour and a day, so it felt like forever. I thought I could do anything and everything, just like before, but the simple tasks that I undertook each day left me exhausted.

I was angry with Bruce most of the time. I knew at one level that he was doing his best to be supportive, but I found myself bristling with annoyance anytime he stepped in to help me complete a task. I was offended, rather than grateful, when he took a coat hanger from my hand and hung up the garment I had been struggling with for ten minutes. The tension between my understanding as a therapist that I was supposed to be independent, my fiercely independent nature and frustration at being able to do so little boiled over frequently, and poor Bruce was the undeserving butt of much of my ire. He was supposed to be retired, but after I came home from the hospital, it seemed that whenever the phone rang, it was either a patient or another doctor calling about a patient.

Aware that he would have to take on the role of primary breadwinner again, Bruce had been purposefully rebuilding his practice, limited—because of his age and moral inclination—to people who could not afford private practice fees. Not wanting to put pressure on me, he had not discussed his plans to share space, coincidentally, with the dentist who purchased his office equipment the first time he retired, when Sarah was a baby.

"You don't even have an office anymore, so how can you be seeing patients all the time? What are you doing that keeps you out of the house and away from me all the time?" I ranted.

"I'm taking care of the patients in the operating room," he said. In an attempt to commiserate, he added, "Look, this awful thing happened to both of us, you know. We are in this together."

"That's just not true," I responded resentfully. "I'm willing to concede that a bad thing happened to you, that the past months have been awful for you too, but this thing didn't happen to both of us. It happened to me. You are free to leave the house any time you want. You can walk. You can drive. You can read. You can use both your hands. You don't look like a freak."

"You don't look like a freak either, but I know how you feel—"

"You don't know how I feel! You can't have the first idea how I feel!" I snapped.

Sandy, a silent witness to the conversation until then, appeared next to my chair with a cup of tea in her hand. She waggled her forefinger at me and said in her inimitable way, "Don't bark at the hand that feeds you!"

Bruce thought "we" should talk to someone. He found a psychiatrist who specialized in counseling couples who had been through traumatic events. It was a dismal failure. I sat through the session, steaming because I did not want to be there and was extraordinarily resistant to what I dismissed as psychobabble. I distrusted psychiatrists and knew there was a reason for that but I couldn't recall what it was. Later, I would piece together the story of how a family friend had murdered his wife, the mother of two children for whom I had baby-sat as a young teenager. As an occupational therapy student doing clinical practice in a hospital for the criminally insane, I had come face-to-face with him and learned from his chart that he had committed the crime while in a fugue state, thought to have been caused by treatment with an experimental drug for depression. Shortly after I finished my rotation, I read in the local paper that while home on a weekend pass, he had committed suicide by putting his head in the gas oven and turning the burners on full blast.

Bruce was left with no choice but to talk about the impact of my stroke on *him* and *his* life. I was irrationally angry at him for making my misfortune all about him.

Holidays came and went without much impact on my routine. First was Halloween. With help from Sarah and Sandy, I was done up as a hippie. I had a long flowery dress from Mexico, a wild rainbow acrylic wig, heart-shaped sunglasses, a bandana, beads, and peace signs all over. As friends and neighbors came by, it was clear that the younger kids had no any idea who the hippie was. I didn't care. It suited me to be anonymous, as unrecognizable to others as I was to myself. Trick or treat? Definitely trick!

Thanksgiving and Christmas came and went, and I was there but not present. Christmas wasn't Christmas that year. I was not running around, driving myself and everyone else in the family crazy.

The shopping, wrapping, hiding, writing cards, mailing cards, and invitations all fell to others that year.

In adulthood, I have not pursued the strong religious tradition of my upbringing. My life experiences and choices have rendered it impossible for me to believe that there is one true church, or that my way is right and all others are wrong. That said, I did conspire with the two churchwardens of Saint Nicholas Church—my uncle, Arthur Rimington, and the general, Sir Christopher Welby-Everard—to have my two daughters baptized at Sapperton; Sarah as a baby and Sandy as a tiny, obstreperous five-year-old. I was anxious to keep their options open.

I have lived and worked among Muslims, Buddhists, and Hindus. I married a Jew. I no longer knew how to be exclusively one thing. Nothing, however, has shaken my belief in a power greater than myself, an architect of destiny who shapes my life. His name is Archie. I made up the term "faithalism" to capture my belief that things happen for a reason, that we are each given the opportunity to live out the life we are intended to live, and it is a good life. Our responsibility is to make the best choices we can and follow the golden rule of doing unto others as we would have them do unto us. Everything happens for a reason, but this particular Christmas, I was not yet able to see a higher purpose for my current predicament. It was what it was. Christmas still was, however, my favorite time of the year, and we were all going to be together. It would not be the same as other years, but we would make the most of it because I might not have been here at all.

Sarah was working at Bloomingdale's in New York for the Christmas rush and came home on Christmas Eve, laden with gifts and Christmas tree ornaments, in time to take over the cooking. She was working as a special assistant to the store manager. He was trying to recruit her into their executive training program. Sarah was flattered but holding out for an internship with the United Nations. Sandy was working as a live-in nanny and would be home late on Christmas Eve.

Midnight Mass was out of the question. It was too cold, and I was too tired to go. My homage to the spiritual side of the holiday would have to be paid via Mass from the Vatican and Andrea Bocelli's Christmas special on PBS.

In my part of England, we had taken a long time to break ties with Rome. We had bells, candles, and incense (referred to as Holy Smoke), so the Mass was comfortably familiar. Bruce and the girls came to join me and as we watched, he reminded us of the time we had attended midnight Mass in Great Gonerby, the village where I was born. The congregation had swelled to standing room only, as the village pubs emptied out at midnight. We had no need of a choir as the voices, a four-octave span of inebriated good humor, swelled in joyous renditions of "O, Come All Ye Faithful," "Silent Night," and "Joy to the World."

For many of the throng, this was the only time in the year that they would enter the church, and the sip of Communion wine was nothing more than a nightcap to top off an evening of boozy celebration. As voices soared in massive, quavering crescendo, accompanied by the triumphant roar of the organ in the last verse of "Joy to the World," someone detonated a stink bomb. At first, no one knew what it was, and people looked surreptitiously at their neighbors, fearing it was the effects of too much rich food.

It quickly became apparent that this was not flatulence but sabotage, if not outright terrorism. It was probably the Methodists down the street. The rivalry had been fierce for generations.

The great, studded wooden doors of the church were thrown open and the cold night air quickly sucked out the foul smell. Extra incense was burned around the aisles as the rector attempted to regain control of his unruly flock. It took him several minutes of tapping the pulpit with his palm and clearing his throat to snuff out the ribald laughter that erupted once people realized it was a prank.

Sarah reminded me of another midnight Mass in England when, aged six, in a full-throttle rendition of "Hark! The Herald Angels Sing," she had swallowed the front tooth that had been hanging on by the slenderest of threads.

On New Year's Eve, Bruce surprised me by saying that he was taking me out. I was very surprised and not altogether pleasantly so. I had not been anywhere since leaving the hospital and I did not want to be in a fancy place with food on my face. He was so enthusiastic about his surprise that I had to go along with it.

The girls helped me to get as ready as I could get. A pair of pants with an elastic waistband and a plain but nice sweater would have to suffice. Bruce helped me stand, pivot, and swivel into the car and then put a scarf around my eyes. I had no idea how long we were in the car or how far we traveled. When the car stopped, Bruce took the blindfold off, and I saw he had parked outside the house of our friends, Kass and Mike, who lived less than a mile from us.

I was relieved and pleased beyond measure because I was *out* of the house but not out in a place where I was surrounded by strangers and unknown hazards. Bruce was pleased and relieved because he had done something right. It was a gamble, but it had paid off. I enjoyed the meal and the company, but my head was drooping impolitely toward my chest and my eyelids were in need of toothpicks to prop them open long before midnight struck.

The New Year brought changes to my routine. I was discharged from home therapy and had orders to go to the hospital three days a week as an outpatient.

But first, I was going on a road trip. My stepson, Cliff, now a successful anti-tobacco lawyer/lobbyist, and his wife, Martha, his dark-haired, dark-eyed college sweetheart, had told us a year or so before that they had completed all the paperwork to adopt a baby. If ever a couple appeared qualified genetically, educationally, and behaviorally to become parents, it was Cliff and Martha. Years of trying and fertility treatment had produced no results.

They did not know when their baby would come but expected to hear early in 2003. They had returned from spending Christmas in Sweden with Martha's sister, to find a voice mail informing them that they had been selected by the birth mother to be the parents of a boy, due to be born in Ohio in early January.

Before they had unpacked their suitcases, the call came, notifying them that that the mother was in labor, and they were to go to the hospital in Toledo to pick the baby up immediately. They arrived at the hospital shortly after the baby arrived but could not take the baby son, Sean, home to Michigan until all adoption formalities were completed. All three were taking up residence in a motel in Toledo to wait for medical and legal clearance to go home.

Bruce announced that he was going to Ohio to see his new grandson, and my immediate response was, "Not without me!"

There was a fair amount of discussion about whether I could make a five- hour car trip, but I was extremely motivated and ready to go. We made the trip. I did not share the driving, as had been our custom in recent years, but sat in the passenger seat and didn't eat or drink for the entire journey, so there was no need for me to get out of the car.

A mixture of fear and exhilaration to be going somewhere different and with the end point of meeting a much-wanted and long-awaited baby boy carried me through the discomfort of the long, tedious drive. He was tiny and perfect. It was the first week of January in the Midwest—cold, dark, snowy, and bleak. Sean warmed our hearts. I was exhausted from the trip and too afraid to hold him with my one arm but could revel in the feel, the smell, the beauty, and the transcendent allure of a newborn baby. It was Christmas all over again!

Back at home, Sandy was not happy with her nanny job and volunteered to stay home and be my caregiver. This would involve driving me to and from the hospital for therapy. I wanted the girls to go on with their lives, but the reality was that there was no good alternative. Bruce could not drive me because of his work schedule. We struck a deal. Sandy would receive a salary for her work until I could drive myself. I assumed that might be in a month or so.

I had no idea that my driver's license was suspended, and I would not get it back before undergoing a rigorous testing and retraining program. Sandy informed me that I should not expect any special privileges and that if I criticized her driving, she would consign me to the bus that took all the other people suffering from "old-timers' disease" to their institutions on a daily basis. That was a threat that I had to take seriously. She would not be known as "Sandy" while she was working for me but would have the honorary title of Mrs. Bloom. We borrowed the name from a radio show that Bruce listened to as a boy. "Yoo-hoo, Mrs. Bloom" was a catchphrase of one of the characters and would be the way I would summon Sandy when I needed her. "Bloom" soon became her enduring nickname.

Our trips to the city were hilarious! Mrs. Bloom behind the wheel was a sight for sore eyes. She was what we, within our nuclear family, lovingly described as "vertically challenged." Barely five feet tall, she positioned her seat as close to the steering wheel as possible, gripped the wheel as if it were trying to run away from her, put the ferocious expression of an Inca warrior on her face, and set off to conquer all before her. She did not engage in road rage but kept up a steady monologue of muttering about the shortcomings of every driver she encountered. I started to laugh, and in those days, once I started, I could not stop. I laughed until the tears ran down my face, and because laughter is contagious, Bloom started to laugh too. Because Bloom was laughing, I laughed some more.

Sometimes laughter was not the appropriate response to something that happened, but I laughed anyway. A friend told me about a loss he had suffered, and instead of commiserating, I acted as if it were the funniest joke I had heard in years. Sometimes I cried. It was not proper crying; there was no emotion attached to it, just tears and a clown-sad, contorted face.

By the time we arrived at therapy, I was already tired from the journey and not at all enthusiastic about what awaited me. Outpatient therapy at the hospital was very dull. I was evaluated, given goals, met the goals, and then was evaluated again to prove I had met the goals. The therapists were friendly and competent, but I was far from an ideal patient. I did not like being on the receiving end. It seemed to me that so much time was spent on evaluation that there was precious little time for therapy. The evaluations themselves seemed pointless. There were lots of questions about whether I could use a broom or vacuum cleaner or wash dishes.

Could I unlock the door with my left hand, comb my hair, and brush my teeth? Why would I? I didn't do that before; why would I do it now? Show me a right-handed person who can brush her teeth with her left hand. There were lots of tests that didn't seem to relate to me at all. They must have been for patients with serious disabilities, not for someone like me.

Nothing in my therapy was markedly different from my training thirty years before. We made patients stack cones then. We made them push blocks covered with sandpaper along boards carefully clamped to angled tables. We made them wave their arms about in slings. I didn't see much point in it then and saw even less now that the tables had turned.

After a few weeks of this routine, I saw the physiatrist for yet another evaluation to determine whether further therapy could be justified. Asked if I were independent in all the atrocities of daily living, I replied that what he saw before him—me, fully, if shabbily, clad—had happened without benefit of assistance from anyone. He appeared to be working his way down a list of criteria: The patient was ambulating short distances with a straight cane; independent in ADL; appeared to be coping with her disability.

"What disability? What are you talking about, and why are you wasting time restating the obvious? By the way, I am neither disabled nor handicapped. I'm just having problems with my left arm and leg."

Then he stunned me by saying, "You are just about ready for discharge from therapy. It appears you have met the goals that were established for you when you first came here."

"What? I am nowhere near ready to be discharged! What about my ninety percent recovery?"

The doctor reminded me that it was now five months since my stroke, and after a certain point, recovery would slow down, and eventually I would plateau.

I had thought that if I worked hard enough, I could get there. Whatever it meant, I knew I was nowhere near that number. Panic bubbled to the surface, my eyes stung, and a lump crowded my throat. This could not be all that there was.

What is ninety percent of what I was? Can ninety percent of me walk normally without a cane; use two hands; stand without constantly reminding myself to keep my leg straight so I don't fall down; drive a car: ride a horse; and take care of a foal? Could ninety percent of me work in my garden: hold my baby grandson; or go to work? Could ninety percent of me be the queen of the Starlight Ballroom?

At that moment I could do none of those things, yet he was threatening to discharge me. I was sure I was no more than forty percent of what I was— fifty on a good day, maybe.

That was one time when I did not feel like laughing. I felt like sobbing, howling, and throwing myself on the floor, but that is not what I did. I got steaming mad instead. I would tell Bruce; he would be even madder than I was.

I would go somewhere else where there was better therapy and a doctor who was not ready to give up on me. I truly believed that if I worked hard enough and pushed my body hard enough, I could force myself to get to the point where life would be recognizable again. There were many days when, despite my intellectual grasp of the fact that I was lucky to be alive and to have the family, friends, and pets I had, I questioned whether I could settle for this new reality. I was depressed but not so anyone would notice, least of all me. My mind swung back and forth, a grappling hook trying to catch emotions that had been pushed down for too long—fear, pain, and sadness.

Growing up, we four children were never allowed to own our fears, pain, and sadness. They all belonged to Mum: my brother Don's back injury in the navy; Tony's army combat tour in Malaya; Keith's TB; my orthopedic surgeries and sleepwalking. They were all stitches in the melancholy mantle of matriarchal martyrdom that Mum donned in her dark moods. They were things that "frightened her to death" and caused her to have gray hair and not to be able to sleep "a wink." Our problems were things for which we should be chastised, things for which we should be blamed, and things for which Dad would be held accountable in a high-pitched, whining, hand-wringing, pacing diatribe.

Many nights the lamentations continued after I went to bed. Most of the time, Mum was sunny-side up outside the house—talented actress, president of the Mothers' Union, leading light in civic affairs. Her dark side was reserved for her family. Occasionally, there was a perpetrator other than one of us—an uncle, an aunt, a neighbor, the butcher, a canvassing politician, someone who did or said something to offend. The sin was recounted in great detail, and if Dad was not suitably sympathetic, he became the villain. "Those who are not for me are against me," was Mum's favorite refrain.

One particularly chilling night, I was the perpetrator. A neighbor had come to the door after I was in bed to complain, "Your Janet has half killed our Patty." I could hear it all clearly as I cowered under the sheet. As the story was recounted, I shuddered to think of what would become of me if Patty were dead. While leading the boys next door on a digging expedition, in which I had promised them that if they dug deep enough, we would reach Australia, I had thrown an excavated brick over the neighbor's hedge and hit Patty Fotherhay smack in the middle of her forehead. She went home to get her wound cleaned and planned to return and help us dig. Unfortunately for me, she was intercepted on the way by her grandmother, Nell, the bicycle-riding chief scold of the village. Nell demanded to know who had inflicted the grievous wound that, by then, was gushing blood as scalp wounds tend to do. Patty, to her credit, did not rat me out immediately. Later, under intense questioning, she broke. That explained the visit. While the conversation was taking place, my thoughts jumped from what was in store for me to speculation about whether it was actually possible to half kill someone and what that would look like. Patty had not looked half dead; she was bloody and tear-stained but very much alive. Is the top or bottom half dead, or is it one side if a person is half dead?

Wow, I thought as my adult self, *That's what stroke does; it half kills a person.*

Back in childhood, the tongue-lashing that came my way focused on the sin of causing grievous bodily harm to a friend and embarrassing the family, something about which the neighbors would cry "Shame!" for months. It also included mention of my every infraction, going back at least six months.

Mrs. Bloom drove me home that day in silence. I told Bruce, tearfully, that I had been discharged or, as I phrased it, "kicked out of rehab."

"Nonsense," he said. "We'll get another opinion."

The other opinion was that I should receive a further period of outpatient therapy at a facility that specialized in stroke rehabilitation. I was making a full circle and coming back to the Rehabilitation Institute of Chicago, my first employer in the United States, the employer that had sponsored my entry into this country almost three decades earlier.

I would not be going to the towering edifice on the lakefront where I'd worked but to an outpatient facility that used to be a restaurant, much closer to where I lived. The drive was much shorter. We would not laugh as much, but I would get more skilled therapy. Bloom, famous for her malapropisms and mixed metaphors, announced she would be able to "kill a bird with two stones" and do the grocery shopping while I was at therapy.

The evaluations began yet again, and a program was designed that focused on improved use of my left arm, independence, and ambulation. I was still wearing a brace on my left leg, but orthopedic history invaded the present in a very painful way. My left knee was not normal before the stroke, so it would be unreasonable to expect it to be normal afterward. With increased walking, the knee became extremely painful. I did not yet know exactly where the leg was but my pain sensation was not diminished at all. Jenny, my PT, noticed one day that my knee was very swollen. I went to an orthopedic surgeon, who used a huge syringe to withdraw fluid from the joint. I was surprised to see the super-sized syringe fill up quickly with a yellowy red- streaked fluid.

My knee had one large and four small scars on it. The doctor asked me what they were from. I was able to pry open the vault of my memory wide enough to tell him I'd had three knee surgeries, one in my last month of college and two subsequently, to remove fragments and a horn of cartilage that had regenerated into the joint.

My left ankle was not normal before either. The tendons that should have stabilized the joint were lax, and the ankle turned over frequently. As a child, I was constantly falling down and was seldom without a scabby graze on one or both knees. I wore orthopedic shoes—ugly, uncomfortable, expensive, and consuming more points in the rationing system than I had any right to expect. The doctor asked more questions. As I started to formulate an answer, grappling with blank spaces in my mind, I was immersed in sights, sounds, and smells from another time and place: disinfectant, paraffin wax, and sizzling water.

I was in Grantham, the town closest to my village, at the hospital physiotherapy department. There was a powerful, pungent, clinging odor of paraffin wax. My feet were soaking in a tray of water, and I had wires attached to my feet and ankles. Electric shocks made my feet turn outward. It sent powerful tingles through my toes and up my legs.

The therapist's name was Mr. Fairbrother. He was tall and handsome, with one distinguishing feature—burn scars on his face and hands. His eyes, always hidden behind dark glasses, were sightless. He was blind. I was eight and could not imagine how he did everything by feeling with his hands. He was so kind and gentle. I heard a woman tell Mum, quietly, that Mr. Fairbrother was training to be a doctor before the war.

He had been shot down in a fighter plane and was badly burned. Then, after the war, he had trained as a physiotherapist. Before and after the war was my parents' generation's schism in time, their marker for filing collective experiences and memories. I was developing my own "before" and "after." The stroke would be the event that forever divided the two halves of my life.

I wish I could say that I could trace my desire to become an occupational therapist back to the inspirational Mr. Fairbrother, but that would be dishonest. I never forgot him, however, and maybe some of his kindness and patience rubbed off on me and made me a better therapist.

My focus returned to the doctor examining my ankle. Without the hated AFO, I tripped over my foot. If I started to fall to my left, I just kept going, having no righting mechanism. I was averaging a fall a week since leaving the hospital. I never knew I was falling until I hit the deck. With the AFO, I had a big, fat, swollen, painful knee, but I could walk. Without it, my knee didn't hurt, but I fell down.

The orthopedic surgeon did not mince his words. My knee was shot and should be replaced. He understood that I was recovering from a stroke and now was not a good time. He was right about that! Wait—I thought the other doctor said I was as good as I was going to be.

The words *knee replacement* filled me with dread, as I recalled screams from behind closed curtains on the inpatient rehabilitation floor. I was not going down that road for as long as I could avoid it. We made a deal.. I would get a shot of cortisone in my knee and physical therapy to strengthen my quadriceps and other remaining leg muscles to relieve some of the pressure on the joint. I would have to continue to wear the brace. I had my own name for the brace now, never to be spoken aloud—"Abominable F—g Outrage."

Depression and anger are first cousins. I got angry a lot, not so much at people, except for Bruce, who got more than his fair share of abuse, but at inanimate objects, situations, and world events. My source of information was television news. Newspapers were delivered to the house, but I could not manage them. They were too big, refused to stay in one place, and covered me with black ink. They made me angry. If

I actually could have read them, they would have made me even more angry. I watched cable news and continued to read with my ears. There was not much good news. We were bombing Afghanistan, bombing Iraq, shock and awe! There were dots to be connected between the awful thing in New York and the bombing, but that was for another day.

I could relate to bombing—boarded-up craters in the ground on my first visits to London in the 1950s. In the early 1970s in London, because of the threat of IRA terrorism, you couldn't go to a movie, go shopping, or even go to work in a hospital without alarms sounding and bomb threat announcements requiring everyone to evacuate.

I remember Beirut in 1970. My brother Tony, who served in the army, told me once that if you hear it with your ears, it is gunfire; if you feel it in your feet, it is a bomb. I felt it with my feet that night. The next morning, what had been a building was a heap of rubble across the street from my hotel. Dust and smoke rose in billowing clouds, and the acrid smell of burned and burning metal, wood, and plastic made it hard to breathe.

In Bangkok in 1973, I did not feel it with my feet, but the huge planes flying over my room in the Swiss Guest House on Convent Road, *en route* to deliver their deadly gifts to the people of Cambodia, made my bed shake and kept me awake with their incessant nightly thrum. I owed my name to a bomb—two, actually. Born in August 1945, shortly after the bombing of Hiroshima and Nagasaki, I was given the name Veronica Janet. My initials reflected my parents' patriotism and recognition of the Allied victory over Japan.

These memories came unbidden, dumped in a heap like rubble. I did not summon them. They were fleeting reminders that there was once more to me than there was now. My life was not always written in present tense. I was not always a "stroke survivor," but that was the mantle I would wear like an old T-shirt for the rest of my life.

I got a call from the doctor's office, telling me that he had ordered a test to see if there were any other defects in my brain waiting to spring nasty surprises on me. The test was an MRA—magnetic resonance angiogram. They would introduce a radio-opaque substance to the arteries feeding my brain. Further abnormalities, if there were any, would be easy to detect.

Bruce drove me to the hospital. I was prepped, connected to innumerable wires, and then fed into a tunnel a millimeter at a time. I immediately began to perspire and feel nauseated. There was banging so loud that it had to be in violation of the Occupational Health and Safety Act standards. If you have to shout to make conversation, it is too loud. According to the yelling nurse, my blood pressure and heart rate had gone sky high. By the time the radiologist appeared, I was drenched in perspiration and extremely agitated, and my head felt as if it would explode.

"What is going on here?" asked the doctor.

"She's claustrophobic," replied Bruce.

I left the present and found myself awake but very fearful in my bedroom in my childhood home—the one that was so cold in winter that ice formed on the inside of the window and so hot in summer that, with windows wide open, moths terrified me as they danced around the light and periodically fluttered against my sticky face. It was the middle of the night, and I awoke with a start because the house was rattling and shaking. I tried to get out of my bedroom to go downstairs to find my parents and brothers, but the door was locked. There was a hook on the outside of the door. I had seen it many times. Every single night that hook went into an eye so I could not get out. I didn't understand it, and no one ever talked about it. That night, terrified, I banged and shouted until eventually my eldest brother Don, my hero, came to explain that there had been a minor earthquake and that was why the house shook. Everything was okay, he reassured me, sitting on the edge of my bed and telling me a story, so I could fall back to sleep.

"But why am I locked in?" I asked.

"To keep you safe," he replied, stroking my hands with his own larger, smooth, white version. He was not freckly like Tony, Keith, and me. His funny story lulled me first into my bunker and then to sleep. The incident quickly receded into nothingness, as often happens with childhood scares.

Sometime after the incident, I thought about the hook on my door again and asked Keith, the brother next in line to me, "Why am I locked in my room at night?"

"Because you are mad," he replied.

I was all of nine years old at the time and have no doubt that I accepted his explanation without question. I learned over time that the very fact of my existence was of great concern to him. He had been sent away to stay with an uncle and aunt as the time for my arrival drew near. As was the custom in the 1940s, he was not made aware of the imminent arrival of a new baby. Upon his return from vacation, he was mortified to find that his six-year reign as the youngest and favorite child was over; he never quite recovered. Not only was he displaced but much worse, he had yielded his throne to a baby sister!

Not only did Keith tell me I was mad, but he also convinced me, for most of the first decade of my life, that I was Chinese. "Every fourth child born in the world is Chinese," he read aloud from the newspaper when I was about four. "You are a fourth child, and you were yellow when you were born, so you must be Chinese." The yellow skin tone was accurate but due to neonatal jaundice, not to having been rescued from an alien spacecraft that landed on Gonerby Hill, purchased from a band of gypsies, or of dubious parentage— explanations that he gave me at various times as I tried to press him further on the origin of my Chinese-ness.

I continued to be locked in my room every night until the Asian flu struck, and I had a nosebleed so severe that I believed I was going to bleed to death. I jumped out of bed, terrified, soaked in blood, and wailed and banged until Don, home on leave from Germany, where he was completing his national service, decoding Russian messages, came dashing to my rescue once again. Having come home late after a night on the town with his pals, he was still wearing his Royal Navy uniform and looking every inch the handsome hero as he surveyed the bloody scene. He grabbed cotton balls from my dresser, made swabs, stuck them in my nostrils, and pinched the top of my nose until the bleeding stopped.

I was eleven and refused to be placated with childish stories about why I was locked in my room. I demanded an explanation. He sent for Mum and Dad, who quickly arrived, rubbing sleep from their eyes. Mum took one look at my blood-soaked sheet and pillowcase and shrieked hysterically, demanding to know what I had done. As she was informing me that I would be the death of her, Don bravely took her arm and led her away from me.

"It is time for her to be told the truth," he said, looking at Dad, the uniform adding gravitas to his adult and forceful tone. "She needs to be cleaned up, and she needs to be told why she is locked up in her room, and if you won't do it, I will!"

In an unprecedented power grab and with all the authority of a naval commander, despite his lowly rank and minimal experience, Don took command of our family ship, sent Mum to get fresh sheets and a clean nightgown, and ordered Dad to explain everything to me.

Dad, almost as shocked as I was by Don's outburst, suggested gently that I get out of the messy bedroom, wash my face, put on a clean nightgown, and join him in the kitchen. He would make me a cup of tea, and we could talk while Mum cleaned up my room.

After I had changed and made my way shakily downstairs to the kitchen, I found Dad, still wearing his rumpled pajamas, his feet stuffed in a decrepit pair of slippers, sitting at the kitchen table with two large cups of tea and a plate of ginger biscuits, my favorites, laid out in front of him.

"Sit down," he said, nodding toward the chair opposite him. "Drink your tea. I've put extra sugar in it because you've had a shock, and you've lost quite a lot of blood. Eat a couple of biscuits, and I'll tell you about the lock on your door."

Not sure whether I wanted to hear what he was going to say, I scraped my chair along the red-tiled kitchen floor to get closer to him. He inclined his head toward the tea and biscuits to signal that he wouldn't start until I ate and drank. I took a big gulp of the sickly sweet, milky tea and lunged for a bite of biscuit to take the taste away.

He took a deep breath and pushed a crumb away from the side of his mouth. He reached over to poke the dying embers of the coal fire that was still giving off a little warmth, cleared his throat, and began.

"It wasn't our idea," he said gruffly. "It was the specialist that Dr. Hopper, the family doctor, brought to see you. (The newly minted National Health Service provided house calls for just about every malady.) "When you were very small, about four, you started sleepwalking. We put you to bed in your own bed at night and found you asleep somewhere else in the morning. At different times, we found you in the kitchen, in the living room, and on occasion, outside the front door. We took you to doctors, but they could not find anything wrong with you. But it kept happening."

He paused to reach for his pipe, scrape out the bowl with the pocket knife he always carried for the purpose, took his tobacco pouch out of his pocket, filled the pipe, lit it with a spell ignited from the embers, and began puffing clouds of smoke across the room. I hastily stuffed two more ginger biscuits in my mouth and took another gulp of the cooling tea.

"We were terrified that you would get hurt, fall down the stairs, stumble into the fire, or fall out of a window. Finally, Dr. Hopper brought a specialist to the house, a psychiatrist. He examined you and asked you a lot of questions and said you showed signs of an anxiety disorder."

"What's that?" I asked.

"I'm not really sure, but he said you seemed to be worried about things."

"How old was I?"

"Four."

The doctor also said that under no circumstances should they wake me if they found me sleepwalking. The effect of such a rude awakening could be very damaging to my psychological health. The doctor advised them to protect me by keeping me away from stairs, where I might fall, and from doors, out which I might wander into the street, by confining me to my room. The best way of doing that would be to put a simple lock on the outside of my door. They also were advised not to tell me anything about my nocturnal wanderings.

"Now that I'm eleven, can the lock come off?"

"If the doctor says it's okay, we'll take it off."

Many years later I would learn that living with a bipolar mother and trying to fend off the unwanted attentions of an overly affectionate uncle could indeed produce anxiety in a young child.

The MRA was canceled that day, and I was referred to another facility that boasted of open MRI facilities. The test was conducted a week or so later, and no further abnormalities were detected. Except for what appeared as a large black hole in my brain, everything was normal. I could continue with my rehabilitation without fear of further strokes.

When I got back to OT and PT again, I was doing a combination of neurological and orthopedic programs. In PT, I lifted weights with my leg and walked as fast as possible. A turtle could easily have overtaken me.

In OT, there was something called "forced use" or "constraint-induced" therapy. The therapist thought it might help. My right arm was tied behind my back, and I was given tasks to perform with my left. The theory was that if the unaffected arm was not able to move, the brain would force other, unused pathways to open, and the delinquent limb would have to cooperate. It was a new concept to me, one that was not around in my therapy days.

There was even talk of climbing the stairs in the gym with only my left arm to save me if I started to fall. Not even the threat of falling headfirst down the stairs would excite my left arm! The funny thing is that my arm looked normal. I saw other stroke patients whose fingers were bent, their nails clawing into their palms. My fingers opened and closed, and my wrist moved in every direction. It could move, but it did not unless I was looking directly at it. I worked at keeping the range of motion in my fingers and wrist. I was ahand therapist, after all. I would not allow contractures to develop if I could prevent them. Maybe if I kept the fingers in good shape, one day there would be a cure. I was starting to feel like those people who have their bodies frozen so they can come back to life when a cure is discovered. An added complication was that my leg and arm were often wracked by crippling, agonizing spasms, making it impossible for me to perform any exercises at all.

On the days when there was no therapy, I often talked to people at work. Periodically we had staff meetings at my house. I found the work-related conversations interesting and reassuring; they anchored me in a world that was not all about strokes and rehabilitation and my limitations

I was surprisingly lucid when it came to anything to do with my job. I had not lost my grip on the details of the consulting practice for which I was responsible. I could engage freely in conversations about clients, revenues, margins and all the verbal and numeric paraphernalia that goes along with running a twenty-plus million-dollar business unit. I just could not voluntarily recall much of my personal history, nor could I read.

After performing my own status update, my prescription was that going back to work would be the best way to pull myself together again.

BIBLIOGRAPHY: CHAPTER 5

Wikipedia. "Lesch-Nyhan Syndrome." Accessed July 10, 2018. https://en.wikipedia.org/wiki/Lesch%E2%80%93Nyhan_syndrome

CHAPTER 6

The Elusive Ninety Percent

A HIGH PERCENTAGE OF PEOPLE WHO HAVE THE KIND OF STROKE I had, maybe as many as ninety percent, do not survive. They fall asleep and never wake up—a startling and sad statistic that fixed the words *ninety percent* firmly in the forefront of my consciousness. As I have already mentioned, ninety percent sprang reflexively to mind, as my target for recovery though I had no clear picture of what that would look like or how it would be measured.

For sure it would include regaining my former leadership role in the family, work, and travel. At a visceral level, I felt that being one of the ten percent of lucky ones who survived carried a burden of responsibility to live as large as possible. It was the least I could do to honor those who did not survive. Lollygagging around at home was not living large, and I was finding the confinement increasingly irksome.

I started thinking more and more seriously about going back to work. I was sure I was capable, though little details such as how I would get there, what I would wear in my business-formal work environment, and how I would cope with the logistics of laptops and other technology had not entered my mind.

The most recent evaluation in both therapies showed me meeting all of the goals they had set for me, with a few exceptions. I could not stand on one leg (I am neither a stork nor a flamingo), and I could not climb stairs without holding on to a handrail. In OT, constraint-induced therapy had made me more resolutely one-handed than ever. What I could not do, I would not do, or I would get someone else to do it for me. It was as simple as that.

In a conversation with the doctor, the issue came up again of whether the insurance company would continue paying for therapy since it was now five months after the stroke. I raised my hand to halt the discussion, saying that I would not need therapy because I was going back to work. The doctor looked a little startled and asked if I was sure. I mustered the biggest grin possible and told him I had never been surer of anything in my life.

"Okay, then," said the doctor, still looking doubtful, "but you'll need another thirty days to get everything set up, and I do want you to continue with outpatient OT and PT twice a week."

Sarah won a coveted internship with the United Nations in New York and was getting ready to leave. Sandy started looking for jobs again. Bruce was busier than ever, with patients booked months in advance. Everyone was getting on with their lives, so it was time for me to do the same.

At work, I had a dual-reporting relationship. The company was divided geographically and by practice. Both of my bosses visited me at home when talk of my returning to work became serious. Both asked if I thought I could do the job. I assured them that I could. The company had treated me extremely well. Starting from the time I was in Oxford, when Bruce was assured that my medical expenses would be covered, and continuing to arranging for transportation home, they had been supportive. I was treated as a managing director on a business trip would have been, despite the fact that the trip to England was for pleasure. I felt an obligation to repay their kindness by doing my job.

April 1, 2003, was set as my return to work date. Who was the April fool? As the date approached, I began to think about logistics. Taking the train to the city, as I had before, was not an option. Even though the walk from the station to the office was only a few blocks, I knew that such a hike would consume my energy ration for the day. I thought I could drive but was told by the doctor that because of my brain injury, my license was suspended. A car service would pick me up on Tuesdays and Thursdays and take me to and from the office. It was the same car service that I had used to go to and from O'Hare Airport for years, and I knew many of the drivers. At the other end, Bill, my administrative assistant, would meet me and help me up to my office. A car would pick me up and deliver me to therapy late in the afternoon. Bruce or Sandy would collect me from there and take me home.

Some pressing practical questions still had to be answered. What was I going to wear? I was accustomed to baggy sweat suits and sneakers large enough to accommodate the AFO. Work attire was business formal. Inspection of my closet revealed a row of suits, mostly skirts but some pants. Each garment displayed zippers, buttons, or belts. Stylish, maybe, but they were as far beyond my current ability as wrapping a sari!

The skirts would require pantyhose and pumps. That clearly was not going to happen. I experimented with pantyhose a few times but had thumbholes poked in them before they reached my knees. And what about shoes? Much like the suits, there was a regiment lined up in my closet, standing at attention, mocking me with their straps and buckles. There was no way the AFO was going to squeeze itself into them and no way my cranky foot could teeter on even a modest two-inch heel. I felt a frisson of sadness when looking at the shoes. On recent, pre-stroke trips through international airports, I had upgraded more than my seat, buying designer shoes in Duty Free whenever I had a chance. The Ferragamos frowned at me, forlorn and forgotten, disappointed in their former general. The lone pair of Chanel pumps silently sneered, shiny, smug, and superior. I slammed the door on them, traitors all!

Another issue to contend with was that the skin on the entire left side of my body was extremely sensitive, and fabric that was hard or rough set off a chain reaction of prickling, burning, wriggling, and fidgeting that would not be seemly in a professional environment. Picture Houdini trying to escape a straitjacket lined with burrs.

We planned a shopping expedition to a nearby mall. Bruce, anxious to help, said he would push me around the mall in the wheelchair. Shopping bags could be hung on the back of the chair or wedged in beside me, he rationalized. I could not think about trying things on. I would not know where to start! Bruce could not come in the changing room, and I could not cope with a pushy sales lady saying, "You look divine in that and the darling gray pant too." *It is pants with an "s" on the end! Is that woman saying "pant" because she too knows that I only have one leg?*

"No, I can't just drape a silk scarf over my shoulder, change from a flat to a 'chic little pump,' and be ready to go from the office to dinner. No! No! No!"

The walls of the tiny changing room started closing in on me; the clothes stuck to me. I had to get out of there. I felt as if I were drowning, and my face was burning hot. I wanted to throw up. I pushed with my foot against the seat and thrust myself out backward through the curtain, practically pulling it off its flimsy rod. I told the sales-witch that nothing worked and scooted the wheelchair backward, out of the changing area.

"How did you get on?" Bruce asked.

"I didn't like anything," I lied.

We tried again another day, and I was thrilled to find myself looking at a display of Eileen Fisher clothes that met my criteria. The pants had elastic waists, the tops had one or two buttons, or none at all, and they were "business appropriate"! I had worn her stuff before so there was no need to try things on. I was elated! I had my uniform. We bought shoes at the "Sensible Shoe Shop," not its real name but a shop that caters to problem feet. I did not have *problem feet*; I had *problem* shoes and a *problem* AFO.

On my third shopping trip, I looked for something a little dressier for a couple of events to which I wanted to go but not looking like a frump. My closet at home contained some clothes that were way above my pay grade by designers so famous they only needed one name—Armani, Missoni, Escada, and Prada. These were from parts of stores through which I sometimes wandered *en route* to the children's clothes, but I never lingered, having glimpsed price tags with more zeroes than my budget could support. These I had not purchased; they had come in large boxes, as gifts from my sister-in- law, Gladys, who lives in a different universe from ours. When clothes had been seen too often or were too "last year," they were dispatched to me, for a second chance at life. Since Gladys and I are approximately the same size, slight alteration rendered them perfect. The boxes yielded clothes and purses that become known affectionately as Glad-Rags and Glad-Bags.

Gladys's supreme generosity was also much appreciated by a couple of my same-size friends. The girls were sometimes beneficiaries too. Sandy won first prize in the Halloween costume contest in the seventh grade when she went as Tina Turner, wearing a large wig and a spectacular gold lame evening gown. None of the participants, judges or parents, would have believed the label on the inside of that dress or that it had cost more than the teachers earned in a month, though many commented on how beautiful it was and wondered from which costume shop I had acquired it.

Gladys helped me in my early days in America to transition from my "London shiksa" look of Laura Ashley and Marks & Spencer and become a little more sophisticated and assimilated into my new, mostly affluent Jewish world, although I still often felt like a pork chop at a Bar Mitzvah.

I scooted myself into the shrine of Saint John, patron saint of professional women and ladies who lunch. There, I selected a couple of things that almost fit but would be made perfect by the tailor promised by the frothy, fussy, friendly salesperson, with whom I was now on first-name terms. She assured me, in a very matter-of-fact way, that the tailor could make my shoulders appear to be the same height and shorten the sleeve on the right more than the one on the left to allow for the bend in my elbow. She lifted my spirits and a sizeable stash of cash from Bruce's wallet, but the outing was a success.

During my last couple of weeks of comparative freedom, I had one special medical appointment. It was with a doctor Bruce wanted me to meet, a Chinese American trained in both Western and traditional Chinese medicine. He was an anesthesiologist who also practiced acupuncture.

A friend had told us that acupuncture might help the droopy left corner of my mouth and help me regain some feeling on the side of my face. I asked the doctor to explain to me how it worked. He said it was very hard to explain to someone who had training in traditional anatomy, physiology, and kinesiology. It was a different paradigm, one based on meridians, not the anatomical systems with which I was familiar. His simple statement that it would do no harm and might help made a lot of sense, so I signed up for a few sessions. It definitely helped!

Whether the improvement in my face was a result of the acupuncture or spontaneous recovery that would have happened in any case is a matter for speculation, but the sensation that I experienced while lying on the bed with those tiny, sharp, pulsing needles in my face was extremely pleasant. People close to me said that I looked better and my lip was not so droopy, so I also felt better.

One night, shortly before I was due to start work, I awoke in a cold sweat, sat bolt upright, and blurted, "Bruce! The car!"

"What car? What are you talking about?" he grumped sleepily in response.

"The rental car, the Mercedes. I parked it outside the hotel in Oxford. I never took it back. It will cost a fortune. How are we going to get it back to them? What if it has been stolen?"

"Calm down. They picked it up while you were in the hospital. It was already taken care of. Go back to sleep."

With a pang of painful if misguided association, I asked, "Were they the same people who stole my jewelry?"

It had taken a long time for me to realize that the few items of jewelry I had taken to England and left in the hotel room on the day I set off to the wedding had not reappeared and most likely had been stolen. A loud snore was his only response.

The night before my first day of work, I set my alarm for six a.m. The car was not coming until nine, but I did not want to be late. It took me a very long time to get ready. I was awake long before the alarm went off. Anxious, excited, scared—a potpourri of emotions crowded my conscious thoughts as I donned the carefully selected outfit and asked Bruce to make sure everything was on correctly.

He made sure that my pants were not twisted, the back of my hair was not standing up, and my makeup was applied evenly on both sides of my face. He patiently reassured me that everything was fine and that I looked nice. Then, giving me the look of an anxious mother seeing a child off to school for the first time, he asked, "Are you really sure you want to do this? You don't have to, you know. It's awfully soon after the stroke. It has only been seven months."

"It's now or never," I said with more confidence than I felt. "If I don't get on with my life now, I could get used to lazing around, and then I'll never go back at all."

The car arrived fifteen minutes early, as always, and I was, uncharacteristically, ready at the door, coat on, bag packed. Before, I would have been flying around at the last minute, one shoe on, one shoe off, eating a piece of toast with one hand while stuffing my briefcase with the other. Makeup and jewelry would have been applied in the car, again with one hand, while I poked a number into my cell phone for a last-minute call with the other.

On that momentous day, I sat sedately on the leather seat with Bruce's help, swiveled my legs in, hoisting my left leg with my right arm while he fastened the seatbelt around me. After a brief, anxious kiss, he laid my bag on the seat beside me, closed the door, and wished me luck. For the duration of the ride, I had nothing to do but poke through the contents of my bag.

There was a large black-leather organizer that started its year with three blank months; lunch, consisting of a granola bar and a banana (there wouldn't be time to go out); and a spare pair of shoes. The extra shoes were because the ones I was wearing, the most comfortable I owned, squeaked when the AFO was in them. I doubted I would be able to stand it all day. There was a mirror, so I could check to see if there was food or drool on my face. That would go in my desk drawer. There was no book because it would be too much to carry, and anyhow, I was still struggling with books. The fact that I still could not read properly had not yet registered. There was no laptop in my bag because I couldn't open it or see the tiny letters on the tiny keyboard.

I was using the desktop computer at home, at least for email, and this was how my typing came out: *IA miss wuite d fer lettrs.* I only used one hand and could not see all of the keyboard. I always hit the A on my way to the caps lock and added commas everywhere in my haste to bang out a sentence. It was a start, though, and I did not need to type anything important at work. Bill did that.

All the way to the office through heavy traffic on the highway, the driver chatted amiably, reminding me that he had driven me to the airport many times—pregnant pause—"before."

When the car pulled up outside the massive office building I had last seen seven months before, Bill, crisply turned out, grinning broadly, was standing by the curb to help me out and up to my office. I swung my right leg out, and he grabbed the left one, lowering it gently to the sidewalk. We set off at a slow pace, with me hanging on to his arm and him carrying my bag. I joked that I was glad his shoes matched the bag. I fervently hoped there was no one I knew in the elevator. I wanted to get to my office with the least amount of fuss and as unnoticed as possible. Was I kidding? If John Cleese of Monty Python fame could see me ambulate, he would immediately appoint me Permanent Under-Secretary in the Ministry of Silly Walks. My shoe squeaked like a lovesick mouse, and my metal cane tapped and rattled with every step. I did meet a few people on the way. Seeing people for the first time was hard for me and for them. It was obvious from their uncomfortable expressions that they didn't know where to look or what to say. The ones I met head-on, the ones I couldn't avoid any more than they could avoid me, bore an expression that was part curiosity, part pity, and part embarrassment. Some said it was good to see me; others said I looked good. I could not relax my concentration long enough to reply but fixed my best bunker smile on my face and moved self-consciously in the direction of my office.

Once there, I found it was overflowing with floral arrangements, almost like my hospital room. A momentary flash of terror assailed me. I hoped Señora Lopez was not around! From the moment I arrived, there was a steady, dizzying stream of visitors and phone calls.

I sat behind my desk, trying to look as normal as possible. The mirror was quickly stowed in my desk drawer, and I consulted it frequently to make sure there was nothing on my face that did not belong there. My visitors told me I looked great; they were happy I was back; they had missed me. They asked me how I felt. I was in bunker mode again, so I smiled my crooked smile and answered platitude with platitude but mentally muttered, "How the hell do you think I feel?" Embarrassed, humiliated, sad, mad, and, on one side of my body, not much at all!

Despite my efforts to catch up from home, I still had over four thousand unopened emails and my voice-mail box was full. Between interruptions, I started poking my way through the emails, deleting all but the most recent in any given chain. There was no quick, easy way to dispense with the voice mails, a mixture of ancient history and messages of encouragement and support, so I just listened and deleted long enough to create space for new messages. I resolved to listen to a batch every day until I caught up.

When lunchtime came, Bill brought food. The banana and granola bar would wait for another day. We began a tradition of Bill bringing lunch to my desk. There were not a lot of choices. There was a sandwich shop in the building, a convenience store, and a Mickey D's around the corner. We settled on a salad from Mickey D's, and another tradition was born. I had a habit of eating the same thing every day for weeks or months, which predated my current state. I chose a crispy chicken ranch salad. I am not fond of chicken, but the unhealthily tasty crust made it unrecognizable, and I stuck with it.

The car was due to pick me up at three. By the time three o'clock came, I was so worn out, I could hardly walk. I squeaked, rattled, and—hanging on to Bill's arm—took the shortest route to the elevator. The car was waiting. I held on to the door, pivoted, and swung, sinking gratefully into the plush leather lining of the car. The next I knew, the driver was politely informing me that I was in front of my house.

For the rest of 2003, all of my energy went into getting through the day— going to work and then to therapy or the health club, when my insurance ran out. Work went remarkably well. I found the discipline of a structured day helped to ground me. I had not been out of touch with the office, except for the weeks of coma and semi-consciousness and was current with just about everything going on, thanks to the regular visits and phone calls with my colleagues.

I still struggled with reading. I compensated by grimacing with frustration at documents handed to me in my office or in meetings and saying, "Oh boy, I'm so backed up! I don't have time to read all that right now. Can you just give me the gist of what it says?" It worked every time.

A lot of frustration resulted from having to move around the multistory building to attend meetings. This felt like the naked supermarket walk of dreams gone by. I was painfully self-conscious, embarrassed, and felt all eyes upon me as I tried to be as inconspicuous as possible, wanting nothing more than to go unnoticed.

Walking with other people was uncomfortable. They would be six lengths ahead of me within two minutes. Some colleagues attempted to go at my speed, but that actually made me feel worse and created awkward silences, as I was unable to walk and talk at the same time. Others brusquely let me know that they needed to get going and sped ahead. I could not manage a stack of papers, an organizer, and a notebook along with my cane and frequently scattered my goodies all over the floor. In order to keep my fingers closed, I had to tell myself, *Close your fingers, close your fingers, close your fingers.* If I lost concentration for an instant, the fingers opened and dropped whatever I was carrying.

Eventually, I figured out that an oversized cross-body bag could accommodate everything I needed. It became my constant companion. I just had to be careful not to overload it or the weight would upset my balance. I figured out ways of getting to meetings unobserved, using different routes from everyone else and leaving a few minutes early to do so. Sometimes Bill sneaked my papers into the meeting room ahead of time, so I just had to get myself there and not carry anything.

I wanted to drive, go to meetings by myself, and carry my own stuff. I became increasingly disenchanted with the physical and occupational therapy services I was receiving. The therapists who tried to help me with care and compassion always seemed to be mired in an endless cycle of justification so that more visits could be authorized. I felt that momentum was continually lost as an inordinate amount of time was devoted to testing things that did not change. As a therapist, I had performed many of those same tests and wondered about their value. As a patient, my perspective was different. I had been warned from the beginning that recovery would slow after the first few months, and I knew enough to accept that some of my deficits would be permanent. I also knew that function could keep improving indefinitely, as long as muscles were used and strengthened. As far as I was concerned, there was no expiration date on my supersized box of recovery potential.

Standing on a box on one leg did not fit into my plans, yet every evaluation called for me to try. I was acutely aware that falling off that box could leave me without a leg to stand on, and that thought triggered spasms that left me unable to lift my leg at all. Stacking a pile of pennies or turning a key with my left hand did not appeal to me as a way of expending precious energy, nor did folding clothes or—worse yet—trying to don a pile of particularly unappealing clothing, snatched from the jaws of the Salvation Army.

After about a month of therapy, the physician at the outpatient rehabilitation facility once again raised the issue of how long my insurance would continue to pay for therapy. My reaction to the question was to assume he thought I had been taking up space long enough, and it was time to make room for another patient. It was not what he said, and, looking back, I can see that it wasn't what he meant, but in my tinderbox of contradictory emotions, it was enough to start a fire. Much of the time I didn't see why I needed all this therapy, but on the other hand, I did want to do 90 percent of what I used to be able to do, and I was not even at 65 percent. I left stroke rehabilitation that day in high dudgeon.

When Bruce arrived to pick me up, I asked him to drive me down the street to Athletico, an orthopedic rehabilitation facility. Without question, he drove me there and helped me through the front door. I asked if they could treat my unstable ankle and arthritic knee and shoulder. I spoke the language of orthopedics fluently. They gave me a cursory glance and said they would be glad to help, as long as I got an order from a physician. I got the order from a doctor friend and embarked upon an entirely new course of treatment. I was assigned to a physical therapist who, as it happened, specialized in neurological conditions as well as orthopedics. Her name was Galina.

Galina, a recent Russian immigrant with jet-black hair and eyes, told me in heavily accented English that she had very little experience dealing with strokes.

"Good," I responded. My order from the doctor was for treatment of an arthritic hip, knee, and shoulder and gait training.

"What are your goals?" asked Galina during the inevitable initial evaluation.

"I want to be able to do 90 percent of what I could do before."

The words rolled off my tongue, but her quizzical look let me know that she needed a little more specificity.

"How about if we put down that you want to increase strength in your lower extremities in order to ambulate independently and to improve your core strength and balance and to facilitate return to work?"

"Oh, I'm already back at work," I said.

She looked a little surprised. "What about your arm? Any goals for that?"

"Not really. I'm doing everything one-handed now, so I'd rather concentrate on my leg."

Truthfully, I was finding it much easier and faster to do things one-handed than to cope with the frustration of fumbling, dropping, forgetting to close my fingers, and then forgetting to open them. Getting the job done was much more important to me than trying to connect with uncooperative, disconnected digits.

In my few weeks with Galina, I made some remarkable discoveries. One revelation was that I could walk better and faster backward than forward. Who would have thought? We toyed with the idea of making this my norm but soon realized that while this might work really well within the safe walls of the gym, it might be more than a little hazardous on the street. The vision of a lopsided middle-aged woman careening backward along the streets caused us to subside in heaps of laughter and resolve to keep trying to pursue improvement in the more conventional manner of ambulation.

The other discovery we made was that Galina did not like the AFO any more than I did, and we made it a goal to try to wean me off it. As a first step, I would wear an orthopedic ankle brace that was softer and kinder to my knee. We did a lot of work with ankle-strengthening exercises and electrical stimulation in an effort to try to resuscitate those weak muscles that allowed the strong ones to pull my ankle in the wrong direction.

Between work and therapy, my days took so much out of me that I was in bed by eight o'clock most days, docked in a deep and dreamless sleep by a pill and the television until the alarm sounded at six thirty, and the cycle began again.

As I was reaching the end of the authorized sessions and had reached most of the goals set by Galina, Bruce embarked on a fitness campaign of his own and joined a gym. We didn't know for how long his passion would persist, but just then, he was highly motivated. He came home one day and enthusiastically told me he had met an exercise physiologist who, he thought, would be able to help me.

At the appointed hour, I arrived at the health club to meet Cheryl, the exercise physiologist who was going to work with me. She was a bright and bubbly brunette with startling blue eyes fringed with enviable black lashes and wore a navy track suit and pristine white athletic shoes. Cheryl greeted me warmly. If she was surprised by the gimpy apparition in front of her, her face gave no hint of it. I had squeaked and tapped down the ramp to the gym, wearing my best burgundy workout suit, now a little the worse for wear, with the soft brace squeezed into oversized red-and-white Sketchers. We sat and talked for a little while, and then Cheryl took me on a tour of the gym. After we inspected all the standard gym equipment, stationary bikes, elliptical machines, treadmills, and such, she told me that she had set up a test to determine my level of fitness so she could plan my program accordingly. She confessed that she had never worked with anyone like me and that her test might be a bit ambitious. She escorted me into a small, mirror-lined room, bare except for what appeared to be a very complicated obstacle course set out in the middle of the room.

There were several beams, about five inches wide, upon which she clearly intended me to walk, putting one foot in front of the other, high-wire style, to test my balance. There were obstacles designed for me to climb over or under. A daunting pile of weights stood at one side of a bench, and I inwardly marveled at the complexity of it all. It looked so artistic and so totally disconnected from my reality.

Cheryl had obviously invested a lot of time and effort in preparing for my arrival. I surveyed the scene, looking long and hard at the obstacles. My tilted, twisted torso was reflected multiple times in the mirrors. I looked at Cheryl and said, "You are joking, of course!"

She looked at me, her face a study of conflicted anticipation. I saw the consternation in her eyes as she waited for me to react. "Don't be mad," she pleaded. "I had no idea how bad you were. Oh, I'm so sorry.

I didn't mean that to come out the way it did. I didn't know you couldn't really walk. I didn't know your arm didn't work."

Poor girl; I felt her concern and embarrassment.

"Cheryl," I said, "when you are in a hole, stop digging!"

We looked at each other and burst into peals of laughter, unbridled mirth at the very thought of my doing any part of that routine. To quote Robert Frost, "If we couldn't laugh, we would all go insane."[7]

That was the start of a long and productive relationship in which Cheryl diligently worked with me to improve my strength, balance, and coordination. This new regimen gave me a big psychological boost and improved my general fitness. The parts of me that did not work were assisted immeasurably by strengthening the parts that did.

Bruce and I attended the club at least three times a week. He worked with his trainer, while I found myself on a mat on the floor doing sit-ups and all kinds of exercises that I would have considered beyond my reach a short time before. I got down to the floor easily. I had had a lot of practice falling and knew that getting down was, for me, nothing more than a modified, controlled fall.

Getting up, however, was a whole other challenge. Cheryl, despite my concerns for her back, insisted that it was a piece of cake to get behind me, put her arms in my armpits, and lever me up to my feet. My job was to know at what point in the process I should nail my landing, knees braced and weight on my feet, to avoid tipping forward and ending up back on the floor, supine to prone in one simple move. We used the Olympic gymnastics scoring system, with the Romanian judge frequently giving me an undeserved perfect ten.

Cheryl was a fabulous trainer, and her joie de vivre was contagious. We spent a lot of time laughing as she gingerly pushed my limits with giant balls, weights, ropes, and elastic bands. I had a lot of moral support from other members of the club. There was great camaraderie, and I was energized by the encouragement I received, especially from the young body-builder Adonis guys with whom, under ordinary circumstances, I would have had very little in common. They cheered whenever I accomplished something new, egged me on to try different machines, and generally made me feel like one of the gang.

One nuisance that persisted was the trigger points around my left shoulder blade that caused a lot of pain and impeded my ability to do many arm exercises. The muscles that stabilized my scapula were paralyzed, causing other muscles to operate incorrectly and become fatigued.

Cheryl mentioned that there was a massage therapist at the gym, who might be able to help with that. I signed up for two sessions a week and found that the massage really helped. I now had something every day after work and on the weekends too. I started to feel like an overextended grade-school pupil, although I had not yet added soccer practice to my routine!

I was feeling much more confident about my ability to get around by myself and realized that from a practical point of view, my biggest handicap was that I could not drive. As kind as everyone was about driving me, I felt that loss of independence keenly. Our house was located where it was impossible to go anywhere sans wheels. I launched a campaign to get my license back at my next doctor's appointment.

"Are you sure?" he inquired. "You will have to go through a rigorous evaluation and training program."

"Absolutely! I need to drive."

There was a brief conversation about perhaps trying one of those powered wheelchairs or scooters first, which I brought to a rapid close with as much good grace as I could muster. I had tried one in the supermarket and succeeded only in going in circles. It was like the hospital wheelchair on steroids. There was the added risk of causing grievous bodily harm to an innocent shopper or demolishing shelves of stacked goods.

There was also the reality that I lived too far from shops or any place I might need to go for me to go by scooter, and I'd need a car to drive the scooter to the mall before I could use it.

After much wheedling and cajoling on my part, the doctor agreed to refer me back to the Rehabilitation Institute of Chicago for a driver evaluation and potential retraining.

The driver education program was at the main building of the Rehabilitation Institute. With Mrs. Bloom now back at work as a nanny,

Bruce agreed to drive me to my appointment. The evaluation was administered by an occupational therapist who had special training in driver education. It was an exhaustive and exhausting process. I recognized the importance of safety and the need to protect innocents on the road from drivers who might not be fully competent. While I did not think that applied to me, I conceded that I was not in the driver's seat with respect to getting my license back, and I would never be in the driver's seat again if I flunked those tests.

Fortunately, I passed, but a couple of adaptations were needed before I could drive my own car—a knob on the steering wheel, known as a "spinner," and an extension for the turn signal so I could operate it with my right hand. The visual/perceptual part of the test revealed a deficit in my field of vision on the left; no big surprise. My lying eyes, however, would not disqualify me from driving as long as I learned to turn my head to compensate for the blind spot.

Next came two two-hour driving lessons with an instructor in a simulated car. That was a lot like playing video games at Chuck E. Cheese! I drove my virtual car on virtual highways and city streets, secure in the knowledge that any accidents I caused would be virtual too. Any casualties would be resurrected in the next game.

The next stop on my road to liberation was driving lessons in a real car. Sitting in the passenger seat with the instructor behind the wheel, it was reassuring to see the duplicate set of controls on the passenger side, knowing that he could steer and stop the car if necessary when it was my turn. I would have to prove that I could compensate for my deficits adequately and would not be a danger to myself or others before I would be set free to travel on my own. I wanted to drive by myself so much that it had become an obsession. It was not that I was in love with driving or cars; in fact, in my lottery-winner daydreams, my shopping list never included a fancy new car. It did include a chauffeur but only for parking. My desire to drive had everything to do with independence and feeling normal again. It was not that I was not a polite or appreciative person, but the amount of gratitude I was having to dole out on a daily basis was getting tiresome. Nobody minded driving me, but I hated having to ask.

On my first real driving lesson, the instructor piloted the car out of the parking lot and drove for a few blocks, explaining to me how the controls worked. In a calm, matter-of-fact manner, he told me he would drive to a large outdoor parking area close to the lake. Then we would change places, and it would be my turn-my maiden voyage as a handicapped driver. He pulled into one of the parking lots, got out, and came around to open the door for me.

"Your turn," he said with a smile.

Gulp, swallow, deep breath—my heart was beating like a caged bird within my chest. Gulp, swallow, deep Pilates breath—in through the nose, out slowly through the mouth. Why was swallowing suddenly so hard? Would it be like riding a bike? Once you have learned to drive, does the ability stay with you? I had already proved that what they say about riding a bike was a myth. I could not even ride the stationary exercise bike in the gym. I tilted so far to the side that the bike would have tipped over, had it not been firmly bolted to the floor. What if I hurt someone—a child, a dog? A confusion of anxious feelings almost caused me to bolt.

The instructor went over the controls one more time and then said, "You'll be fine. Adjust your mirrors, put on your indicator, and when you are ready, pull carefully out into the road."

Deep breath, gulp. I gingerly put my sweaty hand on the wheel and put my left leg over to the side as far as I could so there was no risk of it getting caught under the pedal. My heart was pumping fast, my teeth were clenched, my mouth dry, and I could not move a single muscle.

"Just relax," advised my instructor. "It's just like riding a bike. It'll come back to you."

Oh, bugger! I thought. *I hope it's not like me riding a bike.* I had never been very secure in the saddle of a bike, maybe because I had learned on an antique, sit-up-and-beg model, devoid of brakes or pneumatic tires.

After more deep breaths and gentle encouragement from my instructor, I put the car in drive, used the adapted turn signal, looked in the mirror, and pulled out into the open space. I was not far from the first street when my instructor asked me to turn left. He reminded me to turn my head when I looked to the left. He knew about my lying eyes.

The knob felt strange and unwieldy in my hand as I made my first official attempt at one-handed navigation.

We went around the parking lot making left and right turns, stopping and starting. I followed his prompts to look in the mirror, stay on my own side of the road, not drift to the wrong side of the road, and pick up a little speed. What? I was going fifteen miles an hour already! It felt like a lot more. After a first shaky attempt at reversing into a parking spot, I was done for the day. When I used the spinner for the first time, my turns were ridiculously wide, but I did not hit anything, so allowed myself a little credit.

The second lesson was even more adventurous. Not only was I about to drive on actual city streets, but during the second hour I would have to keep up a running verbal commentary on everything I saw. I learned a new vocabulary. "Stale green light" meant the traffic light was already green as I approached it; same with the red. "Fresh" green or red light meant it just had changed, and I could proceed at normal speed. I had to report on every pedestrian within my field of vision, swiveling my head to catch strays on the left.

"A truck ahead; turning right; a police car in the mirror; a pedestrian crossing; two people in the crosswalk; a car turning right; a motorbike on my right between me and the curb; stale red light; green light; turning left; car in front stops for a pedestrian; stop; move on." The faster I drove, the faster I talked. I was so busy talking I forgot to be nervous about driving. It was a clever diversionary tactic. I was doing fine! It was not like riding a bike; it was like driving a car, and I hadn't forgotten how to do it.

We returned to the parking lot, and my instructor told me he needed a few minutes to write up his report. After what felt like eons, he grinned at me and said, "You have passed, and I'm willing to certify that it is safe for you to get your license back. You'll have to take this form to your doctor to complete, and then go to the DMV and show that your car has been modified, according to the directions on the form, and you'll be good to go. Your doctor will also sign an application for you to get a handicapped placard for your car. Do not forget to turn your head when you look to the left, and be extremely careful. Good luck!"

As I tried to climb out of the car, I felt something pulling me back. I could not get out! *Oh no! Don't let him change his mind.* I looked down and saw that my left arm was still inside the seatbelt. Blood rushed to my face, and I stammered an apology for being so stupid. He told me not to worry about it, that it happened all the time.

It took about a week to have the modifications made. Then the full impact of what was about to happen assailed me. It was a mixture of anxiety and unfettered exhilaration. I was going to be able to go out by myself! No more waiting, no more fitting into other people's schedules, no more apologizing for being a nuisance, no more ... I pulled myself up short. What was going to happen at the other end of my solo trips, when I arrived at my destination? Was I going to be able to walk from the car to my office by myself or navigate the grocery store or the mall? I had not given much thought to that.

Bruce was less enthusiastic about my liberation than I was, so I agreed to practice runs. We went 'round and 'round the parking lot at the mall, just as we had when the girls were learning to drive. I found that a shopping cart makes a good walker, so when there was one available, I placed my cane inside it and pushed. If there was no cart available, I held Bruce's arm. When there was no Bruce, there would be Bill at the office. In my future, there would be countless anonymous knights in shining armor—people I accosted in parking lots, strangers who offered help—but that was not something I was aware of at that time. I just knew that a tiny morsel of my former independence was restored.

After another three weeks of practice in the evenings and on weekends, I was convinced that I was ready to drive to work. I had a phone in my car for emergencies, and Bill would meet me at my parking space. That I had the parking space at the very bottom of the ramp, where the walk to the elevator was akin to climbing the lower foothills of the Himalayas, was a bit of a nuisance, but it never occurred to me to ask anyone to trade places. I had not asked for "reasonable accommodation," and none had been offered. In fact, I had not heard a word from Human Resources since I came back from England. My first solo trip to the office was a big emotional event, exhilaration for me and sheer terror for Bruce, who saw me off like a nervous bird watching the fledglings leave the nest. I promised him that I would be careful, stay in the slow lane, and call him the minute I arrived at my desk.

Exhilaration faded to apprehension as I pulled out of the driveway and turned the car toward the city. I had never liked merging into fast-moving cars at the entrance to the highway, and that morning every car and truck appeared to be going at least a hundred miles an hour. I almost chickened out and went home as I approached the entrance to the ramp. But this was no time for self-doubt. Had I not convinced countless patients that they could do anything they put their minds to? Had their stomachs churned the way mine did now as they set off in their electric wheelchairs or their invalid cars or when they used public transportation by themselves for the first time?

Traffic was moving slowly on the highway that morning, a blessing because I could stay in the slow lane most of the way. My heart lurched when large trucks overtook me, and I felt the push and pull of displaced air, causing me to grip the spinner so tightly that I feared I might snap it off. As the magnificent Chicago skyline came into view, I experienced a pang of panic because I was going to have to exit the highway and navigate the crowded city streets. Again, traffic was moving slowly, so I had plenty of time to position myself to exit smoothly, still swinging wide and overcorrecting. I pulled into my parking space, put my head on the steering wheel, and napped for a few minutes before calling Bill. He arrived promptly and helped me haul myself up the concrete hill. Exactly one hour and ten minutes after leaving Bruce waving in the driveway, I called him from my office to tell him I had arrived safely and to apologize for not waving back when I left. I could not take my hand off the steering wheel to wave without running the risk of driving into the pond!

From then on, the journey got easier every day. As my confidence blossomed, I allowed myself the luxury of listening to a book on tape as I drove. This elixir calmed my nerves if driving conditions were difficult.

About a month after starting to drive myself to work, I decided to take my independence to the next stage and met a colleague, Ann, for dinner after work. Ann lived in San Francisco and had had a similar to experience to mine when an aneurism in her brain ruptured while she was walking in the city a few years earlier. She had been found incoherent and was thought to be a street person before being correctly identified, diagnosed, and treated. I was envious as she walked into the restaurant, where I had arrived early to avoid walking in with an audience. Ann entered the restaurant looking remarkably like her old self, smile symmetrical, no cane, arms swinging in rhythm with her legs. She held out both arms to give me a hug. I responded with one arm. She told me she only uses a cane when walking long distances outside. We ordered a drink, nonalcoholic for me because I was driving and nonalcoholic for her because she was walking and didn't have her cane. The amount of forethought and planning that goes into outings for stroke survivors was not intuitive to me at that time. When dinner was served, we began to eat, and I went automatically into bite, chew, and swat mode.

"There is nothing on your face," she said with a smile. "I used to do that." By the end of the meal, she said a little impatiently, "For God's sake, Jan, will you stop swatting your face with your napkin? You don't have food on your face."

In the course of the meal, she told me about her own recovery, which appeared to me to be almost complete recovery. She had opted for alternative therapies. Because she lived in California, her health insurance covered massage, acupuncture, nutrition counseling, and Pilates. That was how she rehabilitated herself. Wow! I was inspired! She had not folded a single grubby shirt, stacked cones, or worn an AFO. Would that work for me?

My drive home flew by as I contemplated the possibility of maybe even 95 percent. I was not thinking about different strokes for different folks or how the location and severity of damage to the brain influences outcomes. I was just thinking that whatever Ann did was miraculous, and I wanted some of whatever she had in California right here in Illinois. Eat it, drink it, snort it, inject it—if I could do all that she could do, I would try anything.

Once I reached home, instead of falling into bed as I customarily did, I went downstairs to the basement where the family computer resided. It was a long trip down twelve steps, but with newly fitted handrails on both sides, I felt confident enough to do it. I Googled "Pilates."

A prompt asked me for my ZIP code, and I willingly obliged. A screen full of websites and advertisements quickly appeared, and I picked one located close to home and printed off the page, ready to call the next day. I made a snap decision to check my email as long as I was there. Staring at me was an invitation from a cruise line to partake of a much-deserved, hard-earned break from winter blues at bargain-basement prices.

"Why not?" I asked myself. "By the time winter comes, we'll be ready for a vacation. We work hard; why shouldn't we go somewhere nice?"

My cross-body purse was still around my body, with my wallet and a reduced number of credit cards housed within. Before making the trek back upstairs, I signed us up for a cruise to French Polynesia, airfare included, for the following January.

I was still seeing Cheryl, but things were not going well for her at the health club. I showed up one day, and she wasn't there. The receptionist told me, discreetly, that Cheryl no longer worked there. I called her on her cell phone, and she told me she had been fired. She'd had a run-in with another trainer who was higher up the ladder and was shown the door. She hadn't called because she had been told, in no uncertain terms, not to contact any of her clients. I arranged to work with her at home, but there would be minimal equipment and no cheering section.

That was the point at which I called the Pilates studio nearby. I explained my situation, and the receptionist told me there was an instructor who was also a physical therapist, and we agreed that sounded like a perfect match.

I began seeing Wendy twice a week. Wendy, tall and striking with wispy tendrils of blonde hair escaping a ponytail to frame her face, was from New Zealand. She told me in her broad Antipodean accent that she was just emerging from a bad break-up with a *National Geographic* photographer.

Wendy introduced me to weird and wonderful machines with impressive names—a Cadillac that was not a car and a reformer that had nothing to do with social justice. I found myself in some very interesting positions, hanging by my sheepskin bootie-clad feet from slings above my head; dangling from constellations of leather slings, wires, and springs; flapping my wing, while counting to one hundred and performing myriad other contortions aimed at lengthening and strengthening whatever parts of me could possibly be improved. I really liked what we did. The only drawback was that the studio was located awkwardly for me. It was set back from the road with no parking and quite a treacherous walk down an alley to the door that opened outward, posing another hazard. I stuck with it until snow on the ground made it impossible for me to go. Wendy asked me, at my final session, if I would be willing to come to the Lutheran General Hospital, where she worked during the day, and give a talk to the staff of the Rehabilitation Unit. She thought they would be interested to hear from a patient who was also a therapist. I readily agreed, and the date was set for two weeks later. I rushed home and started banging out my talk on the computer. The title was "I've Looked at Stroke from Both Sides Now—with Apologies to Joni Mitchell."

A nurse educator called me a few days before the talk to ask if I had any special needs.

"I won't need a projector or anything. I don't have any audiovisuals. I'm just going to talk," I replied.

"That's not what I meant," she said softly. "I meant how are you going to get here?"

"I'll be driving myself, and if you tell me where to go, I'll meet you there."

"No," she insisted. "It's a really long way from the front entrance to the conference room, and we can't take the risk of your falling."

I caught myself starting to bristle, but after working in risk management for almost twenty years, I understood that I became their responsibility the minute I set foot on the premises. I just asked her what she would suggest. We agreed that I would drive in front of the main entrance and call her cell phone; she would meet me with a wheelchair, the valet would take my car, and we would repeat the process in reverse when it was time for me to leave. My one caveat was that I would get out of the wheelchair at the entrance to the auditorium and get to the podium under my own steam. I asked for a microphone, fearing that because my voice still was not back to full strength, they would not be able to hear me. I also asked for a chair because, if I tried to stand at the podium for thirty-five minutes, I might get carried away with my material and forget to brace my knee, lose my balance, and create another liability for the hospital.

Once introduced, I looked out at a group of about thirty health professionals welcoming me with enthusiasm. I had written cue cards in front of me but found I could not see them. If I put on my reading glasses, I would be able to see the notes but not the audience, so I made a snap decision to wing it.

Since my concept of time was still unreliable, I asked the nurse who had greeted me to give me a warning signal when it was five minutes from the end of my time. I had to clear my throat several times before I began to talk. I felt very vulnerable and exposed and swiped the side of my face with a tissue to make sure there was nothing there. I made a mental note to remember to swallow often so I didn't drool. A few deep breaths, a nod and half smile around the room, and I was off.

Speaking as clearly as I could with my diminished voice and swiveling my head around to make eye contact with as many people as possible, I rattled off everything I could remember. It was in abridged form but included much of what had happened from Jonny's wedding to that moment, sitting in front of them. I highlighted the good parts of nursing care and therapy and mentioned a couple of problems—slow response times to the call button, bad oral hygiene. Likewise with the therapies, I talked about the good parts and the frustrations. The prearranged signal from the nurse alerted me that I was approaching the end of my time. There was a glass of water in front of me, but I did not dare to take a drink in case I set off a coughing fit. Exhausted and parched, I ended by asking if there were any questions. Several hands shot up, and after a couple of throat clearings, I began to answer. Eventually, there was just one raised hand left. The person identified herself as a nurse in neurosurgical intensive care.

"This isn't a question," she said, "but a comment. In my years of caring for acute neurosurgical patients, I have observed that they often have bad breath that persists for some time. It's my guess that the bad breath you smelled was your own."

I saw rows of nodding heads, and as they gave me a hearty round of applause, all I could think was, *I'll be darned! I came here to impart wisdom and just learned that I owe apologies to a number of innocent people. Crow will have to be eaten when I get home!*

Regardless, having successfully delivered a talk to a group was something the old me would have done, and it gave me a boost. I felt the needle on my recovery meter hovering close to 70 percent—heady stuff!

January 2004 rolled around and with it the departure date for the cruise I had booked several months before. I had only been on one plane trip since the stroke, not counting the triumphant repatriation that occurred shortly afterward, about which I remember nothing. After a few months of work, we went to Las Vegas for a long weekend. We stayed at Caesar's Palace, as guests of a friend of Bruce's, who arranged tickets for Celine Dion and Cirque Du Soleil. It was a smooth trip. Bruce had made it a condition that I use a wheelchair for the duration of the trip. I didn't like it, but it was better than not going.

This time there would be no wheelchair. I was at 70 percent, after all. I could use a wheelchair at each of the airports, and all would be well. I was convinced that this vacation was going to be the best ever. Ninety percent of pre-stroke function might still be way off, but I would polish off the rest when I got back.

BIBLIOGRAPHY: CHAPTER 6

Goodreads. Quote from Robert Frost, "If we couldn't laugh we would all go insane." Accessed July 10, 2018. https://www.goodreads.com/quotes/5609-if-we-couldn-t-laugh-we-would-all-go-insane

CHAPTER 7

A Limp Down Memory Lane

It was now eighteen months post-stroke, and we were off to cruise the South Pacific. I had booked this cruise on a wave of assumed invincibility shortly after returning to work. What was I thinking? The simple answer to that question is that I was not thinking realistically at all. I was still unaware of the degree of physical limitation that I had and did not consider myself handicapped. To anyone who might question the wisdom of such a long trip, especially Bruce, my response was that I was perfectly capable, would be sitting down the whole way, and had I not traveled back from England in a lot worse state than I was currently in?

"Travel is what I do and a significant part of who I am," I rationalized to anyone who would listen. "If I can just get back to doing that again, maybe I'll start to feel more like myself."

Travel was also a big part of Bruce and a part of us, as a couple. Aside from our family, one of the most important, defining, positive factors of our relationship was the shared love of adventure, new places, and different cultures. We had been great travel partners. It was how we met all those years ago in Bangkok, when we were both on assignments for the World Health Organization. It was what we had done as a couple and as a family as often as we could. During the years when we both were working hard on our careers and raising the girls, carving out time to be together—away from the hubbub and never-ending demands—by traveling whenever we could kept us grounded.

I hoped this trip would restore some fun and familiarity to a marriage that had been turned upside down and thrown on its head by this new, stroke-induced imbalance in which I had lost my independence and much of my identity and become, in my own words, "a dependent drag."

Bruce is twenty years older than I am. The plan, when we first decided to get married, had been that I would push him around in a wheelchair in old age. We had never considered that it might be the other way around. Bruce, though only recently converted to regular exercise, looked and acted a good twenty years younger than his chronological age. I, on the other hand, was exercising constantly, working myself to a sliver, and still, to my eyes, looked and acted old enough to be his mother. I hated that I felt that way and that we never seemed to have fun anymore. Every conversation seemed to be about the wretched thing that had happened in my head—doctor visits, therapy, degrees of improvement, concessions that had to be made, or medicines that I had to take. This trip was not so much a vacation as a pilgrimage in search of a new, more acceptable norm for both of us.

We flew United from Chicago to Los Angeles, upgraded with leftover miles to first class. I don't know how long the flight lasted, but it was comfortable and manageable. When we landed at the Los Angeles airport, a wheelchair was waiting at the gate, and we were told that we must transfer to a different terminal for the flight to Tahiti.

I noticed uneasily, while waiting to board the plane, that the original owner's name had been painted over with the words "Princess Cruises." As we boarded the flight and turned right, I could tell the plane was old by the configuration of the cabin, the small overhead compartments, and the absence of any form of television screen. The interior resembled a sardine can; the seats were so closely packed together that once occupied, nobody could possibly move. Bruce and I were assigned two middle seats in a row of four toward the back of the plane. I protested to the flight attendant that I would not be able to get in and out to go to the bathroom. She told me there was nothing she could do. There was nothing in my profile to indicate that I needed special assistance.

Why would I even have a profile on this painted-over apology for an airplane? My cane was snatched the minute we boarded, and I had to sidle along the seats, hanging on with my right hand, until we reached our assigned row. Once in our seats, we discovered that the nightmare was just beginning.

Springs poked tauntingly through the upholstery of the seat cushions, and the seats did not recline. The absence of the reclining function had nothing to do with this being an exit row and everything to do with the fact that there was simply no space into which the seat could possibly recline. In coach on an ordinary plane, it can be hard to recline without landing in the lap of the person behind. On this plane, there wasn't even room for the person behind to have a lap. We were all practically standing up, just a slight bend in the middle, and there was nowhere to stow anything under the seat in front. There was barely enough room to accommodate our feet.

Bruce was speechless, an unusual situation for him. He always left the travel arrangements to me, and I never had let him down. He begged and implored the flight attendant to find us different seats but to no avail. His jaw tightened as he segued from sad to mad. In desperation, he offered to pay to upgrade us to first class. There was no first class on this plane. It was an equal opportunity purveyor of misery. We decided on the best course of action we could think of, under the circumstances. I would have to sleep throughout this journey or be overcome by claustrophobia, acute physical discomfort, or both. I had a bottle of sleeping pills in my carry-on bag, which would soon be crammed into the overhead compartment for the duration of the flight. I quickly opened the bottle, clenching the top between my teeth and pushing and twisting with my hand. I removed two pills and tucked them in the pocket of my shirt.

I would kill two birds with one stone—lighten the load and knock myself out. Bruce pushed the button for the attendant and told her I needed to go to the bathroom, urgently.

She wasn't exactly unhelpful but took the opportunity of delivering a rebuke. "It would have been much easier if someone had told us you were handicapped."

Exasperated, I snapped, "Who would have told you that?"

"The person who made the reservations should have," she responded testily.

"I made the reservations, and while I was fully aware that I'm not as fit as I used to be, I've had a problem with my brain. My arm and leg don't work normally, but it would never occur to me to describe myself as handicapped."

Since people were still boarding the plane, I had to swim upstream to get to the bathroom. Bruce went first, holding up his hands to steer people around me, explaining to everyone that his handicapped wife needed to go to the bathroom. I felt like a complete fool and was furious with him.

"Why do you keep telling complete strangers that I am handicapped? If I could get off the plane right now, I would," I grumbled.

Hot, harried, and humiliated, I finally reached the bathroom as the last of the passengers squeezed through, and the crew moved quickly to bar and bolt the cabin door. Slamming the lock on the bathroom door behind me, I fumbled the pills from my pocket, swallowed them, and headed back to my seat, snaking past the crew doing the safety demonstration on the way.

The next thing I knew, Bruce was shaking my arm gently, telling me we were about to land in Papeete. I felt a momentary thrill. I had wanted to visit the South Pacific ever since I saw the movie years before. I looked out of the window, over the heads of the passengers on our side of the plane, and caught a glimpse of a tiny island covered with waving palm trees, white beaches fringed by silver surf, and rolling turquoise waves. It looked like a picture postcard. Soon the flight attendant announced that we should watch our step as we descended from the plane.

"What? There aren't supposed to be any stairs, what happened to the jet- way?" My question was drowned by continuing loudspeaker announcements about baggage claim and ground transportation. I almost choked. The announcements concluded with the flight attendant saying that they looked forward to seeing us on our return journey.

Papeete's airport, as it transpired, was not only devoid of jet-ways but devoid of a terminal, unless you counted the series of thatch-roofed, open- sided structures that housed baggage, ticketing, and a few stalls selling snacks and souvenirs.

Bruce had already summoned the flight attendant again to inform her that the steep flight of stairs that had just been pulled up to the side of the plane— proudly displaying its "Welcome to Papeete" sign, with handrails made of rope that swayed gently in the tropical breeze—was totally beyond the capability of his *handicapped* wife. I shot him a venomous look as he used the H-word again.

"I can do stairs perfectly well, but I need a real handrail, not a flapping, useless piece of string!" I growled, still drowsy from the pills, hungry, dehydrated, and in no mood to be trifled with.

After a somewhat belligerent interchange with a couple of crew members who rejected my invitation to take me back to Los Angeles, a local agent mounted the wobbly steps and announced that there was a solution. With the captain's approval, I could exit the plane the same way as the used catering containers—on the platform of a forklift truck. There was a secret door behind the cockpit, through which I made my descent. Bruce and a crewmember flanked me on the platform so I did not fall off. By means of this unorthodox method of transportation, I arrived on terra firma where, under different circumstances, I might have been tempted to kiss the ground.

We found our bags on the rickety carousel as we inhaled a powerful cocktail of salty ocean water, tropical flowers, and jet fuel. There were many vehicles parked close to the steamy tarmac of the runway, most displaying logos of hotels, resorts, and cruise lines. Our baggage tags identified us as Princess Cruisers, and soon we were approached by a cheery chap wearing an aloha shirt, straw hat, lei, and a huge grin.

"Plincess Cluise," he announced, his handsome brown face split in two by a set of perfect white teeth. Without a word, he grabbed our two suitcases and beckoned us to follow him to a white shuttle van. I was, by now, seated in a decrepit, squeaky wheelchair that made the one I had in the hospital seem like a Rolls-Royce.

As we reached the entrance of the shuttle, already almost filled with passengers, I saw that there was a gigantic step to gain access to the interior of the bus. I got out of the wheelchair and made a move toward the step. Groggy from the long flight and disoriented from the pills,

I could not lift my left leg off the ground. It had become as stiff as an iron poker. The knee joint would not bend. I tried stepping up with the right leg first and then lifting my left leg with my right hand. It was rooted to the ground. Then I tried standing on the right leg, looping my right arm under my knee, and pulling. Nothing happened.

Soaked with perspiration, I experienced a sudden blast of déjà vu. This was not the first time my leg had refused to leave the ground in a sultry, sticky place. It had happened in Singapore, after the plane I had taken from Saigon had depressurized over the South China Sea and hurtled more than twenty thousand feet downward before the pilot had pulled out of the dive just in time to avoid plunging us all into a watery grave. I had taken a cockroach- infested train all the way back to Bangkok, a twenty-four-hour odyssey, rather than get on another plane. Any further attempt to chase that flimsy recollection was forestalled by the van driver saying he would help me. I put my right leg on the step, and the driver started to lift my left leg. It moved forward with a jerk and got caught firmly under the bottom step. I could not go up or down.

Bruce was a mortified and helpless observer. He was as tired and discombobulated as I was. The driver extricated my trapped foot, and I sank down on the dirty, greasy step, facing forward, despairing of ever making it to the ship. The driver then suggested, bravely, that perhaps I could go backward. I could haul myself with my right arm, and he would push my left leg. I had walked backward efficiently enough in therapy. Could climbing steps be that different?

The plan was that he would get behind me, hold me under my armpits, and pull. I would hang on to the side of the bus doorway and step up with my right leg on a count of three. My left leg, we reasoned, would follow. We counted, and on three, he pushed and I pulled. All that happened was that my left leg shot out in front of me like a battering ram and delivered a hefty kick to the thigh of a man who was standing right in front of me. He winced and blanched. In an instant of eye contact, it registered how close I had come to destroying his manhood.

The chap who had greeted us was not quite so cheerful, as he eyed the passengers lining up behind me. To their credit, they were not complaining and were doing their best to be encouraging, but they too had spent the night in Princess Purgatory and were anxious to be on their way.

In the end, there was a consensus that I could not get on this shuttle. A wise man in the audience suggested a taxi might be a better way for me to go to the ship. Bruce readily concurred, with the caveat that the taxi driver must accept dollars, as we had no Tahitian money.

"No plobrem; I will gradry take dorrahs," a driver shouted. Amid the cheers of our relieved fellow passengers, we finally set off to find the ship.

At the dock, we entered a teeming throng of people, vehicles, and carts piled high with bags. Our bags were snatched immediately, and we were told we would see them again in our stateroom. Stateroom sounded very grand! I pictured opulent furnishings in spacious quarters, red velvet, gilt mirrors, a silver tray with martini shaker and soda siphon. I might never have been on a cruise before but I had seen pictures.

The daughter of a friend of Mum's, Muriel Arnold, was a purser on one of the Cunard Queens when I was a young teenager. Muriel, blonde and elegant, the closest thing to a movie star our village had ever produced, showed us photographs of her travels whenever she was home on leave.

The photographs and accompanying stories were spellbinding to someone like me, who had never been anywhere exotic, except in daydreams. I sat for hours on her parents' living room floor, trying to imagine myself inside the scenes so I could smell the aromas and hear the sounds that went along with the pictures. I dreamed of going to all of those places and more. I wanted to see the whole world.

Most of the year, Muriel traveled back and forth across the Atlantic from Southampton to New York, but in winter, she cruised. The crew's uniforms switched from navy blue to tropical white as they forsook the gray Atlantic for warmer, bluer waters. She showed us pictures of tropical islands, natives in elaborate costumes, and fruits I had never seen, piled up in vivid splendor on carts manned by dark-skinned, gap-toothed merchants. There were exotic birds and animals—flora and fauna that, for me, existed only in the pages of well-worn *National Geographic* magazines handed out for us to read at recess on rainy days.

I was ill-prepared for the reality of the "stateroom" that greeted us when we finally arrived at our accommodation. We took an elevator down from the muster area, skidded through a dark, noisy, and very greasy area that appeared to be the engine room, and were shown, with a great flourish by our cabin steward, into a small, dark room, where a bed appeared to occupy about 99 percent of the available real estate.

There was a window, thank God, or I might have expired on the spot, but it was grimy and water-stained and looked as if it might actually be below sea level. Examination of the bathing facilities revealed a configuration of shower, toilet, and sink that rivaled my health club obstacle course. There were high porcelain steps to climb to both shower and toilet; inadequate, slippery handrails; and not enough room in which to turn around. It was awful.

Bruce started to complain to the steward that this room was not suitable for a "handicapped" person. The steward said, predictably, there was nothing he could do. Bruce settled me on the bed as best he could and set off to find the reception area to talk to somebody.

He didn't get very far before there was a loud-speaker announcement of a mandatory emergency drill, and he had to return to the "stateroom." He came back for me and grabbed our two life jackets, and we set off to rock and roll our way to our designated muster station. It was a long walk, but mercifully, there were handrails for me to hold.

On the way back from the drill, we stumbled into the reception area. It was as opulent as I foolishly had imagined our stateroom would be—huge chandeliers hung from several stories up, shedding light into a gilt and glass atrium filled with mirrors and sweeping, elaborately carpeted staircases. Brass stair rods, gleamed from every step, and brass handrails, beckoned invitingly from either side of the stairs. Those stairs even I could manage! In the center of the lobby, a suave-looking man in white tie and tails sat at a grand piano, playing "Some Enchanted Evening."

I hung on to Bruce's arm as we traversed the undulating expanse of oriental carpet to a desk bearing a brass sign announcing, "Guest Services." Bruce explained to the woman in uniform behind the desk that the facilities in our stateroom were inadequate for his "handicapped" wife's needs. I vowed to myself that I would keep quiet and swallow my annoyance, but it wasn't an issue because she never even looked at me. With her perfectly groomed head tilted to one side in a sympathetic manner, she explained to Bruce that the cruise line prided itself on having excellent facilities for handicapped guests. Unfortunately, whoever made our reservations had made no mention of a handicapped passenger. She would be very pleased to show us the specially designed staterooms so we could see the lengths to which the cruise line had gone to meet its obligations under the Americans with Disabilities Act, but, unfortunately, all such staterooms on this voyage were already occupied. In short, there was nothing she could do. We would have to make the best of it.

"Effing Marie Antoinette of the Seas," I mumbled under my breath. "Let them eat cake!"

We did make the best of it. With minimal help from Guest Services, who, we quickly learned, were more concerned with managing the cruise line's liability with respect to any mishap that might befall a handicapped passenger than actually helping that passenger, we resolutely planned our shipboard days. My OT days *and* my risk management days came back to bite me.

We found an area of deck, close to the elevator and not at all crowded, where we staked a claim each morning, with shade for me and sun for Bruce. I would be able to people-watch or daydream, and Bruce would be able to read. Before, I would have read too, and we would have played Scrabble, but my verbal skills were nowhere near ready for either at that stage. I had a plan to use the time spent on deck constructively, to see if I could make some headway with my capricious memory.

I had read a mnemonic that went like this: "Memory Needs Every Method of Nurturing Its Capacity." My theory was that if exercising my body and pushing it to its limit was what had to happen to gain the maximum improvement in physical function, then the same must be true of mental function. I planned to bully my memory into remembering—at my command, not its own.

In the late 1600s, John Locke identified memory as the currency of identity. I needed to take charge and reconnect with mine in a meaningful way. Before the stroke, I would have said that I was the sum of all the people, places, and events that had influenced me—my narrative scrawled on a chalkboard over almost six decades of life. Now my face was pressed against a sheet of glass that separated me from my past. There were crowds of memories pushing and jostling to get out. Those inaccessible memories were what made me *me*, my accumulated life capital. Without them, I really was not sure who I was. I needed to smell the mildew in the vault where my history was stored to get to a place where my identity was more than "stroke survivor" and the primary adjective applied to me was not "handicapped." I resolved to spend as much time as possible trying to recapture as much of my past as I could.

Recalling became an active verb, a heavy-lifting exercise, a conscious act of grabbing at tendrils, fleshing out flashes of familiarity, and letting my mind reach back as far and with as much accuracy as it could.

At first, it was like my early attempts at learning to drive Dad's ancient Morris Minor with manual transmission. It felt as if I spent long periods idling in neutral, with no memories coming at all. Then a sudden lurch backward yielded a result. I spent most of the time in low gear, moving very slowly, and periodically parked somewhere pleasant before engaging a higher gear and surging forward again.

Bruce brought breakfast and lunch to our spot, and we picnicked there. I didn't go to the buffet myself because I couldn't manage to carry my own plate. That was the reason I gave, but it was more than that. I could not bear to look at the vast expanse of every conceivable kind of food displayed in stainless steel chafing dishes on yards of creaking buffet tables. There was something offensive to me about the sight of so much food. "All You Can Eat" buffets trigger an aversion to greed and gluttony that comes from a place deep within my soul. I let the feeling roll to see where it took me. I found myself in my childhood home in post-war England with my parents and three brothers. My time as a small child was divided between two Lincolnshire villages: Great Gonerby, where we lived, and Sapperton, the site of my grandparents' farm. The detritus of war was all around us—craters in the ground; men missing limbs; others, white-haired, hollow-eyed, short- tempered survivors of prisoner-of-war camps. Their appearance and behavior was explained by adults with a sympathetic shrug as being a result of having been in the hands of either the Japs or the Gerries. I had no idea what that meant but recognized that it gave those men license to chase us with a walking stick, shout at us, or just sit mutely in the back of the church and never speak or make eye contact with anyone.

The male pillars of the community were known simply by their military rank—the Major, the Colonel, the Wing Commander, and my personal favorite, the General. There were plenty of fatherless children, some the result of death in action, others by-products of wartime liaisons that had often involved another spouse and family on the other side of the Atlantic. Every square inch of arable land, including lawns, tennis courts, and cricket pitches, was requisitioned to grow fruit and vegetables or graze livestock.

We were not poor, but we did not have *things*, and we did not have much food. Nobody did. Everything was rationed—food, clothing, household goods, gasoline. Every man, woman, and child had a ration book, issued by the Government Food Office, containing coupons that were exchanged for meager allowances of food from a designated grocery store.

Whatever we had was shared scrupulously fairly within the family and the community at large. There was zero waste. Whatever was unfit for human consumption was fed to livestock that would, in turn, produce more food. The concept of wanton overeating or wasting of food was, for us, almost a capital crime. To be accused of being greedy was to receive a dagger to the heart.

Rationing eased off in 1954, when I was nine but we did not go from shortage to plenty overnight. When things started to become available, it was as a trickle, not a torrent. We still had to be very careful. It was another two years before food, clothing, and household supplies were readily available.

I landed back in the present with a start by Bruce asking if I was okay.

"You seemed to be far away," he said.

"I was but in a good way," I responded. "I'm making headway with my memory."

On shore days, we figured out what we could reasonably accomplish. If a water ferry was required to go ashore, we spent the day on the ship, availing ourselves of the never-ending activities or, more likely, just sitting. We skirted the shower issue by means of the spa, where there were accessible showers and a hot tub with good sturdy steps and handrails. I pretended to work out by limping around the walking track a few times, and then, suitably sweaty from the sun, requested a towel and disappeared into the showers. My hair was washed and styled in the salon for the obligatory formal nights. The prices in the salon were usurious, but respectability was a necessity, so I bit the bullet and paid up.

I disciplined myself to spend at least three hours each day—more, if possible—trying to recall a particular period of my life and found that writing snatches of memories in a notebook purchased from the ship's gift shop aided my mission.

Thinking about rationing brought to mind the acquisition of my first school uniform. At the age of eleven, I passed an examination and won a scholarship to the prestigious Kesteven and Grantham Girls School. Clothing coupons had been hoarded for months to cover the extensive list of items deemed necessary for me to join the ranks of what the other children in the village dubbed "high school snobs." The list called for more items of new clothing than I had owned in the preceding ten years combined. There were winter shoes, summer shoes, athletic shoes, hockey boots, a winter coat, a raincoat, a navy blazer with light blue trim, navy knickers for winter and light-blue ones for summer, two summer dresses, two gym slips, two light-blue shirts, a felt hat for winter, and a straw boater for summer—on and on the list went.

Because no one knew when rationing would end, Mum bought wisely. The navy raincoat she purchased for my first day at my new school was the same one I wore when I graduated seven years later, and it was still too big. I never did grow into it, despite reaching my adult height of five foot eight somewhere around the middle of that time.

Bruce's gentle reminder that it was time to get ready for dinner brought me swiftly back to the present. We went to dinner each night in the enormous formal dining room, dressed to the nines. We eschewed a large communal table in favor of a more intimate one for two, close to the water, where we enjoyed magnificent food and wine and chatted comfortably, as we had not for a long time.

My conscious memory string-pulling worked best when I stuck to a chronological path, so my next stop was college. That I was an occupational therapist had garnered a lot of attention when I became a patient, even though I had not practiced for some time. How I became one in the first place was now a matter for much speculation of my own. I knew I had fallen into the profession rather than having been possessed by a burning vocation and had always thought of myself as an "accidental" occupational therapist. But how had it come about? Burrowing back all the way to the examination that determined the course of my education, I remembered that scores achieved at the age of eleven determined not just whether a girl would go to the grammar school but also whether she was academic or practical. Academic girls were bound for university or teacher training college. They studied Latin. Practical girls were bound for marriage and motherhood and learned to type, cook, and sew. I was an academic girl, so Latin it was.

The tenure of Miss Dorothy Jane Constance Gillies, as headmistress of the school, spanned the twenty years that separated the school's most distinguished pupil, Margaret Thatcher, who went on to become the first female prime minister of England, from my classmates and me. Gil, as she was known to generations of girls, never tired of extolling the virtues of her favorite pupil and announcing each achievement to the assembled six hundred light-blue-and-navy-uniformed, quietly groaning girls. But Gil took an interest in lesser mortals too. When I found myself nearing the end of my final year of school, studying advanced level English literature, French, and history without actually having applied to college—due to too many extracurricular distractions and struggling to pass mathematics—she took matters into her own hands.

My exposure to working women had been limited to teachers, nurses, the post lady, the army of colorful village women who set off by truck to pick potatoes in the Lincolnshire Fens on summer mornings, and the eternally glamorous Muriel, the purser on an ocean-going ship. I certainly did not want to be a teacher. I wanted to be a newspaper reporter, but that ambition was met with a lukewarm response both at home and at school. I must have something to "fall back on," they said, to support myself if, as appeared likely, no suitable husband materialized.

Gil came to my classroom one morning and announced that she was taking me to the new Career Testing Center to have me evaluated. I had never known her to leave the school before, except to attend church, and found her personal attention both flattering and intimidating. Stern in starch and tweed, pencil-thin lips etched in deep pink, and thin gray hair scraped into a severe bun, she practically frog-marched me to the office in the center of town.

The test results showed that I was suitable for training to be a physical, speech, or occupational therapist. Why, I could not imagine. I had the beginnings of an excellent liberal arts education but minimal sciences. I had apparently scored well on the parts of the test that related to so-called "caring professions." I had absolutely no idea what an occupational therapist did, but since the science requirements were lighter than for the other two therapies, I decided that if it would get them all off my back, I would be one. It would only be until I could get out on my own and do what I really wanted to do, which was to become a reporter and see the world. I never imagined then that my accidental career choice would be my passport to seeing a lot of the world.

Recapturing pieces of my past was lightening my mood and making the cruise enjoyable in ways that I could not have anticipated. Almost everything we saw and did resulted in the liberation of more memories and a stronger sense of self. My next chronological port of call was at my first job as a junior occupational therapist at the Royal National Orthopaedic Hospital in Stanmore, just outside London. On the steamy, hot deck of a ship in the South Pacific, I pictured myself on my twenty-first birthday, on one of the hottest August days on record in England, equally hot and steamy, making my way from home by train and bus to the hospital for my interview.

Our college principal had drilled us on how to groom, dress, and behave for an interview. Hair must be off the collar, makeup understated, and no colored nail polish. One should always wear a suit and low-heeled pumps. Handshakes should be dry and firm and eye contact maintained when answering questions. That the only suit I possessed was made of heavy brown tweed and my pumps were brown suede had not seemed much of an issue until the heat began to hit me. By the time I arrived at my interview, four hours after leaving home, I was soaked with perspiration, my face was the color of beets, makeup dripped from every pore, and my suede shoes practically squelched. The only way I could be sure my hand was dry for the handshake was to wipe it on my steaming, prickly skirt.

Nothing in England was air conditioned in those days, so I sweltered my way through the interview with the head OT and her deputy, doing my best to maintain eye contact but painfully aware that mascara must be running down my cheeks.

To my surprise and relief, I was offered the job by the hospital administrator, Commander Roantree, a retired naval officer. As it happened, he was wearing a suit very much like my own. He was in similar distress, mopping perspiration from his brow with his handkerchief as he laid out the terms and conditions of the job. I smiled inwardly, thinking of how Englishmen of his generation were caught off guard by a hot summer day. Looking at Bruce sprawled out next to me on the deck of the ship, wearing only swimming shorts, an image of my father on our annual seaside holiday popped up. Dad's idea of informality was to roll up his woolen pant legs to just above the ankle, roll his shirt sleeves to just below the elbow, and maybe, just maybe, take off his tie.

Thinking back over my years at Stanmore, I recognized how extremely lucky I was to have landed that job. I met many remarkable, even great, people there,-surgeons, therapists, and patients—who taught me what it meant to be an occupational therapist and cemented my desire to specialize in the treatment of hands.

It was at Stanmore that my concept of patients as people flourished; it was actually encouraged. Sir Ludwig Guttmann, a pioneer in treatment of spinal cord injuries, had discovered that one of the best ways of making sure that his patients had a place to go when they were ready to be discharged was to marry them off to nurses and therapists. I had done a brief clinical practice at Stoke Mandeville, the National Spinal Injury Center, where Sir Ludwig ruled, and had been made aware of the crowded social calendar and the number of trips to local pubs with patients in chairs, stretchers, and even beds, pushed by a crowd of laughing, eager staff. It was an environment conducive to romance, and it worked.

That same easy familiarity between patients and staff existed at Stanmore. Some patients had been in the hospital for many years, due to chronic disabling conditions, such as respiratory poliomyelitis and Guillaine-Barré syndrome. We thought of them as friends. We knew their families and were involved in their daily lives. One of my colleagues, Maggie, married John Prestwich, a remarkable man, who, as a result of contracting polio at the age of seventeen, was confined to an iron lung for more than fifty years. They had a long and happy marriage, and he lived a full life, despite being able to move nothing but his lips and eyelids. Maggie devoted her life to taking care of John, embodying the best characteristics of human nature, selflessness, and compassion.

Barbara Werndly lived in the hospital all week. Her father, George, picked her up every Friday to take her home for the weekend. Babs, blonde and very attractive with a bubbly personality, lived in the hospital from the time she was a young teenager, when she contracted a virulent combination of polio and Guillaine-Barrė syndrome, until she died in her fifties. She was never medically stable enough to go home permanently She had minimal use of her hands and arms and, because of recurrent bedsores, had to be supported on her stomach in a specially designed corset. During her years in the hospital, Babs ran a successful Avon business and baked cakes in the OT kitchen that fed generations of hungry orthopedic surgeons. She also raised funds to buy a customized ambulance to transport wheelchair-bound patients on outings and to and from their homes. With a pang of guilt and remorse, I remembered that I had crashed that bright blue ambulance emblazoned with the logo "Barbara's Bus," loaded with patients, into a police car in Sloane Square one Friday afternoon. The patients were fine and actually enjoyed the experience, but I was terrified. The officer jumped out of his crumpled car, rage turning his face a vivid shade of puce, ready to drag the ambulance driver out of the vehicle, but he stopped in his tracks when he saw a young woman wearing a white uniform and green belt cowering behind the wheel. It transpired that much of his rage stemmed from the fact that he was off his beat and had a woman, who was not his wife, in the car with him. Although the accident was clearly my fault, I skated without as much as a ticket.

My initial experience of fraternizing with a patient did not involve romance. In my second year at Stanmore, I was asked by one of the surgeons if I would be interested in renting a room from one of his patients, a woman in her mid- eighties, on whom he had performed hip surgery. It would be a mutually beneficial relationship, in that she would have someone in the flat overnight in case she needed help, and I would be living practically rent-free in a very smart flat close to the hospital. I had been residing in the nurses' home on the hospital grounds, and this did indeed seem like an opportunity to spread my wings. I accepted the offer and moved in with my new flat-mate, who, at approximately four times my age, turned out to be a lot of fun. She loved to cook, and I loved to eat. She loved to regale me with tales of old Berlin, and I loved to listen to her refined, slightly accented English; occasionally, I practiced my fading German with her. That must have been part of the reason that I spoke German in the hospital after the stroke!

One morning I was toiling up the hill from the flat to the hospital in a heavy rainstorm, when a black chauffeur-driven sedan pulled up next to me. The back door opened, and a familiar, imperious voice called out, "Get in, madam."

It was Sir Herbert Seddon, noted surgeon and professor of the Institute of Orthopedics at the University of London, housed at Stanmore. Sir Herbert was renowned for having operated twelve or more hours a day on soldiers with severe hand injuries during the war and especially for his system of classifying peripheral nerve damage. The reason I recognized his voice was that I, along with every other surgeon and therapist in training, trailed around after this slight, balding, bespectacled genius on his teaching rounds each week, hanging on his every word.

No mother's warning about getting into cars with men would have dissuaded me from obeying this command. Once I was seated beside him, Sir Herbert said, "You are the young lady who is interested in working with my patients' hands, are you not?"

I stammered that I would like nothing more.

"Then," he said, giving me a long, thoughtful stare, "I must make sure you know what you are doing."

Right then he began a series of personal lessons, each one lasting no longer than ten minutes—the time it took to drive to the hospital and park the car—that went on for several months.

Sir Herbert pulled out a pen and labeled all of the bones on my hand. The next time he started labeling muscles and finally moved on to tracing the peripheral nerves up and down my arm. My short rides to the hospital were filled with lessons that I never forgot. One time he would label, and the next, he would grill me on what he had labeled the time before. I can still close my eyes and read what he wrote. What an honor and how much teasing I endured, though I never actually became the OT assigned to his firm. That privilege was bestowed on people with much more seniority and experience than I had.

Nevertheless, Sir Herbert became an invaluable mentor to me, despite the huge gap between us, with me at the start of my career and he at the pinnacle of his. He played a pivotal role in my early professional life. After a lecture series that took place at the city branch of the hospital in Great Portland Street every Wednesday night, attended by all of the surgeons in training and therapists, it was customary to repair to the pub. If Sir Herbert was in attendance, any ideas I might have had of carousing into the night were curtailed by a tap on the shoulder and the familiar voice announcing, "It's time to go home, madam."

Off I would slink behind the great man, followed by the jeers and whistles of the junior surgeons. He could not hear them because he always turned his hearing aid off after and—to tell the truth—sometimes during the lecture.

The ship docked at the islands of Raiatea, Mo'orea, and Bora Bora. When we were able to go ashore, we hired friendly local drivers, who drove us around in beat-up old cars, free of steps and other nuisances, and gave us enough local color and history to make us feel that we had really visited the place.

While visiting these islands, my memory took another leap back to a tropical island I had lived on for more than a year. At the age of twenty-three, I had obtained a coveted position with the World Health Organization on the island of Mauritius in the Indian Ocean.

Sir Herbert had told me about the opportunity, after I had already applied, as it happened. He gave me a reference and copies of a number of articles he had written about his own work on the island, following an outbreak of poliomyelitis a few years before.

I had arrived on the island as one of six young, single English women brought in to work in a newly built hospital. I helped to establish a hand rehabilitation clinic, where we saw dozens of patients suffering from every conceivable type of hand injury, including hereditary or genetic conditions we'd read about but never saw in the developed world. We worked hard and played even harder during that magical year, and some of my closest friendships date back to then. While details of my time in Mauritius remained skimpy, the associated feelings were as warm and fragrant as the tropical sun and flowers on each of the new islands we visited.

As we sailed back into Tahiti at the end of the cruise, Bruce and I reflected on what we had done and what we would do differently in the future. I really liked being on the water. Contrary to what I might have thought about walking on a moving surface, I found that I was getting more sensory input from my left foot, or maybe I was just more aware of it. Because safety is an issue for all passengers, especially in rough waters, there were sturdy handrails everywhere, except in our shower. I therefore found it quite easy to get around. Bruce and I agreed that we would definitely take another cruise, but next time we would make our own air travel arrangement, and yes, I would request a better stateroom and handicapped accommodation. I would say it was for my elderly husband!

The flight back to LAX was no more comfortable than the outbound one, but it afforded me the time to think about my "elderly husband" and how we had found our way into each other's lives.

When my time in Mauritius ended, I took on an extended trip around India and the Middle East before returning to London. After a few months of temporary work, I found myself back at the Royal National Orthopaedic Hospital, this time as head occupational therapist. It was a great job in a hospital I loved, but I found it hard to settle in drab, dreary, strike-ridden, IRA-terrorized London after the excitement of international work. I missed the excitement, and I also missed the sun. Just over two years after I accepted my new position,

WHO contacted me to see if I would be interested in a short-term consultancy in Southeast Asia. Most of my friends were married by then, and a few had left England with their husbands to begin new lives elsewhere. The most recent of a string of unsatisfactory romances I'd dabbled in had just fizzled out, and the hospital encouraged overseas service and would grant me a leave of absence. I saw no reason not to go.

At the same time as I was making my arrangements to leave England, a woman in Chicago, almost four thousand miles away, was telling her husband that she didn't think their marriage was working out, and she thought they should separate. He, an oral and maxillofacial surgeon, had just accepted a short-term consultancy with WHO in Southeast Asia and had planned to take his wife and three children with him. In light of the new development in his marriage, he initially decided to cancel the trip. Only at the insistence of his thirteen-year-old son did he decide to go ahead, taking his son with him.

Whether by coincidence or the hand of Archie, the two of us landed in the Ministry of Health in Bangkok, Thailand, within a few weeks of each other. Our mailboxes were adjacent to one another.

When I met Dr. Bruce Douglas, it was certainly not love at first sight. The last thing I was looking for was another entanglement. Having resolutely fended off anyone who might have been even remotely suitable as a life partner, I had specialized in *cavaleurs*—the poet, the diamond merchant, the TV presenter—exciting but unreliable and definitely not interested in a future with me. The Vietnam War was going on, and Thailand, Vietnam, and Laos were not easy places to work in 1973.

My country had resolutely stayed out of the war, viewing it as an American folly, but still the BBC airwaves transmitted horrible images to our living rooms nightly. The military death toll, young lives snuffed out way before their time, civilian casualties, and villages bombed with napalm had become the stuff of outrage and protest around the globe.

It was easy to be anti-American as bombers thrummed over our heads on their way to bomb Cambodia, night after night. The English-language newspapers were filled with stories of high-ranking pilots refusing to fly any more sorties. Bruce was the only American

I knew in Bangkok, so I held him personally responsible for everything bad that was going on. That he was even more opposed to the war than I and that we saw eye to eye on most issues gradually emerged, and the power of his good looks, charm, and persistent niceness won me over. People had asked me over the years how I could leave everything and everyone behind in England to move to a country where I had nothing and knew not a single person. The answer was always the same: the choice was between living a rich, full life there without him or coming to America with nothing and building an exciting new life with him. The choice had been surprisingly easy.

It was not an easy path. Bruce's children posed many challenges, and in adulthood, only one of them remained a part of our nuclear family, along with the husband and daughter of another. The other two, of their own volition, did not. Nevertheless, we built a good, happy life, raised two lovely children, and had everything going for us—until the awful thing happened to my head.

This trip had been a great success, despite the physical and mental challenges. We returned with an extensive bucket list of places we wanted to go and things we wanted to see, including all fifty states. Due to my work travel, I had already been in forty-six and Bruce in forty-three. We wanted to see as many wonders of the world as possible, presidential libraries, and national parks. Our list was endless. Most important, I felt that in the course of ten days at sea, I had taken some giant steps toward real recovery.

As the second anniversary of the stroke approached and the memory of the long flight from Tahiti faded, we began to think about going back to England. Bruce had been corresponding with Professor Aziz in Oxford and thought it would be good to have a follow-up visit. My English family and friends had been diligent about visiting us, and it was great to have had their support, but it was time to face the fear and pain associated with not just my last visit but also the ones that preceded it. A black cloud had hung over most of our visits in recent years, and so many people were gone for good that it scarcely seemed like the same place. I had not yet unlocked the door to the room in my brain where all of that pain was stored, so it was in a haze that I made the arrangements.

I rented a cottage in Norfolk and made plans for family and friends to visit us there. Our old habit of traveling around and staying with people had to be abandoned because there were too many uncertainties about accessibility. I had never had to think that way before, and it took some getting used to. I had to know in advance what the terrain was like. Were there steps? Was there a toilet on the first floor? Would I be able to get in and out of a bath or shower? The cottage I found met our criteria for accessibility but not much more. It was cramped, lacking in amenities, and had no view. In hindsight, it was not unlike our stateroom on our infamous South Pacific cruise. I still had a lot to learn as a travel agent.

We spent the last day of our vacation in Oxford, visiting Professor Aziz. As Bruce drove tentatively into town, the sight of a red double-decker bus triggered lines from a poem learned long ago.

What is it that roareth thus?
Can it be a motor bus?
Yes the smell and hideous hum indicat motorem bum
Implet in the Corn and High terror me motoris bi…[8]

Reverend Russell, a temporary Latin teacher, had tried to inject a little humor into our otherwise deadly dull declension exercises by getting us to memorize AD Godley's poem about an Oxford bus.

As we entered the Radcliffe Infirmary, nothing was at all familiar to me, except for Professor Aziz himself. Slender, now with threads of silver around his temples and streaking his mustache, dressed in street clothes, he beamed as I walked into his office and took his outstretched hand.

"Do you really remember me?" I asked, mindful of how many patients he must have treated in the two years since he operated on me.

"I remember you very well," he responded warmly, looking directly into my eyes. "You were at your nephew's wedding when the event occurred. You had a rough time, and it was touch-and-go for a while. I am delighted to see you looking so well."

He asked me about my arm and how much I was able use it. I demonstrated my range of motion and told him the main problem was that the arm still did not seem to belong to me, and unless I could see it, I had no idea where it was.

He said that was normal and might improve with time. He was delighted by the amount of recovery he saw. "I was concerned that because of the location of the bleed, you might not have much recovery in your arm."

The professor asked if I was having any other problems, and I mentioned the wracking spasms that affected both my arm and leg. He told me about a drug with the trade name Baclofen that might help. We walked a short distance from the hospital to a restaurant and enjoyed a relaxed lunch. As we neared the end of the meal, during which I tried to swat my face as little as possible, Professor Aziz asked if I had any questions.

"Just one," I said. "Before the surgery, did you take me into a small room to explain what you were going to do?"

"I most certainly did," he replied, "but I am really surprised that you remember that. You lost consciousness while I was talking to you."

Shortly after returning home, I saw a neurologist, Dr. Munson, who, as Professor Aziz had suggested, prescribed Baclofen. He asked if I was still getting therapy.

I explained to him that based on the prevailing insurance company wisdom, I had passed my sell-by date and was as good as I was going to get. "I'm working with an athletic trainer, a Pilates instructor, a massage therapist, and an acupuncturist," I proudly informed him.

"Very impressive," he said with a smile, "but who is the captain of your team?"

I am the Master of my Destiny. I am the Captain of my Soul. "Invictus" on the tip of my tongue, right when I needed it. Thank you, General Wavell, for those *Other Men's Flowers.* Thank you, Captain Aubrey Booker, harbor master and neighbor in Mauritius, for introducing me to that wonderful anthology, and thank you, Mum and Dad, for sending me my own copy for Christmas 1969. It has been my constant companion ever since.

Dr. Munson chuckled and said he liked my spirit but thought I could still benefit from more traditional therapy. After giving me a thorough examination and talking a little about whether I might have sleep apnea (I do not, but Bruce does), he referred me to a physiatrist.

Dr. Eliades, he said, would make an excellent captain of my team and would manage the gradual introduction of Baclofen into my system. It took a while to get an appointment, but when I met Dr. Eliades, I felt comfortable with him right away. Soft-spoken and relaxed, with a reassuring professional manner, he gave me a physical examination, checked my medication, and watched me walk, both with and without the cane. I was wearing the dreaded brace and confided in him how I much I hated it. He ordered more therapy and gave me a glimmer of hope that I might someday be able to dispense with it.

BIBLIOGRAPHY: CHAPTER 7

Kesteven and Grantham Girls School. History page on school website for prospective students. Accessed July 11, 2018. http://www.kestevengrantham.lincs.sch.uk/history/

Mars-Awe, Mary. "Bruce Douglas: Someone We All Should Know." Blog, website of the Chicago Chapter of Fulbright Association. 2015. Accessed July 12, 2018. https://fulbrightchicago.com/2015/12/01/dr-bruce-douglas- someone-we-all-should-know/

Nimbalkar, Namita, PhD. "John Locke on Personal Identity," *Mens Sana Monogram*, 9(1): 268–275, January 2011. Accessed July 11, 2018. https://doi.org/10.4103/0973-1229.77443

North Shore University Health Care System. Patient website that includes professional profiles. Profile for Miledones Eliades, MD accessed July 12, 2018. https://www.northshore.org/apps/findadoctor/physicians/miledones-n.-eliades

North Shore University Health Care System. Patient website that includes professional profiles. Profile for Richard John Munson, MD accessed July 12, 2018. https://www.northshore.org/apps/findadoctor/physicians/richard- john-munson

Royal College of Surgeons of England. "Plarr's Lives of the Fellows Online." Accessed July 12, 2018. http://livesonline.rcseng.ac.uk/biogs/E006924b.htm

Royal National Orthopaedic Hospital. Business Website. Accessed July 12, 2018. https://www.rnoh.nhs.uk/

Wavell, Earl A.P., Field Marshall. *Other Men's Flowers.* London: Jonathan Cape, 1944.

Wikipedia. Entry for Alfred Denis Godley's "The Motor Bus," first published in 1914. Accessed July 12, 2018. https://en.wikipedia.org/wiki/The_Motor_Bus

Wikipedia. Entry for William Ernest Henley's "Invictus," first published in 1888. Accessed July 12, 2018. https://en.wikipedia.org/wiki/Invictus

Wikipedia. Sir Ludwig Guttmann biography. Accessed July 12, 2018. https://en.wikipedia.org/wiki/Ludwig_Guttmann

CHAPTER 8

A Drawer Full of Troubles

As I continued to cobble myself together, physically and mentally, immersed in my job and my renewed therapy and taking the Baclofen that had conquered the painful, debilitating spasms, I started to feel more normal, more like someone I recognized. But there was still something disquieting eating away at me, an unexplained sense of loss and emptiness hiding behind a veneer of complacent passivity.

Despite my inappropriate mirthful response to Dr. McNulty, the grief counselor who visited my hospital room two years earlier, I knew there was still a lot of baggage buried under piles of denial and that it had something to do with my current predicament. I had neither been able to recall the visits nor find the reasons for why I was referred for grief counseling in the first place.

An innocuous telephone conversation with my brother Keith triggered the opening of a window in my brain that had been painted shut. It opened so wide that the events that had caused me to seek out Dr. McNulty and visit his Highland Park office all those Saturday mornings were suddenly clearly visible and palpable. The force of emotion was powerful enough to knock me off my feet, as wave after wave of released pain washed over me. All these things had happened shortly before the stroke.

On a routine office visit, a new primary care doctor told me that I was taking too much blood pressure medication for a person my age. My blood pressure that day was 150/90, and the doctor told me that was within normal limits, according to the guidelines published by the American Heart Association. I thought it was too high, but he disagreed.

My response had been to burst into tears, a rare phenomenon for me. The doctor asked if anything else was going on in my life that could cause me to be upset. I had pulled myself together as quickly as possible and told him that I had lost a few close relatives recently, and both my daughters had gone away to college. He did not reduce my prescription that day, but neither did he increase it. As I struggled into my coat, anxious to be out of his office as quickly as possible, the doctor handed me a card. He said it was for a grief counselor. I shoved the card in my pocket and fled. I had no interest in talking to anybody. Stiff-upper-lipped English people do not complain; they do not whine if things do not go their way; they suck it up and get on with it. They keep calm and carry on.

Therapy, for me, had always come from such simple things as losing myself in a book, watching an old movie, or working in my garden. Sinking my face into the soft, warm neck of a horse, feeling the gentle beat of its heart, or hearing the rhythmic, reassuring sounds of hay being munched in a quiet stall worked like magic to calm jangling nerves or distract me from disquieting thoughts.

Abruptly, my self-administered therapy stopped working. I started crying at inopportune times, unable to pinpoint a reason. Recognizing that this could not continue, I dug the card that the doctor had given me out of my coat pocket, made an appointment, and started to see Dr. McNulty on Saturday mornings. Over the course of a couple of months, I emptied the contents of my drawer of troubles all over his desk, his floor, and parts of his private waiting room. With mountains of wet tissues and perpetually red-rimmed eyes, I poured out my account of the events that led me to his door.

I started with Mum. After all the strife and turmoil of our growing-up years, she had mellowed and blossomed in widowhood and enjoyed a lifestyle that she could have only dreamed of earlier. She traveled extensively, went to India when she was seventy-nine, and achieved a lifetime goal of riding an elephant. She came to visit us in Chicago every year for at least six weeks and enjoyed the company of a few good friends on both sides of the Atlantic.

As she reached her eighties, Mum's behavior softened quite a bit. There were flashes of her old issues—blow-ups with people, tantrums, grandiosity—but for the most part, she was living a full and independent life. One day, in 1996, just after she turned eighty-six, while shopping in her local supermarket, a display of cookbooks collapsed, and one of the books hit her hard on her left shin, leaving a gash about three-quarters of an inch long. She went to the doctor, who assured her it was nothing to worry about; that she should keep the wound covered with a clean dressing and carry on with her usual routine. Eventually, a scab formed, and the wound appeared to be healing. While she was staying with us, a nurse friend changed the dressing every few days.

Mum went back to England and continued her life as normal, except for debilitating pain from the wound on her leg. In the fall of 1997, the scab fell off to reveal a foul, purulent ulcer. This spelled the end of her living independently. The doctor admitted her to the geriatric ward of the local hospital. Visiting her there, I was appalled to find her the only lucid patient, apparently, in a sea of skeletal, white-haired, pink-beribboned, vacant-eyed crones.

A physician friend intervened and got her transferred to a nursing home, where both the environment and the care were vastly improved. Despite the improvement in care, the wound on Mum's leg continued to deteriorate. All the anger, poison, and tumult of her life seemed to be pouring out of this gaping wound.

For her eighty-eighth birthday in March 1998, I traveled from Chicago to organize a small party. As the junior sibling, the only one with any form of medical training, and one of only two with whom she was on speaking terms, I asked to meet with the doctors. Mum was quite lucid but angry. She stated that if she had to have a birthday party in such a place, at least there should be sherry. I requested and obtained permission to serve sherry. All of the patients were allowed a taste; even the stroke patients, who had problems with swallowing, got theirs, mixed with food thickener and slurped through a straw.

Mum was in queenly form, receiving the salutations of her guests, smiling broadly while letting me know, through clenched teeth, the shortcoming of every item of food, the dismal selection, and the way everything was presented. She also expressed her displeasure with my attire. My skirt was too short, my shoes were ugly, and my haircut did not suit me. I should be ashamed to call myself a daughter when I had abandoned her in such disgraceful circumstances.

"Don't think you are going to be prancing around, playing Lady Bountiful at my funeral," she scolded, a long, freshly manicured finger wagging in my face. "I won't give you all the satisfaction of fawning and fussing over me when I'm dead. I'm leaving my body to science!"

The next morning I met with the doctor, who told me that the only thing that could help Mum would be to amputate her leg below the knee. The infection had penetrated the bone and become full-blown, antibiotic-resistant osteomyelitis.

"Would the stump heal?" I asked.

"Probably not," replied the doctor.

"So how will that help her?"

"Our only other option is to control the pain with morphine, but that will almost certainly shorten her life."

"What sort of a life would an eighty-eight-year-old amputee have?" I asked.

He shrugged compassionately and said, "It's the only hope of prolonging her life."

I followed up with the age-old question: "What would you do if it were your mother?"

"Give her the morphine," he said.

"Give her the morphine, then." I breathed heavily, heart beating fast, palms sweating, acutely aware that I was handing down a death sentence.

The day after her birthday, I got permission to load Mum into a rental car and drive her around her childhood haunts. We visited the house where she was born, her first school, and the graveyard in Sapperton where so many of her forebears rested and, more recently, where Dad's ashes had been buried. She was nervous at first and acted like a truant, sliding down in her seat, not wanting to be caught outside on a school day.

"You have permission to be out today, so it doesn't matter if someone sees you," I tried to reassure her.

"But I'm in my nightgown. What will people—" She stopped herself in mid-sentence and, with some of the twinkle of old in her still-vibrant blue eyes, said, "I don't care what the parson says. Let's have a pub lunch!"

And so we did. I parked outside a pub that had a beautiful garden already full of spring flowers—snowdrops and daffodils—and we shared a plate of crusty bread, Cheshire cheese, and a half pint of beer mixed with fizzy lemonade.

"I wandered lonely as a cloud," she quoted Wordsworth, reminding me from whom I got my love of poetry. *"When all at once I saw a cloud, a host of golden daffodils."*

She lasted a few more weeks but never was able to go outside again. In early May, I got the call that it was time to come. Accompanied by Cliff, my stepson, I made another transatlantic dash to her bedside. By the time we arrived, she was burning with fever from the septicemia that had come from the infection in her leg; her eyes were open but sightless.

I never knew for sure that she knew we were there, but I suspect that she did. We left to take a break and went to Don and Sheila's house nearby. No sooner did we sit down to have a bite to eat than the phone rang, and a nurse informed us that she was gone. True to her word, she had bequeathed her body to science, but since she died on a holiday weekend, the hospital informed us there was, unfortunately, no way to make that happen. She could not refuse to be the corpse at her own funeral, after all.

We buried her ashes next to where Dad's had been interred, almost fourteen years ago to the day, and around the corner from her parents, grandparents, great- and great-great-grandparents in the Sapperton churchyard.

Dr. McNulty helped me release and sort through the cornucopia of emotions that had flowed from my subconscious to consciousness as a result of the loss of this complex, difficult and yet luminary parent. I couldn't grieve when it happened. I didn't have time, and I didn't know how.

Together, we identified the conflict. There had been two people in one skin. I loved one and feared the other. I was angry that she had not been a mother to me in the way I had wanted her to be—nurturing and warm and interested in me and my life, hopes, fears, and dreams. Rather, she had wanted me to live out her hopes and dreams. I regretted that I had never really told her how much I respected her intellect, acting talent, wit, and knowledge and also that I had never told her to cut the crap, stop yelling at me and everyone else, and be the person that she was capable of being and that we needed her to be. I had never had the courage to tell her not to waste the precious time we had together by railing about whoever she happened to be angry at on that particular day. I regretted that I had never been able to talk to her as an adult about her disappointment that she had not had the life she wanted, that she had felt trapped by an unplanned pregnancy into a marriage with a man she considered her inferior (though that belief was not shared by anyone else). Winning national crossword puzzle competitions had not compensated for not getting a PhD and pursuing a career in research; she wasn't satisfied to be a wife and mother, and her family could never live up to the high expectations she had for them, no matter how hard she pushed.

I felt personally guilty that I had not had the courage to confront her about her mental illness, to tell her she was sick and needed treatment. Fearing the wrath that such a statement would unleash, I had, instead, opted for appeasement—diplomacy and self-preservation. I had learned to navigate minefields stocked with emotional explosive devices by hiding in my bunker, keeping my expression neutral, using diversionary tactics to steer conversations away from people or events that could trigger outbursts, and tamping my own feelings firmly down into my subconscious, where they caused stomachaches, nightmares, sleepwalking, and high blood pressure. All this I learned in Dr. McNulty's office. Furthermore, I began to understand that living with Mum's bipolar disorder might have caused me not to be two people living in one skin but one person living in two skins—one visible to the world, the other hidden from view.

There was a large dose of grief in the knowledge that the good times, of which there had been many, would never come again and a substantial measure of relief that the bad ones would not either.

Mum's passing should have brought a degree of freedom for Don. As the oldest son and the only one living close by, he had borne most of the burden of her declining health, and over the years, he had been the target of much of her ire. This was not in the cards. A few months after Mum died, I received a letter from Don, in which he stated simply that he had been diagnosed with prostate cancer. His odds, he wrote, were excellent. What he did not know then was that the treatment for his prostate cancer would unleash a beast within his body. Sadly and tragically, he had smoking-related lung cancer that had already metastasized to his brain, and in less than a year, he would be dead too.

At first, Don seemed to respond well to treatment for his prostate cancer, until one day he fell down while gently rolling a ball across a velvet-grass bowling green. They said he had suffered a stroke, a mild one, and that he should be back to normal quickly. He didn't recover quickly; he didn't recover at all. He began a steady decline that robbed him of everything. My handsome, popular, brilliant, funny brother; father of six; talented athlete; decorated by the Queen for his service to education; president of every society or group to which he had ever belonged just evaporated. By the time the brain tumor was discovered, he had lost his ability to speak. An operation to remove the tumor provided relief for a brief time. Bruce and Sarah were lucky enough to make it to see him while he could communicate. Sarah was doing her junior year at the University of Sussex, and Bruce was visiting her when the short-lived improvement occurred. I wasn't so lucky. My job required me to make regular trips to London, and I went to see him as often as I could. Once I made two round trips across the Atlantic in a week. An important meeting in New York required my presence there during his brief period of lucidity, and I was never able to have a conversation with him. I believe he knew I was there. The bleak expression in his blue eyes, Mum's eyes, communicated everything.

After receiving the dreaded but inevitable phone call, we made plans to go to the funeral. Riding in the black car from the standing-room-only church service to the crematorium, searching for a sliver of levity, I said to Tony, "Please take care of yourself. If you die, I'll be left with him"—I pointed to Keith—"and you know he has been trying to get rid of me since the day I was born."

Tony smiled as I reminded him of some of Keith's exploits. He had tethered me to a tree so he and his friends could use my stroller to take hair-raising rides down a very steep hill near our house; and bound me hand and foot to railroad tracks with straw until I could feel the vibration of the oncoming train, in order to ensure my silence about other misdemeanors.

Tony swore he would do his best to stay alive and protect me. He gave me a droopy, watery, lopsided smile. He had had a stroke a couple of years before that reduced him from a fiery, creative executive in the movie industry to an emotionally labile shadow, old beyond his years. It hurt to see him in this state, but he was doing his best to carry on.

He did not keep his word about staying around to protect me. Almost exactly a year later, we received a phone call from Sandy, who was attending Princess Christian College in Manchester, training to be a nanny. It was about midnight on a Friday night—six o'clock in the morning in England. I knew before I picked up the phone that something was wrong. Prickling neck hairs, sharp intake of breath, and nagging dullness in the pit of my stomach only intensified as I heard her voice. Through sobs and gasps, she told me that Uncle Tony and Auntie Sheila had been in a bad car accident. They were both in intensive care, and I had to come as soon as possible. She had been trying to call us all evening, but we had not answered the phone. We had been out for dinner with friends, oblivious to events unfolding overseas. I reassured her that I would come. I set about calling airlines to see when I could get on a flight. It took most of the rest of the night to complete arrangements.

Manchester was the closest airport to the hospital to which Tony and Sheila had been admitted, so I flew there. My niece's husband, Tim, met me at the airport. Sandy, Keith, and his wife, Jane, were waiting for me at the hospital, with the rest of the family. Tim filled in the details as he drove consciously, carefully, to the hospital.

Sheila was out of intensive care with serious injuries to her foot, but they expected her to make a full recovery. Tony was another matter. He had sustained horrendous head and facial injuries and had suffered cardiac arrest shortly after arriving at the hospital. He was on life support and in need of major surgical reconstruction to his face but not medically stable enough to withstand general anesthesia at this time. His legs were smashed, and he had other internal injuries. I asked Tim what had happened, though I could barely hear his answer over the banging of my heartbeat in my ears. Sheila had been driving at the time of the accident. Perversely, I was relieved to hear this, fearing that Tony's stroke damage might have played a role in the accident. She didn't know whether she fell asleep or was blinded by the setting sun on a country road, but she had encountered a sudden, unanticipated turn and had been on the wrong side of the road when they were hit head-on by a truck. Tony, in the passenger seat, had taken the brunt of the impact.

On legs of jelly and with butterflies as big as crows flying in my stomach, I was led into the Intensive Care Unit. Tony was unrecognizable. What was visible of his face was the color of raw liver. His features were displaced, his nose flat and his jaw bandaged, holding his mouth shut as though he were already a corpse. A breathing tube inserted in his throat powered the only motion his body was capable of, a slight rise and fall in his chest as the heart- lung machine thrummed in its mechanical attempt to keep him alive. That image of Tony's demolished face was behind my eyelids every time I closed my eyes for months to come and is what first drove me to the doctor to ask for sleeping pills.

My instantaneous reaction as I struggled to take in the scene was that there was nothing of my brother in that room. I couldn't give voice to my thoughts because outside the rubber door, his nearest and dearest were clinging to the slimmest of hopes that he would recover, that somehow, miraculously, he would wake up and be the Tony of old. A nurse infuriated me by saying that he would have been in better shape, had he been wearing his seatbelt at the time of the accident.

"You don't know him," I snapped. "He is the most safety-conscious person you have ever met. He would never be in a car without his seatbelt." Indignation at this perceived insult drowned out all other emotion for an instant.

Sheila's foot had been was crushed, and a surgical team had worked for hours to reattach blood vessels, nerves, and muscles, and while the prognosis was uncertain, there was reason to believe that she would make a good recovery. Shocked and groggy from surgery and a mild concussion, her concern was all for Tony. We took turns sitting by Tony's bedside, stroking his hands, kissing his battered face, for almost a week. Nothing changed. We learned that a team of plastic and maxillofacial surgeons was waiting for the right time to intervene and repair Tony's face.

I talked to Bruce on a nightly basis, filling him in on what was happening.

Facial reconstruction being his specialty, he requested permission to talk to the surgeon in charge. Sheila willingly gave her blessing and the conversation took place. When I talked to Bruce later that day, he outlined the plan and said gently, "You know the prognosis is poor."

"I do," I replied, tears coursing down my cheeks then, as when I was recounting the story to Dr. McNulty. "I think he is gone already."

The next morning, the doctor informed us that they would take Tony to surgery that day. The family gathered in Sheila's room to sit and wait for word of how the surgery had gone.

We waited many, many hours, trying to keep up cheerful banter, forcing down tasteless sandwiches. I snapped at Keith for putting too much salt on his food. "You know with your high blood pressure that can kill you!" I snarled.

He looked at me, shocked and wan, misery oozing from every pore. "Not today," he pleaded. "Don't lecture me today."

Eventually, the gaunt-faced lead surgeon, still in scrubs, his head covered, came to the room and beckoned for Keith and to me to leave with him. I knew by the grim expression on his face what he was going to say, but his words stung like a swarm of bees. "I'm so terribly sorry, but we lost him. He's gone."

My ears shut down; all the blood drained out of my head. I tried to force myself to listen but only caught snatches of the rest of what he said; my thoughts focused on the word *gone*. Not Tony! I had suspected it but the cold confirmation in the doctor's words still came as a shock.

"Cardiac arrest. Table. Couldn't revive him." He continued spouting a string of irrelevancies. "Completed the restoration of his face. Thought he would pull through. The operation was a success. Too much for his heart to withstand." Then he ventured, "Perhaps this is for the best?"

"I know you mean well, but how dare you?" I cried.

Another doctor took my arm and walked Keith and me stiffly back down the hallway to Sheila's room. Various family members came toward us, wooden, pale-faced, and anxious. One by one they heard, each reacting in his or her own way. Sheila, still in her room, was the last to hear. She vomited. Still fragile from her own injuries and the guilt of being behind the steering wheel, her retching and sobbing filled the air with heart-rending grief. Tony's children encircled their mother, offering what comfort they could, while struggling to hold themselves together. Keith and Jane stood ashen-faced, trying to hug each other, while offering hugs to Sandy, their other nieces and nephews, and me.

Before long, another doctor came and said that we could see Tony before his body went to the mortuary. In a sad procession—Sheila in a wheelchair and the rest of us walking—we made our way into the recovery room. The room was silent, no whirring of life-support machines, no clanking of carts, no blood pressure cuffs hissing and sighing, no sound at all. Behind a curtain, Tony lay on a bed, completely covered by a pristine white sheet. A nurse turned back the sheet so that we could see his face. I felt my breath squeeze out of my chest and my throat knot as I saw Tony's restored face. It was *him* again. His handsome face bore rows of tiny black stitches, but his nose, cheeks, and forehead looked much as they had looked before. The deathly pallor muting some of the bruises gave me a moment's pause. Vain as he could be about his appearance, he would be pleased that he had gone to meet his Maker looking halfway decent. I also noted the purple outline of a seat belt etched across his chest, angry proof that he had indeed been wearing it at the time of the accident. I wanted to find that nurse and show her how wrong she was.

That week between the accident and Tony's death was a poignant illustration of the difference between being killed in a car accident and dying as a result of injuries sustained in a car accident—the horrible, shocking certainty of one and the minute-by-minute roller coaster of hope, despair, and fear of the other. The ultimate outcome is the same in both cases: the victim is gone; the torment for the family unbearable. But it is not just the family that suffers. I had seen firsthand the toll that losing a patient took on the medical and nursing team—the guilt, the shame, the self-doubt—not just in that situation with Tony but many times in my professional life. I had given up my office at Grant Hospital to Father Croak from DePaul University, so he could inform parents that their second son had been killed in a car accident less than a year after the first. This after the surgical team had worked all night trying to save him.

The hospital chaplain came and offered a prayer and words of comfort. "These things," he murmured, "are not God's work. They arise out of chaos." I would have words with Archie about that later, but there were things that I had to do. I had to let Bruce and Sarah know, and I had to book a flight home. I was back in Chicago only long enough to make travel arrangements for all of us to fly back to England, stop by my office, catch up with work, and get back on the plane to go for the funeral.

Tony had chosen to be buried next to his infant granddaughter, Leeza, who had succumbed to SIDS at the age of seven weeks, a few years before. As they lowered his coffin into the ground, I was horror-stricken and asked Bruce to promise not to let anybody do that to me because of my claustrophobia.

Tony had a wicked sense of humor, and I could not help thinking of his story about participating in the funeral of one of his employees, who was Jewish. He and a colleague had been asked by the family to participate in the ceremony by using shovels to heap soil onto the coffin. They were required to wear black hats. Since neither Tony nor his colleague possessed such a hat, the bereaved family offered to lend one to each of them. Unfortunately, neither of them fit very well, and just as Tony, anxious not to miss a beat, discharged his shovel full of dirt into the grave, his colleague's hat fell off his head, into the hole, and was buried. He told that story, as he always did, with so much theatricality, emphasizing his and his colleague's struggle to maintain their composure out of respect for the solemnity of the occasion.

As is typical when someone dies, I did not think of Tony as he looked and acted in later years but as he had been as a suave, debonair executive in the theater business on that night in 1963, when he introduced me, a gawky, spellbound seventeen-year-old, to the Beatles and Roy Orbison. How proud I was to claim that handsome young man, dressed in a perfectly tailored tuxedo, his black hair gleaming, as my big brother.

We all stayed at a hotel in Newcastle the night after the funeral. Keith complained of not feeling well before going to bed. No one paid much attention, attributing his illness to the stress of a horrible day. In the morning, however, he said he had some symptoms that made him think he was having a stroke. Numbness, tingling, headache—he listed them all. As he walked away from us to get in the car, I saw that his leg was swinging in an arc from his hip to clear the ground. He had not mentioned foot-drop, but he had that too. Instead of leaving to go home, he went directly to the hospital.

As I poured out this story to Dr. McNulty, I told him of the anguish of trying to figure out what to do next. I wanted to be with Keith with all my heart—to go to the hospital, sit beside him, and help him through the maze— because despite elevating sibling rivalry to an art form, there was a deep bond between us that could not be broken. I wanted to stay, but there was no way I could. I was terrified that he was going to die too, that I was going to be the sole survivor of our nuclear family of six. I simply could not deal with losing him too.

I am not proud to say that I bolted, but I did. I just could not handle another blow. I was barely hanging on as it was. I had to hurl myself back into my busy life. I had a husband and two daughters who had to get back to their lives, and I had to get back to work. I had seen the looks on the faces of some of my coworkers as I took off this last time. The number of flights back and forth was straining my credibility. How many sick and dying relatives could one person have? All of my sick days were exhausted and most of my vacation days too. With heavy heart but defiant conviction that Keith would be all right—that he *had* to be all right—I gathered up my clan and set off to drive to London.

By spring, Keith was doing much better. He had some residual disability but was able to return to work as an accountant. He called one day and said he and Jane would like to come and visit us and bring their daughter, Suzanne, and son-in-law, Sean, with them. We set the date for the first and second weeks of September.

By this time, I had stopped seeing Dr. McNulty. We had agreed that I was coping much better, and things in my life were on a more even keel. I went back to Saturday morning riding lessons. With the girls away and horse shows being a thing of the- past, I was concentrating on

French classical dressage. The girls had loved jumping, but I had always preferred riding on the flat in as close to total harmony with the horse's movements as I could get. My new passion added music to the routine so that the exercise was, in essence, dancing on horseback. What I did not know at the time was that the core strength built up while riding would someday make the difference between walking and not.

By the time Keith and Jane came, we had planned a couple of weeks' worth of activities, mostly around Chicago, because I had no vacation time left and would have to work. On the first weekend they were with us, we went to the Galena Territories on the Mississippi River.

It is a beautiful area, steeped in history. General Ulysses Grant, Civil War hero and eighteenth president of the United States, had lived there. I had rented a fancy townhouse on a golf course to serve as our base for wining, dining, and sightseeing. On a tour of Grant's home, we encountered a docent, immaculate in period costume, who gushed and raved about every detail of "our dear, late president," causing Jane to whisper in my ear, "How can she be so truly, madly, deeply in love with someone who has been dead for 115 years?"

I snorted and had to leave the tour for a few minutes to attend to a feigned coughing fit. As I rejoined the tour, Jane said in a stage whisper, "You didn't miss much. We just learned who is buried in Grant's tomb."

On Monday, September 10, 2001, I left everyone at home and took off for a quick trip to Dallas. I was going to make a speech on absence management at a risk-management conference.

Ironically, I was advising employers on how to keep their workforce on the job and productive when I had barely been able to keep myself on the job, let alone productive, in recent memory.

Representatives of most of the large employers in Dallas, including United Airlines and American Airlines, had signed up for the conference that began with breakfast, followed by a morning of presentations and discussions. As we gathered in the lobby before going in to the meeting, due to start at 8:00 a.m. central time, a small crowd was gathering around the television blaring in the corner.

Someone shouted over to us, sounding alarmed, "A small plane has crashed into the World Trade Center!"

"How awful. Do you know which tower?"

"Not sure," came the response.

It made a difference because we had offices in the North Tower. The conference organizer called us together and said it did not seem to be a big deal. It was most likely an accident, and we needed to get started.

I was the first speaker called to the podium after the introductions. As I began my presentation, automatic pilot kicked in. I was delivering the right words, but my thoughts were far away. I was wondering where that plane hit. Could it have been our offices? What about Tom, Ruth, and Adam/ Were they okay? I had brought Adam and his family here from England to join our practice. Ruth and Tom were colleagues and friends of mine.

It was not the usual receptive, attentive audience. People were fidgeting and looking at their Blackberries. I noticed the representatives of the airlines hurriedly leaving the room. I started to feel like the orchestra leader on the Titanic. I kept talking but more and more distractedly, alarmed but ignorant of the magnitude of the disaster unfolding, as more and more people left the room, phones in hand and intense, disbelieving looks on their faces.

The head of our Dallas office entered the room and addressed me directly, saying, "I'm really sorry, but I must ask you to end your presentation now." Then looking at the audience, he continued. "The rumor we heard of a small plane hitting the World Trade Center was false. Two towers have been hit by passenger jets and the Pentagon has too. There is at least one plane still in the air. There might be more. This is a terrorist attack. Under the circumstances, I am sure you would prefer to get back to your offices."

People literally ran out of the room, a blur of gray and navy suits. Those of us left behind sat or stood stupefied, bewildered, and unable to comprehend the horror of what we had just heard. We drifted slowly, numbly, toward the lobby and the television, now tuned to CNN and surrounded by an ever- expanding crowd of guests and hotel workers, each of them looking as if they were staring down the barrel of a loaded gun pointed in the direction of their heads. Everyone looked scared, frozen, and paralyzed by what they were hearing. As I drew close enough to hear, it was to learn that the first tower hit had collapsed. My brain could not wrap itself around the words. Then the second tower collapsed.

"How could this be?" we asked each other. Large steel and concrete buildings do not collapse! Then names started pouring through a tiny aperture in my steel-clad brain: Adam, Tom, Ruth, Harry, and on and on. My friends, Sue Sauer and Kathy Bantis, who had left for New York the day before at the same time I left for Dallas—were they in the building? We had made a hurried plan to meet for lunch on the Thursday after we all got back.

The main thrust of information coming from the television was that other cities might be attacked, and no one knew what had become of the plane they had believed was on the way to the White House or Capitol building.

There was an air of generalized inertia, as no one knew what to do, where to go, or how to act. Everyone was ghostly pale, disbelieving, quiet. There were long lines forming at reception, at the pay phones, at the car-rental desk. Just about every person had a cell phone pressed to one ear. Shock, fear, and bewilderment in equal measure registered on every face. My heart and head pounded, and I felt adrenaline streaming through my body like hot oil. Flight, fright, or fight? I was preparing for all three.

People were trying to get news of loved ones, trying to find a way out, trying to let loved ones know that they were safe. Word came quickly that all commercial airlines were grounded. There were no private rentals of automobiles, and even the Greyhound buses were frozen in place.

It took several hours to make any sense of what was happening. Sense? There was no sense to any of this. I had checked out of my hotel room and left my overnight bag with the bellboy. I had planned to grab it and run back to the airport as soon as the conference ended, but the hotel manager announced that those of us who had checked out were welcome to return to our old rooms because no new guests would be arriving. There was a doomsday resonance to his words.

Once back in my room, I was able to use the phone to call home to let them know that I could not get back, which, of course, they knew.

Sandy had left a couple of days before to go to college in England, but Sarah still had a week to go before she was due to leave. Bruce was at work; they would let him know I was safe but marooned.

Next, I called Bill. He told me that evacuation of the Chicago office had been ordered because of the possibility that there were more planes in the air, more attacks in the offing. Heavy losses to our company were expected, but there were no details. He was trying to locate Adam, Tom, and Ruth. There was no phone contact, and the internet was down.

The television continued to release more and more information. Another building had collapsed, and a fourth plane had crashed in Pennsylvania, downed by passengers, they said.

Back in the lobby with a small crowd of colleagues, time stood still. We could not begin to comprehend the magnitude of what was unfolding. I found myself unable to look at the television screen, unable to watch a plane hit a building. It was just too ugly to comprehend.

I could not open my brain wide enough to give even a hint of credulity to the theory that they were advancing; that this had been done on purpose.

"Is the human spirit capable of such raw evil?" I pondered aloud.

If Tony's accident had not been the work of God but of chaos, then surely this chaos must be the devil incarnate, roasting innocent people on the end of his fork, spitting them like toasted marshmallows into the great fiery beyond.

A Dallas-based colleague came to the hotel and invited a group of us to his house to while away a few hours. His wife was out of town on business, and he was not able to contact her, so he could use some company. We gladly accepted, each feeling a strong need to be with others, to keep each other going, to blunt the pain, to row as a team across the river of uncertainty.

By late afternoon, I was able to reach my boss on his cell phone. In flat, colorless tones, he told me the New York offices were gone. They did not know for sure who was out of the building, but anyone who was inside was gone for sure.

"What about Sue and Kathy?"

"Gone." That simple word was loaded with so much past, present, and future. We had been at dinner with them both, at Sue's apartment, not two weeks before. We were going to have lunch on Thursday. Now we were not. Now, they were dead.

A list of names trickled thickly down the phone and hung in the air, as he confirmed their presence in the building.

"Adam? Tom? Ruth?"

"Not accounted for."

That evening and the following morning, we tried diligently to find a way out of Dallas.

Meanwhile, as we got an ever-lengthening list of colleagues confirmed lost, we got miraculous news that Adam, Tom, and Ruth were all alive. Bill told me over the phone, relief palpable in his voice, that each had had a reason not to go to the office that day. It was not their destiny to die in the World Trade Center.

There was no way out of Dallas. Planes were not allowed to fly; buses were parked in garages. Back at the hotel, a colleague, William, and I added our names to the list for a rental car. He had to get home to San Francisco, but we figured that if we made it as far as Chicago by road, he could at least work in the office there until he could get on a flight.

On the morning of Thursday, September 13, we received word that a rental car was available for us. So began our marathon trip home on empty roads under cloudless skies, devoid of planes and the customary trellis of vapor trails. Our monotonous, surrealistic journey was punctuated only by brief snatches of radio news and conference calls, updating us on the number of dead and missing. We got to almost four hundred confirmed dead before we reached the Chicago suburbs.

I made it home around dinnertime on Friday evening, exchanged tight embraces with my somber-faced family, and shared what I knew of the fate of my friends and coworkers.

Keith, Jane, Suzanne, and Sean were due to return to England, but international flights were still suspended. Jane suggested a barbecue. From there, a bonfire seemed like a logical progression. Before we knew it, we had consumed a serious amount of alcohol, burned Osama bin Laden in effigy, with an elderly scarecrow playing the lead role, and sung every patriotic song we knew. We did not quite know the lyrics for some, but we improvised as loudly as possible. It was a cathartic experience, and Jane, after leading a rousing chorus of "Rule Britannia," threw up her arms toward the sky and yelled to no one in particular and the universe in general, "We'll show the bastards who is boss!"

Over the next few days, they managed to get on flights and go home, and Sarah left for the London School of Economics. It was so hard to watch her board the plane and know that in this time of extreme uncertainty and danger, where the rules we had lived by suddenly didn't exist anymore, that I would be separated by the Atlantic Ocean from both of my children. I did not want her to go. Could she not wait and go when the world was a little more settled? Bruce sided with Sarah, who could not wait to be on her way.

"If we let them disrupt our lives, they have won," he said in his matter-of- fact voice. "If we carry on as before, we win."

"Screw winning! I just want my girls where I can see them and hold them!" My protests were washed away by a tide of opposition. I was an obstructionist, a defeatist. I was not the person they thought I was.

"No, I'm just their mother!" I snorted to myself.

Right after they all left, I put in a call to Dr. McNulty to see if I could come in and talk. "I thought I was done with the bad luck," I said, "but apparently not."

He gave me my old spot and said he had heard that my employer had been hurt badly by the terrorist attacks.

Dr. McNulty asked me what I felt when we learned about the attacks. "Nothing," I told him. "I couldn't feel anything. We were like boa constrictors trying to digest an elephant. It was just too big. Normal feelings didn't apply."

We attended funerals and memorial services until I was certain that if I had to sing or hear "Amazing Grace" or "America the Beautiful" one more time, I would lose control of what remained of my sanity. I only went to a couple of funerals, but some of my colleagues in New York went to scores.

Somehow, the days went by, and we grabbed any bit of normalcy we could, going about our business. We had daily national conference calls and rowed together across a river of uncertainty.

I learned that "liking" is not a prerequisite for either missing or mourning someone, and people who could irritate and annoy the most left just as big a hole as those who pleased. I did my own head count. As the list of names, along with photographs, was released, I built a pyramid. Those I knew, sixty two; those I had worked closely with, twenty-eight; those I knew well, sixteen; those who had reported to me, eight; close friends, six.

The company reorganized in the wake of the disaster, trying to compensate for huge losses in economic as well as human terms. I was asked to take to a management job in the Chicago office and assume responsibility for all lines of consulting for Chicago, Milwaukee, and Indianapolis.

As Thanksgiving approached, I suggested to Bruce that we go to London to see the girls. He readily agreed, and we rented an apartment in Canary Wharf, with enough space for Keith and Jane to join us. Having lived for seven years in New Jersey, they felt enough solidarity with the United States to participate in the Thanksgiving holiday, especially that year.

I noticed from the moment they arrived that Jane did not look well. Her face was pale and drawn, and she complained of pain in her hips and back.

In April 2002, I was on my way to Washington to attend a global managing directors meeting. While waiting to board the plane, I answered a phone call from Bruce. "Jane just called," he said.

I caught a hint of a somber tone in his voice that gave me chills. "And?"

"She asked if you could call her as soon as possible."

I tried to pump him for more information, but he clearly wanted to get off the phone as quickly as he could. I ran from the gate to the Red Carpet Club. Fingers trembling, I punched in the interminable list of numbers required to use a telephone credit card to make an international call.

Jane answered the phone on the first ring. There was no greeting, no preamble. "I've got cancer."

I wanted to throw the phone to the ground, rip it out of the wall, and stomp on it. "What kind?"

"Gall bladder, but they think it has spread."

"I've got to get on the plane," I said when I could find my voice. "I'll call you when I get to Washington." I punched in our home phone number as I dragged my bones back to the gate. Bruce picked up right away. "Did you know why Jane wanted to talk to me?"

"Yes," he replied softly, apologetically, "but she asked me to let her tell you herself."

When I finally reached the gate to board the plane, a colleague greeted me with the words, "You look as if you've seen a ghost."

I had.

However disposed I might have been to be against Jane when Keith first brought her home (I was very possessive of my brothers), I could not dislike her. Her charm brooked no opposition. An only child, she lost very little time in telling me that she believed I had the potential to be the sister she never had. As the only girl among boys, I had long fantasized about having a sister too and saw qualities in her that would make her the ideal candidate. I was thirteen and she was sixteen at the time.

We forged our alliance over a nefarious business deal. This involved my selling to her, for an extremely reasonable price, one at a time, love letters written to Keith by the Irish girl he had met on his first summer holiday with friends instead of family, a few months before. I sneaked a letter out of its hiding place, smuggled it to her to read, and then she would pay me. I smuggled that letter back and took another one. Unfortunately, I was caught red-handed one day, and our enterprise ended. Their relationship survived, and so did our friendship, and Jane was my constant companion throughout my teenage years. When they eventually married, I was the chief bridesmaid and listed in the newspaper announcement as sister of both the bride and the groom.

After the first phone call, we kept in touch regularly, and the news just kept getting worse. I reminded her of her words at our 9/11 bonfire—*We'll show the bastards who is boss!*

"Cancer is just another bastard. Show him who is boss!" I urged.

The cancer spread to her liver, and they were going to do surgery that she was not sure she wanted.

"What's the point? I'm not a brave person. I don't have a high tolerance for pain. It will just show up somewhere else."

I couldn't stand the bland resignation, the acceptance in her voice. I wanted to throw myself down the phone line and shake her. Who was this person telling me that she did not want any heroic measures, that she was at peace, that she had had a good life? She was not even sixty years old. Where was my sister, the one who would start a conga line at our dance club and take it outside into the street to pick up all the kids who could not afford the price of admission? Where was the sister who was elected to political office and also served as a governor of the school?

Despite having no business reason to go to London, I made reservations to go for Jane's birthday on July 25. It was another gut-wrenching, heart-aching trip across the Atlantic. I suspected that it would be the last time I saw her.

Sarah met me in London and said she would have to forgo the birthday party because of tests at school. I was disappointed not to have her with me but also relieved. It would be all I could do to cope with my own pain. My head was pounding pretty much nonstop the whole time I was on the train. I have no doubt my blood pressure was high, but that was the last thing on my mind.

When I arrived at their house, Jane was upstairs, resting on the bed. I could barely recognize the person I knew and loved. How could a few short months have wreaked such havoc with her appearance? She was yellow, bloated, and wearing an oversized flowered, button-through old-lady dress, in which my sister would not have been seen dead. She could hardly move because the pain was so intense. I recognized the look and the odor of someone who was taking high doses of narcotics. When she spoke, it took enormous effort, and her words were slightly slurred. She had something she wanted to show me.

I squeezed myself onto the couch next to her as she handed me a brochure to read.

"It's what I want," she said, her voice scarcely above a whisper. I glanced down at the glossy paper and saw that it was advertising meadow burials. "I've picked a plot in the country, away from noise and pollution, where I can have everlasting peace among the trees, wildflowers, and birds. Can you think of anything better?"

"You are not going to need this for a very long time" was all I could manage, knowing that neither of us believed that.

She gave me a long, wistful look and murmured so quietly I could barely make out her words, "You know that poem we like—*"When I am dead, my dearest, sing no sad songs for me"*? That's what I want."

I did not want Rossetti; I wanted Dylan Thomas—*"Do not go gentle into that good night."* There was no good in that night. I wanted her to *"rage, rage against the dying of the light."*

I left her on Sunday afternoon to go home, with promises that I would see her in a month for our nephew, Jonny's, wedding. I was standing in that meadow two weeks later, as she was lowered into the ground. I was unable to appreciate the serenity and beauty of the location because of the rage burning inside me at the unfairness of it all. Bruce and I bade farewell to the girls, yet again, and went home.

August 23, 2002, was my fifty-seventh birthday. I was not much inclined to celebrate. My soul was too heavy. To my surprise, Ruth and Janis, another friend from New York, decided that after what we had all been through, we should not miss an opportunity to celebrate a happy occasion. They flew in for the weekend, and with a few friends from Chicago, we ate, drank, played loud music, and toasted better times.

By then I could only describe myself as punch-drunk. I remembered watching boxing matches with Dad, the heavyweight, welterweight, or bantamweight men teetering, tottering, taking punches on the chin, slashing wildly, dancing, and falling into the ropes. After a second on the ropes, they lurched forward into the fray to slash, dance, crack, and fall back again to await the final blow to the chin that would end the fight. I knew how they felt.

On the Wednesday after my birthday, we flew to England for Jonny's wedding, spent a couple of days with Keith and his family, still reeling from Jane's death and throwing themselves into planning a memorial concert, featuring Jane's favorite music.

"Of course!" I said. "Nothing will keep me away."

From Keith's house, we set off to drive to Oxford, by way of Newton Blossomville, determined to focus on Jonny's happy day.

Exchanging honey- colored cottages and blooming gardens for spires and grassy quadrangles, we pulled into Oxford just in time to dress for the wedding.

With a blast of sickening insight, I recognized the relationship of all of these events to the stroke. Dr. McNulty had said during one of his strained visits to my hospital room, "It's not surprising that this happened to you after all that you had gone through, leading up to it."

I had no idea what he was talking about then. Now, I saw clearly that my stroke had not happened in a vacuum or out of the blue, as I had previously thought. The pressure had been building—blood pressure, fueled by stress, pounding against an ever-weakening artery wall until it simply exploded.

BIBLIOGRAPHY: CHAPTER 8

9/11 Memorial & Museum Website. Alphabetical list of names on the 9/11 Memorial Wall. Accessed July 12, 2018. https://www.911memorial.org/names-memorial-0

Ferris, Paul. *Dylan Thomas, A Biography*. New York: Paragon House, 1989.

Wikipedia. Entry for Dylan Thomas's "Do Not Go Gentle into that Good Night." Accessed July 12, 2018._https://en.wikipedia.org/wiki/Do_not_go_gentle_into_that_good_night

Wikipedia. Entry for William Wordworth's "I Wandered Lonely as a Cloud." Accessed July 12, 2018. https://en.wikipedia.org/wiki/I_Wandered_Lonely_as_a_Cloud

CHAPTER 9

Subject Matter

JUST AS MY PAST LIFE WAS STARTING TO STUMBLE OUT OF STROKE SHADOWS, my work life began to fall apart. I had been back at work successfully for more than two years when I noticed a subtle change. At first, I could not put my finger on the problem, but there was definitely a shift in attitude toward me. No one said anything, but the signs were clear. I learned about meetings after they had taken place, not before. Some people I met in the hallway averted their eyes, pretending they had not seen me. Conversations ended abruptly when I rounded a corner or entered a room. People stopped calling or stopping by to ask what I was doing for lunch. I offered to give people a ride to an outside meeting, and they told me they were looking forward to the walk.

The post-9/11 corporate reorganization had taken me out of my global practice leader role and placed me in an executive position, where I had significant management responsibilities but little direct client exposure. Had I still been working with clients, mostly large multinational companies, my limitations would have made it difficult, if not impossible, to do my job. Flying around the country, visiting all kinds of workplaces, while evaluating the employer's practices relative to human capital management, including pre- and post-injury and disability management, required being able to navigate difficult terrain and maintain a grueling schedule. It often involved hours of meetings, sitting at the end of a table with management lined up on one side and union representatives on the other, as contracts were hammered out, disputes resolved, and service providers selected. Visiting worksites like meat-packing plants, factories, and mines required greater physical mobility than I could muster. My previous job had also involved a great deal of writing. We had to submit a proposal to win the business and present detailed reports of findings and recommendations at the end of projects. Often, several months of work had to be distilled into an executive summary, consisting of two-pages of bullet points because such was the attention span of senior executives of companies we served. While I estimated that I had reached about seventy percent of my pre-stroke capacity, as much as I loved the work, I could not have continued to do it.

But that was not what I was doing at the time of the stroke. I had a desk job. Admittedly, it was one that carried a lot of management and budgetary responsibility, but it required minimal travel, and client work was handed off to others. In accepting that position, I unwittingly signed my death warrant with the company. A second reorganization had effectively eliminated my position, but no one wanted to put it into words. I had always been successful in my professional life, a trailblazer, a pioneer, whether in hand therapy or consulting for large companies.

I had never wanted to work for this particular division of the company. I had worked happily and successfully for another division and had quit rather than accept the mandatory transfer that was offered to me. The president of the company had flown in from New York, asking to meet with me on very short notice. It happened to be a day when all of my senior colleagues were at an offsite meeting. He explained that corporate chiefs had determined that it was in the best interest of the company to move my practice to the other division. He hinted that the other division had a practice he would like to get in return. So there it was—an asset swap. After careful consideration, I told him politely that he could decide what was in the best interests of the company, but only I could decide what was in my own best interests, and making that move was not. I resigned and accepted an offer on behalf of my team to join one of the "Big Six" accounting firms.

After a brief period there, it became clear that it was not a good fit, and a group of us left to start our own company. This launched one of the happiest and most successful periods of my career. We built a small but very talented team, with support from the public accounting firm and the owners of a thriving small business, who sublet office space to us. They helped us navigate the turbulent waters of cash flow and attract major corporations, for whom we were able to pull off major consulting projects at a fraction of the cost of our major competitors.

Things went very well for a few years, until all my family health issues began. I struggled to combine the responsibility of leading the small business and being its primary business developer with flying back and forth to visit my sick relatives. The business grew to the point that we either had to raise more capital and hire more people or be acquired by a larger organization. We chose the latter and entered into an agreement with a company to acquire the business. It was a disastrous mistake. In a matter of days after the contract was signed, that company was acquired by the one for which I had declined to work before, and I found myself exactly where I did not want to be. At first it had worked out better than anticipated. I was appointed business leader of a consulting practice that was a joint venture between two sister companies, and then after 9/11, I had transferred to a leadership role locally. I had done well in that role both before and after the stroke, but suddenly, I was experiencing a precipitous fall from prophet to pariah that was as unnerving as it was unexpected. Was it because of the stroke that there were now two people—another woman and me occupying what used to be my position?

Did I have food on my face? Did I drool? Was it the way I walked? Was it because I was always dropping things that someone else was taking over my responsibilities? Was I an embarrassment? Those questions poked at me as I tried to make sense of what was happening. The fragile tissue of self- confidence in which I had wrapped myself began to crinkle around the edges. Conversations with the two people to whom I reported were disconcerting, vague, and innuendo-filled.

"Are you sure this job isn't too much for you?"

"What are your long-term plans?"

One day while walking back to my office after leading a staff meeting, one of my senior direct reports, a physician, told me he thought I should know that my being around was really bad for morale, as the staff didn't know who to suck up to—me or the other person. I should leave, he added, for everyone's sake, including my own.

I was stunned! I had done the job well, grown the business, and balanced the budget of $25 million with a profit margin greater than 25 percent. I had been popular with the staff and was respected by my colleagues, though apparently not all of them. Why should I leave? I was not ready to retire. Not yet sixty years old, I was battered and bruised but not finished. What I overlooked at that time was that my base of support within the company lay in New York and around the country and not in Chicago. When the national consulting leader requested a private meeting and suggested it should be at my house, I should have smelled a rat immediately.

We settled on a date and time, and I made sure that I was home in plenty of time. I answered the doorbell at the appointed time, and oozing charm from every pore, he oiled his way across the floor. The speech he delivered had apparently been well rehearsed, but I was taken aback, not for the first time, that he did not seem to grasp the discriminatory nature of his comments and actions. I was by far the most qualified person for the job and was already doing most of it. Why was he now telling me that it would be too much for me to do the job I was already doing successfully? The simple answer was that there was someone else he wanted to promote. My disability had become a convenient excuse.

We were just finishing paying for the girls' education. We had supported my mother for seventeen years after Dad died, buying the smaller house for her and subsidizing the mortgage. The last few years of work and saving were going to be for us. What would I do about health insurance? I was not old enough for Medicare, and with a preexisting condition such as I had, I would not be able to get private insurance. When the meeting ended, I needed a bath. As I wrestled with how to handle this uncomfortable situation, Archie intervened. He had another plan.

At a follow-up appointment, Dr. Eliades, captain of my therapeutic team, told me about a research study at the Rehabilitation Institute of Chicago, for which they were seeking subjects. The study would require attendance at RIC three days a week for a total of twelve weeks and would involve therapist- assisted treadmill walking. I would be in the control group, comparing the benefit of this kind of treatment with that provided by the Lokomat, the robot made famous by Christopher Reeve, a superman both before and after his horrific accident.

If accepted, I would be in the study with the primary purpose of contributing to data collection that would eventually help other stroke survivors receive more and better treatment in the early stages of recovery. There also would be two potentially beneficial side effects for me. The additional intensive exercise could strengthen my ankle to the point that I could dispense with the brace, and my removal from the workplace for a few weeks would allow the current ambiguous situation to sort itself out. At the very least, I would be removed from the contentious work environment and resulting stress to which I was reluctant to expose myself.

Sarah, employed by the United Nations and living in New York, was traveling back and forth to various parts of the world, mainly Africa. Sandy had a new job as a nanny, taking care of two little girls. She had a new boyfriend, Reni, who shared her Hispanic heritage, and she was giving indications that this relationship might be serious. She believed a proposal might be in the offing.

I was accepted into the study and received approval for a period of short- term disability insurance. My blood pressure was already trending up and I could not allow myself to ignore the significance of that. With encouragement from both doctors and family, I took advantage of the opportunity to focus once more on my own recovery. This time, I was able to participate mentally and physically in the program in a way I had not in my original post-stroke rehabilitation.

Returning to the Rehabilitation Institute of Chicago was a bittersweet experience. I had enjoyed my time working there immensely but my passion for rehabilitation of the hand had evolved into a desire to work on prevention of industrial accidents that resulted in the devastating injuries that I had seen. I had left RIC to go back to school to get my master's degree in public health, and that had taken me in a different career direction, but I retained enormous respect and affection for my first American employer.

I was surprised to find that even after being gone for thirty years, I recognized and was recognized by some people who still worked there. Entering the soaring lobby, I recalled my first day of work in this building in September 1974. The building was brand new then, as was the transatlantic phase of my life. I had come to Chicago, knowing only one person on an entire continent, to be with the man with whom I had fallen in love, Bruce. I interviewed at the original RIC, located in a repurposed warehouse, in January of that year. I walked from Michigan Avenue to RIC wearing a thin trench coat, the warmest garment I owned, and thought the wind blowing off Lake Michigan would slice me in two. On a couple of occasions, then as now, I had grabbed a door handle or drain pipe, to avoid being blown off my feet. By the time my green card, which actually was blue, came, allowing me to report for work, the move to the new building was completed.

I entered the elevator wearing a sticky label that identified me as a "research participant" on the sweater of the loose, comfortable outfit I had been directed to wear. I stopped myself from pushing the button for the sixteenth floor, where my office had been when I was Director of Occupational Therapy Education. Instead, I pushed thirteen, where the study would take place.

As I met the team of researchers who were running the research project, I noticed that their name tags identified them as physical therapists, occupational therapists, or engineers. There was one marked difference from my clinical days: These therapists all had doctoral degrees or were on their way to obtaining them. As I waited, my mind wandered back to my own training.

I received a diploma in occupational therapy for psychiatric conditions and physical dysfunction after three years of training at a college located on the grounds of an exclusive, private psychiatric hospital. We students essentially lived with the patients, attending classes for part of the day and spending the rest working on patient activities. The hospital was located in Northampton, a medium-sized manufacturing city, the main product of which was shoes. The city gained renown later as the home of the factory that was the inspiration for the play and movie *Kinky Boots.* It was also home to a large Avon cosmetics factory that made our part of town smell like a tart's handbag when the wind was blowing in the right direction.

Our training in OT for physical dysfunction took place during three consecutive periods of three months; we worked under the supervision of qualified therapists in hospitals around the country. Our clinical practice included both orthopedics and general rehabilitation.

In orthopedics, we served as indentured laborers, checked patients in, loaded them in and out of wheelchairs, ran back and forth to the x-ray department, removed smelly casts and bandages, and comforted terrified patients. In return, the surgeons taught us to read x-rays and to recognize various fractures and conditions affecting bones and joints, particularly those of the hand. This was the genesis of my fascination with the hand, as we observed intricate reconstructive surgeries following industrial accidents, and we became involved in postsurgical rehabilitation.

In general rehabilitation, the patients were mostly stroke survivors My one prior experience of stroke, my grandmother's, had been very traumatic, and I was not predisposed to enjoy the work.

Thinking about Grandma's stroke brought the taste of maggoty bacon to my mouth. I was sitting at the large pine table in the kitchen at Sapperton, where one of my aunts was serving lunch. My mother and her sisters took turns taking care of Grandma after her stroke, and one of their major responsibilities was to make sure lunch was on the table for my grandfather, uncles, and the farmhands at one o'clock every day. The fare that day included boiled bacon, potatoes, and cabbage. Grandma was sitting in a large cane-backed chair at the head of the table. She was unable to speak because of the stroke, and as I lifted the first forkful of bacon toward my mouth, she began gesticulating at me with her good hand, grunting, wheezing, and uttering incomprehensible sounds. She frightened me, and I stuffed the forkful of food in my mouth. The taste of that food was utterly disgusting, and I wanted to spit it out but that was not a viable option. Such a breach of good manners would have been unacceptable.

Grandma's red-rimmed eyes filled with tears, and she pointed wildly at the platter of bacon on the table, uttering her nonsensical words with increasing volume. Before I knew what was happening, one of my aunts grabbed me off my chair, stuck two fingers down my throat, and carried me outside into the yard where I emptied the contents of my stomach all over the cobblestones. There had apparently been two platters of bacon in the larder, one good and the other riddled with maggots. When I returned to the table, the only food put in front of me was a slice of bread and butter. Grandma continued to weep and utter strange words, and the association between stroke and maggoty bacon was cemented in my mind.

As students, we struggled gamely with the tools at our disposal—slings and springs, dressing aids such as buttonhooks and long-handled shoehorns—to help them regain movement and independence. It was an uphill battle. Had I known then that my life would include becoming an "old hemi" myself, it would have been an extremely dismal prospect.

One of the researchers pulled me back to the present by asking me to sign a stack of papers attesting to the fact that I understood that this was a research project. No therapeutic benefits from the exercise were guaranteed. I had the right to leave the study at any time. My personal information would not be shared without my consent, and my right to privacy would be protected.

"Right to privacy," I repeated to myself. "What privacy?" After spending much of the past few years in and out of hospitals and doctors' offices, I did not know what privacy felt like. I signed the papers and then walked over to the treadmill.

I was relieved to hear that I would not be walking by myself on the treadmill but would be supported in a harness, so that my feet just touched the track. After my experience on an escalator, no matter how competent I might be on a stationary bike or elliptical, I avoided having anything to do with earth that moved under my feet. A therapist supported my left foot, and together we performed the motions of walking while the treadmill operated at different speeds. Several monitors were attached to my arms to track my blood pressure and heart rate.

As the therapist indicated we were ready to begin, the treadmill lurched forward. Dangling in my sling, I struggled to find a rhythm with my right leg, while the therapist lifted and moved my left in a synchronized imitation of a normal step. At slow speed, we did all right, but as the speed increased, my left leg flailed and my left arm waved about in uncontrollable sympathy. I glanced down at the therapist and saw that she was working so hard to manage my foot that she was dripping perspiration on to the rubber track of the treadmill. I felt bad for her and feared that while I performed my hamster- on-a-wheel routine, she would expire from dehydration or cardiac arrest. She was the one who should be wearing the monitors. When my allotted time was up, I was required to drink a bottle of water and rest for thirty minutes before I was able to leave.

While I was resting, another of the researchers came over and introduced himself, saying everyone was pleased to have an occupational therapist in the study. He asked if I would be willing to participate in other studies, as I was "interesting subject matter." My perspective, as someone who had looked at stroke from both sides, would add a different dimension. I told him that at the end of this study, I would have to go back to work and may have a wedding to plan, but time permitting, I would be more than willing to do anything I could that might help future stroke victims recover faster.

As the study wound down, I started making inquiries about returning to work. I was unable to get any clarification about what my job would be or, indeed, whether I actually had a job. I heard nothing from the company and— more disturbing—nothing at all from the people at work whom I had considered friends.

I was still more comfortable reading magazines than books and came across an article in *Vanity Fair* by one of my favorite writers, Christopher Hitchens. He quoted something he had read about the French and their refusal to become involved in the Iraq conflict following the attack on the World Trade Center: "You can always count on the French to be there when they need you." It struck me that this was an accurate description of some people I had thought of as friends. They had always been there when they needed me but were conspicuously absent when I could have used support from them.

Maybe it would be best to look for another job, and maybe it would be better to stick to old friends—real ones. I repeated my hamster routine three times a week for twelve weeks. On off days, I was stiff, sore, and exhausted but fully occupied with planning Sandy's wedding, the proposal and acceptance now a matter of history. I eschewed any suggestion that we should hire a wedding planner. For what? I had plenty of time on my hands; I could do this. While my ideas about what I could and could not do by myself were more realistic than before, my judgment was still flawed, and I still tended toward grandiosity.

The wedding would take place in our garden, with food and music reflecting the couple's Latin heritage. Bridesmaids' dresses, flowers, tablecloths, and flowers would range from the palest lavender to deep purple, shades of Sandy's favorite color.

We planted flowers in the garden and in containers in the same hues and created a lovely backdrop for the occasion. We rented a huge cathedral-ceilinged tent to house both the ceremony and reception. It was an afternoon wedding, and Sandy wanted to honor the English tradition of ladies wearing hats. Wear hats, we did! Sporting large hats, small hats, simple hats, outrageous hats, or fascinators, everyone got into the spirit and had fun with the theme. I was a little spooked while donning my cream, wide-brimmed straw confection, when secondhand nausea and a phantom worst-headache- of-my-life briefly overwhelmed the joy of the moment.

We were expecting about 120 people. A number of my family members were coming from England—Keith and his partner, June; my two surviving sisters-in-law; my cousin Shirley and her husband. A private plane load of Bruce's New York relatives; a few of the groom's family members from Puerto Rico and Ecuador; and my friend Carole from Mauritius also would be flying in. In fairness, the groom's grandmother did warn me that their family did not subscribe to the custom of replying to invitations.

"We have different customs," she told me. "You won't hear from them, but they'll come, and they might bring a couple of extra people." She then added, "Don't worry; they'll bring money for the bride and groom."

I passed on the warning to the caterer, who said he would add 20 percent more food, and to Sarah, who already was struggling with the seating plan.

The day of the wedding arrived, and all was ready. The weather was hot, as befitting a summer weekend in Chicago. I was not planning to be part of the bridal procession, afraid of the risk of catching my foot in the white, flimsy carpet spread out on the grass and doing a nosedive in front of the assembled guests. I had asked my stepson, Cliff, to walk me to my seat when the time came, entering from the back of the tent, sheltered from public scrutiny.

As the tent started to fill up, and we women started to feel the weight of our hats, Sarah asked me to step in to the kitchen. She was looking lovely in her lavender bridesmaid dress but had a panicked expression on her face.

"Have you seen how many people there are out there?" she asked. "There are at least 150 already!"

Before she could say anything else, our attention shifted to the kitchen window, from which we saw a medium-sized bus with the words *Iglesia Pentecostal* emblazoned on its side, pulling up to the front door.

"Oh my God!" Sarah choked on her words, "More people!"

"*And thick and fast they came, at last, and more and more and more.*" It appears that the only people missing at this stage were the Walrus and the Carpenter themselves. The whole affair was taking on a *Through the Looking Glass* surreal aspect.

We watched in jaw-dropping disbelief as the groom's uncle Angel, a part- time pastor, descended from the bus, followed by a flock of parishioners. We had known him longer than we had known the groom. As a day job, he ran a furniture upholstery business. He had recovered practically every piece of furniture in our house at one time or another. Angel did not follow the large, carefully placed purple arrows pointing to the back garden, where the wedding musicians were warming up. He paused at the front door only long enough to gather his flock and shepherd them into the front hallway. From there, he led them on a guided tour of his handiwork—the couch in the living room, specially recovered for the wedding; the chairs in the den; the couches in the family room that had been delivered by none other than the groom himself before Sandy met him.

Sarah regarded her seating plan with grim surrender written on her face. Then, with a great sigh, she ripped it into tiny pieces and threw it into the trash.

"They are going to have to fight it out among themselves. Apart from the bridal party, it's strictly open seating," she proclaimed.

"Does that include the mother of the bride?" I asked. "I don't do well with mob scenes, what with the cane, the hat, and all."

"You'll be okay," she reassured me. "I have reserved a large table for all the elderly rellies." Whether her term of affection implied relatives or relics was uncertain. At the time, I definitely felt more like the latter.

A signal from the musicians let us know that it was time for me to get to my seat. The judge was in place, and the bridal party was ready to go. As Cliff guided me to my seat, one of the guests, a man to whom I had been helpful on many occasions and who never failed to call me when our practice was handling a piece of business he wanted, seized the moment to let me know there would be no place for me in his organization. If things did not work out for me to return to my job, he would have nothing for me. Immaculate timing—at my daughter's wedding. *Merci beaucoup!*

The ceremony was beautiful. The bride looked radiant in her handmade gown. The bridesmaids and flower girls were picture perfect. The men of the wedding party were wearing summer cream tuxedos with lavender ties and cummerbunds. Apart from looking a little hot around the collar, they were straight out of *The Great Gatsby*.

Nonny and Poppy's daughter, Joanie, a professional singer, performed music from *West Side Story*, and the rivulets of perspiration appearing from under the brims of hats, comingled with trickles of tears, as the romance of the moment overtook the heat and discomfort.

At the end of the ceremony, everyone came out into the garden, where servers were passing out drinks and hors d'oeuvres. Guests mingled while the official photographer, a friend of the family, took pictures of the bridal party, and the catering crew busily rearranged the chairs and tables for dinner. As the last few quests stepped out of the tent, a torrential downpour engulfed everyone.

Two rolls of thunder and two flashes of lightning were all it took to get the stampede started. Cordons, temporarily erected to keep the guests out of the tent, pending dinner, were pushed aside as a throng of soggy, be-hatted, and dripping women and sweaty, be-suited gentlemen strove to find shelter from the downpour anywhere they could. I found myself asking Archie why he had chosen this precise moment to open up the heavens.

"Couldn't you have waited until they were seated in the tent?" I asked, looking up at the sky, which was brilliant blue again, with no sign of the evil, black storm clouds that had done their damage and fled.

To their everlasting credit, the caterers kept their cool. The manager approached me as mountains of hors d'oeuvres disappeared in record time and told me that they did not have enough food. "There are at least twice the number of guests we planned for," he said plaintively. "Can I see what's in your freezer and pantry?"

"Of course," I said. "Take anything you can find; just make it look nice."

A definition of hors d'oeuvres that I'd heard on the radio years ago—"dirty great dollops of dodgy doodah on doilies"—made me smile in spite of the gravity of the situation. Whatever we had—hot dogs, hamburgers, chicken breasts, chicken wings, chicken nuggets, veggie burgers, mini pizzas, salsa and chips, bagel bites, cold cuts, cheese slices—were rapidly transformed to bite-sized portions, placed on crackers, garnished with parsley from the garden, and added to the buffet table. No sooner did the food arrive than it was consumed by a swarm of human locusts. I had to admit, if only to myself, that the occasion was totally out of control. Maybe a wedding planner would not have been such a bad idea! My post-stroke grandiosity had gotten the better of me, not for the first and certainly not for the last time.

After the DJ announced the couple's first dance, the wedding cake appeared for them to cut. It was a massive three-tier affair, decorated with purple flowers and ribbons, in keeping with the theme. The top layer, we thought, would be frozen for the christening of the first baby, in keeping with English tradition.

As the dancing got under way—a mixture of disco, rock, and salsa—I did not leave my bunker. I wanted to dance so much, but I dared not. I did not want to fall on my face. I could not take the risk. I looked around at the crowded tent filled with family and friends and bleakly pondered on how many of those friends were real and how many were "French." With my smile Super Glued on my face, I sat at one of the tables and observed Bruce dancing with everyone he could persuade on to the floor. I felt an aching loneliness for the time when I was the one in his arms from opening chord to last man standing.

I saw myself throughout my all-girls schooling, always dancing the part of the man because that was what the tall girls did. Bruce and I had struggled in our early years as he, at first politely and later more belligerently, asked me to stop pushing him around the dance floor. He had finally patiently taught me to dance backward in heels, the lot of the female partner. I had taught him the joys of such dances as the Gay Gordons, a name he thought politically incorrect but a dance he thoroughly enjoyed, Highland yells and all, once he got over his American inhibitions.

I started to feel sad, uncomfortable, bereft. My mind was wandering down a rock-strewn path, and my hat felt tight and heavy, as if my neck could not support it anymore. Bile rose in the back of my throat. I grasped the lavender tablecloth in my clammy right hand and pulled on it to steady myself in my seat. I had not wanted to think about work, let alone talk about it, on this special day. I should not let the intrusion of work and all that meant at that point in my life spoil Sandy's day for me, but in the midst of all of those people, including those closest to me, I had never felt so alone.

Carole caught my eye, and she must have spotted something in my expression. She came over to where I was sitting. "Let me take your hat," she said. "You must be boiling."

"Melting, like the ice cream!" I replied, glad of the chance to be distracted from peaking pangs of paranoia about what had happened the last time I put on a hat to go to a wedding.

The following day, when I asked where the top layer of the cake had been stored, I learned that there was not a crumb left. There was good news for the bride and groom, though. When Bruce tallied the crumpled checks, bank notes, and gift cards, brought largely by the unexpected guests, it amounted to several thousand dollars. This was on top of the mountain of boxes piled up in the front hall, bearing such labels as Crate and Barrel; Bed, Bath and Beyond; and Marshall Field.

Sandy and Reni went off on their honeymoon; Sarah and Bruce went back to work. The out-of-town guests dispersed, leaving me at home with nothing much to do.

Shortly after the wedding, I received a phone call from RIC, asking if I was available for another study. Having heard nothing from work,

I agreed to participate. One study led to another and another, and for several weeks, I went to RIC to do battle with robots just about every day.

I found the research projects very gratifying. Even though it had been twenty years since I'd treated a patient, I recalled being bothered in my early days in the United States that we charged patients a lot of money for treatment of neurological conditions, the benefits of which were never proven scientifically. It was different with hand therapy—on both sides of the Atlantic. Hand rehabilitation was much more quantifiable by increases in range of motion, strength, and function than are most other forms of rehabilitation. That was one of the reasons I chose that field. Most of my patients would get better and go on with their lives. I served my time working with patients with severe spinal cord injuries and degenerative neurological disorders. I have profound respect for them and the therapists who take care of them but found the emotional toll too draining to make a career of it.

I found myself drawn into this brave new world of robots. Could a robot take the place of a therapist? One of the realities of this modern medical economy was that research showed that patients could benefit from more therapy than their insurance would cover.

A research therapist attached my useless arm to a robotic one. The study required me to reach toward a target on a screen, with and without both assistance and resistance from the robot. It was not a fair contest. I got tired way before the robot did. I spent hours hooked up to the Lokomat, pedaling in the air, trying to move faster than he could. I never won.

In one study, I joined a group of stroke survivors in a street-walking exercise. We went to a high-rise building down the street where we were timed at the beginning of the study as we walked around the first floor. We then engaged in a few weeks of strenuous therapy and returned to the original building to see if our times had improved. Mine had, dramatically, rekindling my conviction that there was no expiration date on potential for improvement.

I was recruited by Northwestern University's School of Physical Therapy, because of my background as an occupational therapist, to take part in another set of studies. I participated in two that involved wearing a bionic glove on my left hand. I was attached to a nerve stimulator that I wore on my belt, with two electrodes stuck on my arm. The glove transmitted a tingling sensation to my hand and fingers. I wore the glove while performing normal activities for certain periods every day. I wore it to the health club when I went to work out, much to the amusement of my exercise buddies. The glove made me aware of my hand in a way that I had not been since before the stroke. I was much more inclined to use the hand when I knew it was there. I wondered how different my outcome might have been, had I been able to wear this glove in the early days, before I learned to cope so effectively without a left hand.

For a few weeks, I wore a pedometer to keep track of how many steps I took during the day. My competitive spirit ignited as I tried to outdo myself. My speed of walking was measured at the beginning and at the end of the study, and once again, I had improved markedly. Bruce asked to borrow the pedometer and found, to his chagrin, that he did not take nearly as many steps as I did in the course of a day.

I was invited to give an address at the PT students' graduation at Northwestern University and found myself on the dais with distinguished guests and faculty, standing for just about ten minutes to deliver my remarks.

I spoke without notes, with half of my mind focused on my speech; the rest focused on bracing my leg, steadying myself against the podium, and remembering to swallow the pooling saliva in my mouth. After my talk, a physician approached me and asked if the Professor Aziz who treated me was Tipu Aziz. When I answered in the affirmative, he let out a soft whistle and said, without irony and with no pun intended, "What a wonderful stroke of luck! I am familiar with his work, and you could not have fallen into better hands!"

To that point, *lucky* was not a word that I would have chosen to describe much about my experience in recent years, but I found myself wondering for the first time whether, beyond falling into Professor Aziz's brilliant hands, there might be other aspects of having this stroke that might turn out to be lucky. Was I lucky that I had been an occupational therapist? Was it helpful to my recovery? It was still too soon to tell.

After the intensity of the summer and with the studies and the wedding behind us, I started making more inquiries about going back to work. My initial calls and emails went unanswered. I learned that the Chicago office head had left the firm, along with a group of other very senior colleagues and as many clients as they could grab, to join a start-up competitor. The company was in turmoil again.

No one contacted me until one day in mid-August, when I heard from Human Resources in New York. They said they very much wanted me to return to work but not until mid-September. My job would be exactly what it had been before. I just had to find something to do until then.

On another late-night excursion on the internet, I found an email that offered last-minute deals on cruises to Alaska. I asked Bruce what he thought, and he was guardedly enthusiastic. "Don't take a cheap flight," he said, "and remember Tahiti. Get us a decent cabin!"

The cruise ship would sail from Vancouver, so I booked us on United for the day before the ship sailed. This time, I knew what I was doing and got us a stateroom with a balcony. I found a hotel, located right across the street from the harbor, and this cruise was as smooth as the waterways of the Inland Passage through which we sailed. We spent most of the time on our balcony, drinking wine and reveling in the sheer splendor of the view of the mountains and glaciers. One morning, we saw a flotilla of icebergs passing by. I had no idea that icebergs were blue—glaciers were blue too! I had expected them to be white.

Shortly after we arrived home, I received another message from Human Resources in New York, confirming that I should return to work on the last Monday of September. My job would be exactly as it had been before, and if that did not work out, there was a possibility of another one. I was highly respected, and they definitely did not want me to go away. They looked forward to my return. The Chicago office apparently never got that memo.

My second return to work was very different from the first. There was no Bill to greet me at my car. He had retired, remarried, and moved to Maryland. There were no friendly faces waiting at my office, although it was once more filled with bouquets of flowers from family and real friends.

The "Frenchest" of my friends, the only other managing director in the practice, a woman for whom I had put myself out on countless occasions ever since she was a bubbly, curly-haired, young OT, greeted me with a single sentence: "What do you want?" An angry look hardened her now middle- aged countenance and hit me in the face like a pitcher of ice water.

"What do I want? What do I want?" Words failed me. I did not say anything, but my thoughts seared as they formed in my brain. *My arm and leg back would be nice. My life back would be even better. I would like to retire with dignity, closer to my actual retirement date. Failing that, I want nothing more than to be treated with the kindness, respect, and professional generosity that I have extended to you over the last almost thirty years.*

I pondered what the term friendship really meant. I was blessed to have a group of real, close friends—from college, from my workdays in London, from my time working in Mauritius, from the horse world, neighbors, and a handful picked up here and there. My definition of friendship involves loyalty, reciprocity, trust, shared meaningful experience; being there for people when they need you; knowing they will be there when you need them; being able to pick up where you left off, sometimes after not seeing each other for years.

I realized in a moment of crystalline clarity that there had been no reciprocity and very little trust in my relationships with those people I had allowed myself to think of as friends at work. It was always about me doing things to help them. Sometimes it was because they asked for help—a promotion, a preview of a proposal that might give them a leg up in obtaining new business, more billable hours. In other cases, I felt I was paying forward my appreciation of treasured mentors in my own career by offering a helping hand. Being helpful apparently could be interpreted as being manipulative. I saw now that these people did not meet the basic criteria for anything but faux friendship and never had. The relationship they sought was not with me, the person, but with the position of influence that I held. They were not friends at all but habits. It was a tough, painful realization but also a liberating one.

My bunker was now submerged. I was underwater, confronting one of the hardest, loneliest, most painful periods of my life. I felt as if I were drowning, losing myself again, this time in a sea of human flotsam and jetsam. With greater clarity than before the stroke, I observed what the corporate landscape looked like. It was awash with white, mostly male faces. The men— guffawing, nodding, and winking at each other—stuck together. Nothing united them faster or firmer than opposition to strong, successful, independent women. The women, however, did not stick together. Mostly, they hitched their wagon to the star of whoever could carry them farther and faster, male or female. There were exceptions, but they were few and far between.

In *Little Dorrit*, Dickens used sea creature metaphors to describe the business world of his time. I found his concept amusing and enlightening as I detached and assigned sea creature roles to those around, above, and beneath me. There were plenty of barnacles; their only mission in life was to hang on to their jobs—any job within the company, regardless of their qualifications or ability to do that job. Their weaker cousins, limpets, attached themselves to any smooth surface, sheltered from the direct line of fire. There was the Italian blowfish, a true ultracrepidarian, who could talk up a storm on any topic but fell short when it was time to deliver. He was particularly adept at promoting himself at the expense of his female colleagues. There was the hillbilly stingray, smooth on the surface but possessed of a deadly barb. His attack was always from behind, and his word was never his bond. There were innumerable barracudas, who snapped up anyone who got in their way, octopi, and sharks. A whole flotilla of Portuguese man-of-war floated by— nothing more than puffed-up jellyfish.

I assigned myself the character of sea turtle, reluctant to poke my head too far out of my shell for fear that it would be stepped upon or, worse, bitten off. My fears proved legitimate when I poked my head out far enough to try to do my job, to exercise authority, or to make decisions and found myself publicly rebuked and accused of insubordination by the loquacious limpet who wanted me gone. I was also reprimanded for forwarding work emails to my home computer to work on in my own time, instead of using a company laptop. I wanted to scream, *"Have you ever tried to manage a briefcase, a purse, a laptop, and a cane with one hand? Have you tried to operate a laptop with one hand? I can't even open the damn thing, let alone find those tiny keys."* Instead, I said nothing and sucked it up because I did not want to give them the ammunition they sought to brand me as disabled.

A lawyer friend advised me to get legal advice. Bruce advised me to quit. I could not quit. I am not a quitter, stroke or not. They wanted me to go on long-term disability. The consulting practice I led specialized in disability management. I knew I was not a candidate for this. My doctor said he would not put his license on the line by certifying me as disabled when I had proven myself capable of doing my job. Long-term disability insurance is not intended to be a benefit of convenience for an employer who wants to downsize at the lowest possible cost.

The lawyer advised me to show up for work every day, and I did for eight and a half months. I sat in my office all day long, despite having a minimal amount of work to do, in order to prove that I really did not have a job. I didn't entirely give up on looking for another job, but organizations that had sought me out before pulled up their drawbridges, rolled up their sidewalks, or let me know that honestly, they would love to hire me but didn't want to offend the corporate giant for whom I worked.

I spent those eight and a half very long months pretty much in solitary confinement, except for a couple of male colleagues who took the risk of remaining loyal when most didn't want to be seen in public with me. The role of pariah was a new and painful one—salt rubbed into as yet unhealed wounds.

Where are the friends of yesterday?
What do they say that jolly crew, so new and brave and free and easy?
What do they say that jolly crew who must make even Judas queasy?

Borrowed from Osbert Sitwell's "Rat Week," these words played though my head on a continuous loop.

Lunch was a break that I cherished, not for the food but for the escape from isolation and monotony. There was a convenience store in the building where I could buy my lunch *du jour*, string cheese, a banana, a granola bar, and a lottery ticket. I have never won a penny on the lottery, except in England—once a family syndicate won ten pounds and split it four ways. Still, on the journeys to and from work, between my purchase and the drawing, I distributed my future fortune between family members, worthy causes, and people who had shown me random acts of kindness.

On days when I decided to go out for lunch, I was usually alone and drove my car to one of two restaurants that I liked in Greek Town. There was valet parking, a necessity for the walking impaired, and very friendly service at both. I was soon on first-name terms with the maîtres d', several waiters, and valet parkers. In the restaurant, ordering food as a one-handed eater consumed quite a lot of time. My concern was less about taste and more about manageability—what I could eat without making a mess or shooting food items, missile-like, across the restaurant.

When alone, I used my cell phone as a prop, checking voice mail at home and at the office, where there were seldom any messages. I wanted to create the impression of connectedness so that other patrons could not see the pound puppy inside me, desperate for attention, desperate to please, desperate to be adopted and taken home. I continued to experience random acts of kindness from total strangers, in stark contrast to the studied indifference or outright meanness of the people among whom I spent my days.

There were days when I was in particularly low spirits and wondered about taking my hand off the spinner on my steering wheel while passing through Hubbard's Cave, the labyrinthine tangle of highway that burrows under the soaring skyscrapers of Chicago's distinctive business district, around which the elevated railway wraps to form its iconic Loop. The brick walls of the underpass seemed to possess a magnetic quality. I wondered what it would feel like to stop trying, to give up and settle. I wondered if it would have better if I had not survived the stroke. It might have been easier—definitely for me, but maybe it would have been easier for Bruce and the girls too. I wondered about a few more Temazapam at bedtime to extend my dreamless sleep to eternity. I could only give headroom to these thoughts as long as I did not allow myself to think about the impact of my actions on my nearest and dearest. Could I leave them to ask, for the rest of their lives, why they had not been enough?

These thoughts, black as skid marks on the road, were fleeting, born of a desire to turn back the clock, to be free of the weight that slowed my progress, the physical chains that made me feel like Houdini in his underwater escape routines. I was desperate to escape the chains that prevented me from doing the things I had planned to do in retirement—breed more horses, become a master gardener, take those ballroom dancing lessons, pick up piano lessons and really learn to play that piano that patiently waited in the family room, or go back to hand therapy. Now, facing forced retirement without the ability to do any of those things, I had no plan. If I left this job, who would hire me? Nobody would! I knew the statistics. A disabled employee's best chance of remaining gainfully employed is with his or her former employer. If people who knew me and knew my work did not want me, why would anyone else? Even though I did not see myself as handicapped in terms of doing my job, obviously others did. They offered me another job that I could have accepted, had I been more of an ultracrepidarian. But it was so far out of my skill set that I could only assume it had been offered as an invitation to fail. My upbringing and clinical training had imbued in me such a strong sense of respect for boundaries that I could not set myself up as an expert in things about which I knew very little. "You can talk the talk," they told me. "You are an excellent consultant and facilitator."

But can I walk the walk? I asked myself. The answer was always the same. I could not walk that walk, not down streets I had never set foot on.

Even on the worst days, I could not completely extinguish my innate optimism. I was lucky, after all—lucky that I could get out of bed by myself, get dressed, and drive myself to work, even if I was miserable when I got there. It had not always been so, and I would eventually be able to think about the good times—the client successes; the strong teams; the retreats in Scottsdale, Galena, and Kohler; the laughs; the songs; the food fights; the adventures. Most of all, I was lucky that I had a husband and family who loved me, and I had enough real friends to mitigate whatever losses I might sustain. I also had Archie.

One morning in May 2006, I received an early retirement package. It had finally become clear to all concerned that my job had disappeared, and the new one offered to me was not a viable alternative. While I still did not want to retire and dreaded being adrift with no reason to get up in the morning, there was clearly no option but to accept the package and move on.

BIBLIOGRAPHY: CHAPTER 9

Chicago Architecture Organization website. Blog dated 9/23/09, "What Is Hubbard's Cave?" Accessed July 12, 2018. http://www.chicagoarchitecture.org/2009/09/23/what-is-hubbards-cave-2/

Gradesaver website. Webpage, "Little Dorrit Metaphors and Similes." Accessed July 12, 2018. https://www.gradesaver.com/little-dorrit

Hocoma, Inc. Lokomat Website. "Relearning to Walk from the Beginning." Accessed July 12, 2018. https://www.hocoma.com/us/solutions/lokomat/

Metrolyrics. Webpage entry of lyrics by Allan Jay Lerner. "My Fair Lady– You Did It Lyrics." Accessed July 13, 2018. http://www.metrolyrics.com/you-did-it-lyrics-my-fair-lady.html

Reeve, Christopher. Christopher and Dana Reeve Foundation Website, "Christopher's Exercise Program." Accessed July 12, 2018. https://www.christopherreeve.org/living-with-paralysis/rehabilitation/christopher-reeve-exercise-program

University of Northampton. University Website "News" page. "We've Been Celebrating 75 Years of Occupational Therapy Education." Accessed July 12, 2018. https://www.northampton.ac.uk/news/75-years-of-occupational-therapy/

Wall Street Journal. Accessed July 12, 2018. https://www.albinoblacksheep.com/text/france.html

Wikipedia. Entry about Allan Jay Lerner. Accessed July 13, 2018. https://en.wikipedia.org/wiki/Alan_Jay_Lerner

Wikipedia. Entry for Lewis Carroll's "The Walrus and the Carpenter" from *Through the Looking Glass.* Accessed July 12, 2018. https://en.wikipedia.org/wiki/The_Walrus_and_the_Carpenter

CHAPTER 10

The Meaning of the Word

I HAD TIME TO FILL BETWEEN RECEIVING NOTIFICATION OF THE DATE of my retirement and actually leaving, so I continued with the new round of therapy that Dr. Eliades had ordered and invested some time in pondering the meaning of the words *handicapped* and *disabled*.

From the time I had returned to work, seven months after the stroke, I had started re-assimilating into so-called normal life. As I did, I encountered all kinds of interesting facts regarding accommodation for handicapped people. A curious dichotomy existed within my head. As an occupational therapist, of course I knew about adaptations and accommodations that were required for handicapped people, but I did not think of myself as one of them. The words *handicapped* and *disabled* did not resonate with me at all.

With the prospect of my work life winding down, I paused to take stock of some of the things I had learned as I went through the painstaking process of expanding my independent horizons. I recognized certain difficulties with my body and their relationship to the environment in which I operated. Certain features were helpful. Rails around the toilet, for example, were very useful. It was advantageous to have something with which to hoist myself off the seat, especially when my left foot persisted in shooting straight out in front of me when I attempted to put any weight on it. There was an ever-present danger of doing the splits when the floor was wet, which, I discovered, it usually was. This I did not understand. Why was it necessary for grown women to pee on the floor? Men, I understood, but women? What was their excuse?

"Whose bright idea was it," I mused, when going to the bathroom in a public place, "to situate the handicapped stall at the farthest end of the restroom?"

I suppose if you are on wheels it does not matter quite so much, but if you are on shaky legs with a cane or crutches, it can be treacherous. Crossing the River Hades in front of the sinks adds an element of adventure to this most basic of needs. I also wondered who was the bright architect or designer who decided to make public bathroom stalls so small that it is impossible for a normal-size person to turn around in them? I have been required to lift my leg over the seat in order to get in and out on numerous occasions. That is no small feat when carrying a purse, a cane, and a coat. I actually had a couple of claustrophobic meltdowns when I could not get out because my purse strap had caught on the hook on the back of the door as I attempted to maneuver my way out. Why do they make the doors so heavy that it requires herculean strength to push them open?

I was amazed at how many public places had flights of stairs with handrails only on one side. If the rail was on the right side, I could go up just fine. When it was time to come down, it was another story. One of my therapists taught me that if there was no handrail on the right when coming down, I should just sit on the steps and bounce down on my rear end or walk down backward. While efficient and safe, neither option is compatible with maintaining the kind of dignified front I prefer in public.

"But what about going up if the rail is on the left?" I inquired.

"Same thing in reverse. Just sit on the step and haul yourself up backward, one step at a time. Practice a few times. You'll get used to it."

I had tried that in Papeete without success, but I did practice and became quite proficient. It is not something I recommend. There is the ever-present problem of how to stand up once one reaches the top. I have done it several ways, most commonly a strong pair of arms under my armpits, hauling me to my feet. Once or twice, I tried bumping up two or three steps of the next flight, dragging myself to a standing position, and easing myself onto my feet.

As I started to venture forth alone into Chicago's streets to attend meetings, I began to find the notion of a ramp on every corner as mythical as President Hoover's "chicken in every pot." There are many ramps, but some are so steep that when they were covered in snow, I had as much chance of climbing up them as I would of making it up K2 without ropes and pitons. On one occasion, I executed my own version of a skateless triple axel, double Salchow on the way down a ramp outside a restaurant, where I was meeting a client for lunch. I landed in a gutter filled with ice and slush. Miss Gillies, my headmistress, had prophesied forty years before that we sixth-form girls had as great a chance of landing in the gutter as of ascending to the great heights scaled by our distinguished predecessor, Margaret Thatcher. How right she was! It took three men to pick me up because my feet kept sliding out in front of me, but my heroes stuck with me and did not let go until I was seated, soggy-bottomed but safe, in a booth in the restaurant.

I learned a lot about human nature as I ventured out in public alone, I was touched by how many people offered to help me across the street or held a door open for me. The most unlikely-looking people often turned out to be the most helpful. One day, in a high wind, I was hanging on to a lamppost while waiting for the traffic light to change at an intersection. A young man dressed from head to toe in black leather, sporting a tattoo of a snake slithering from the back of his neck up one side of his face and rings or studs in his nose, his eyebrows, his cheek, his lip, and his tongue, approached me. Under different circumstances, I might have been unnerved by his appearance and turned away, but when he asked if I needed help, I unhesitatingly accepted his arm and walked with him not just across the street but for a further two blocks as he politely told me he was going my way. We must have cut quite a dash, the two of us, and I could not decide whether to be relieved or disappointed that I didn't meet anyone I knew.

My knights included a young man with a mane of dreadlocks and another wearing a gray floor-length fur coat, gray fedora with a black brim, black shirt, sunglasses against the winter sun, and copious amounts of gold jewelry. I never inquired as to what any of them did for a living, figuring I was better off not knowing. All that mattered to me was their kindness and that I arrived at my destination in one piece.

There were other occasions when I was amazed and annoyed by the liberties that some people took. Tapping along a city street, I felt someone I had not seen grab my left arm. The act of grabbing my arm startled me .The resulting surge of adrenaline triggered muscle spasms that upset my precarious balance, causing me to stumble.

When that same stranger looked pityingly at me and told me the same thing had happened to her grandmother, it was all I could do not to snap, "You have no idea what happened to me, and how dare you compare me to your grandmother. You are probably older than I am," but I politely thanked her for trying to help.

When someone I had never seen in my life told me I could get up a flight of stairs with no handrails or hop on the bus, my instinct was to land a right hook squarely on that person's jaw, but that most likely would have landed me in the "big house" for assault. I know what I can do, and if I cannot do something, it is not for the lack of trying.

I became aware of people talking to me at a considerably higher decibel level than was necessary. There is nothing wrong with my hearing. There must be something that handicapped people have in common with foreigners that makes people feel obliged to shout to make them understand.

One of my more annoying encounters took place in a dress shop in Highland Park, when I pulled an earring out while trying on a sweater. I asked the salesperson if she could put the earring back on for me because I have no feeling in my earlobe, and it is hard to find the hole.

Her shouted response was, "Gross! That is disgusting! I can't do that!"

"Then, I'm sure you will find it equally gross and disgusting to touch my money, so you can keep the sweater, and I'll be on my way," was my retort.

She said nothing, but her expression said it all: *"Don't let the door hit you on the way out!"*

That was enough to ensure that I never set foot in that store again, and I did not shed a tear, a few years later, when it was shuttered permanently.

It took me a long time to recognize that I needed help and even longer to get up the courage to ask for it. Once I got in the swing of it, it got progressively easier, and I became skilled at recognizing good prospects. Young men of any stripe were always willing to give me a hand across the street, as were middle-aged men and women of color. White men of any age were generally good, as long as I could get them to slow down and get their attention away from the phone in their ear or their handheld device. I also learned who not to ask for help. Middle-aged white women in fur coats were at the absolute bottom of my list, being the only ones who had actually refused to help on the grounds of being late for a meeting, going in the opposite direction, or pretending not to have heard me.

I was still attending therapy, as prescribed by Dr. Eliades, and there was good news on the ankle front. My physical therapist had taken a course to learn how to use a fancy new tape, developed in Japan that stuck directly to skin. Athletes were using it to support sprained joints and to replace cumbersome braces. She thought it might work for me. I had nothing to lose, so I was game to try it.

Within a few days, the AFO was gone! Hallelujah! My ankle was taped three times a week, either by Sherri, the therapist, or Bruce. Sherri showed him how to apply the tape—where to start, where to end, and the required degree of tension. I was ecstatic! I could wear regular flat shoes, and liberation from the brace meant the stress on my poor knee was relieved too. The tape was miraculous! I covered it with a plastic bag in the shower. It was light and inconspicuous, but there were limitations: it was temporary, had to be reapplied every other day, and I most definitely could not apply it myself.

I realized that the tape mimicked the action of my paralyzed posterior tibialis tendon, the one that would pull my ankle outward and prevent it from turning over, the one that was always lax and had caused me to fall so often as a child.

Surgery would be a permanent solution to my problem, but I had been immersed in the complexities of American health insurance long enough to know there would be many more rivers of conservative treatment to cross before that would be approved. I intended to cross them but meanwhile, the tape was a significant step forward.

Coincidentally, another *Vanity Fair* article by Christopher Hitchens yielded a nugget of information. If travelers reach one million miles on

United Airlines, they become "gold" for life. This status carries such perks as free upgrades, free checked bags, and various other privileges to which the frequent flyer has become accustomed and doesn't want to give up. I consulted my statement and found that I had more than 990,000 miles.

"We need to take a really long trip," I told Bruce.

"Fine with me," he replied. "Just choose somewhere we have never been."

One of the gratis, glossy magazines that crowded our mailbox on their way to Bruce's waiting room bore an advertisement for Argentina on its back page.

"Is that far enough?" I inquired.

"It should just about do it," was his enthusiastic response.

I called a meeting and informed the staff that I would be taking early retirement, not with the intention of quitting work for good but to travel and to see what new possibilities presented themselves. I would be leaving at the end of the month, in my own time and on my own terms, to go to Buenos Aires, and after that, I would return to empty out my desk and then on to something new.

At the end of May, we set off on our much-anticipated trip to Argentina, where I would test the meaning of the words in international waters. This long flight would bring me across the million-mile threshold, and I would be golden for life, at least for traveling purposes. Making our way through the airport and on to the plane, I was reminded of another hazard. People wearing backpacks have no idea what a menace they are to those who are none too steady on their feet. I have come to think of them as " whackpacks" as their owners turn around with no concern for who or what might be behind or beside them. On that particular flight, I was knocked sideways into my seat.

I had made reservations on the internet at a local hotel that looked charming and was centrally located. I swallowed my pride and requested a handicapped-accessible room.

We arrived at our destination by taxi At first glimpse, it looked charming. There was no doorman, so the cab driver took our bags ahead of us. After the long flight, we were both a little groggy. I hung on to Bruce's arm as we activated the electronic glass door. As we were halfway through the door, it malfunctioned and started to close. I could not dodge out of the way fast enough, and the door knocked me sideways. It hit me on my right side, knocking me to the left, so I did not know I was going until I hit the ground. I was not prepared for Bruce to go down too. He said he tried to save me and lost his balance; I maintained that he tackled me.

Regardless of how it happened, we arrived in a tangled heap of arms and legs, having slid across a couple of feet of very shiny tile floor, directly in front of a startled front-desk clerk. A few anxious-looking hotel employees appeared, talking to each other in rapid-fire, staccato Spanish, a different accent from any I had heard and incomprehensible at first. Bruce and I looked at each other, reassured each other that we were okay, and allowed them to pick us up. As they did so, we began to laugh at this inauspicious start to our visit. They were obviously very concerned. They must have known about the litigious nature of Americans and were probably already anticipating a lawsuit. They insisted that we sit and drink tea—strong, black, and hot. They asked if we needed a doctor. They produced a box of tissues for the señora to wipe her eyes. They thought I was crying, but it was the opposite; I was laughing so hard that I could barely catch my breath. I could not stop laughing, and tears flowed until the front of my denim travel shirt was soaked.

As soon as we composed ourselves and checked in, one of the staff escorted us to our room. Bruce checked that it was handicapped-accessible. "Of course, señor," the desk clerk said. "It is on the first floor; no need to use the stairs." The door to the room was thrown open with a flourish, and we were shown in to a very elaborate space. Marble everywhere! The first snag we encountered was a set of three marble steps down to a red-velvet-covered king-size bed. There was no handrail and absolutely nothing to hold on to but Bruce's somewhat unsteady arm. We had just traveled for eighteen hours and taken a spill on a hard floor, so it was not surprising he was shaky. I sat on the bed and looked around before inquiring about the whereabouts of the bathroom. "Up there," said the hotel clerk, pointing to another three marble steps on the other side of the bed. There was no handrail there either.

I was utterly exhausted, and I knew Bruce was too, but there was no way I could stay in this room. It was bright, cheerful, and comfortable, as advertised on the internet, but imagine having to get up in the night to go to the bathroom. It was a deathtrap. I started to giggle again. Bruce looked decidedly unamused and shot me a withering glance as he began to speak in halting Spanish.

There followed a conversation that involved Bruce using the word *pesos* instead of *pasos*, thinking he was asking for a room without steps when he was actually asking for a room without paying. The clerk looked utterly bewildered and began beckoning us back up the steps. By this time, I was unable to contain myself. I was laughing hysterically, part stroke laugh and part genuine humor.

We struggled back up the steps and down the long hallway to the lobby. The manager was summoned and immediately apologized for any inconvenience. He responded to Bruce's request for a different room by telling us that all of the rooms were the same. "But we asked for handicapped accommodation."

"Si, señor," responded the manager gravely. "We gave you a handicapped room. It is on the first floor, so there is no necessity for you to climb stairs to your room." It was pointless to ask about the stairs within the room; we all knew we were not going to stay. It became clear to us that our problem was not that they did not understand our Spanish but that they had a very narrow understanding of the word *handicapped*. So did I, but mine was getting clearer every day.

The desk clerk produced our passports, and again with a flourish and with great ceremony, he ripped up the credit-card imprint taken when we checked in. The manager made a couple of phone calls and summoned a taxi. He explained in clear but heavily accented English that we were going to the Marriott. His hotel would not charge us their customary cancellation fee, and the Marriott would charge us the same rate as his hotel, as a courtesy to him. Smiling and nodding, a couple of hotel employees bundled us into the waiting taxi. I could almost hear the manager's sigh of relief as the taxi pulled away. The Marriott, fortunately, spoke the international language of disability, and we were installed in a very comfortable, safe room within a few minutes.

Bruce faithfully taped my ankle, as needed, and we set out to explore the streets around the hotel. Our mood was festive, as we are never happier together than when scratching the soles of our itchy feet in some new part of the world.

We could not cover long distances on foot, so we interspersed walking with stops to rest in cafes and shops. My favorite shops were the ones that sold leather goods. There is something about the scent of leather that I find intoxicating. The bags, belts, and jackets on display were in bright colors— blues, yellows, greens, and even some floral patterns. They were crafted beautifully and were reasonably priced, even in the most elegant of boutiques. The cafes were clean and bright, with friendly, courteous waiters.

People were polite, especially, it seemed, to foreigners, although an Englishman we met in the hotel bar advised me to downplay the English part of my identity.

"They are not quite over the Falklands War yet," he told me, shrugging apologetically, "and you will see that a lot of the old buildings have bloody great cannonballs embedded in the walls, courtesy of our lot a couple of hundred years ago."

We took a tour of the city in a car, arranged by the hotel, to avoid problems with a tour bus. We saw the infamous cannonballs as well as all of the major tourist attractions.

One of the obligatory sites to visit in Buenos Aires is the tomb of Eva Peron. We went to the Recoleta Cemetery to pay our respects. Seeing Evita's portrait evoked memories of me as a seven-year-old, hearing the news on the radio that she had died. I cried along with Mum that such a beautiful lady was gone. Such is the onion-peeling character of memory that I was put in mind of Sarah's first trip to Paris as a young teenager, when we had been eager to show her every cultural icon that city had to offer. Her only request was to go to the Père Lachaise Cemetery to visit the grave of Jim Morrison of the Doors. We had found the grave replete with beer bottles, peace signs, and cigarette stubs, and her vacation was complete. My trip was enhanced by finding the grave of one of my favorites, Oscar Wilde, in that same cemetery. I had done a better job of planning this trip than the infamous South Pacific odyssey, but it was still ambitious.

We took a side trip to Uruguay. Sarah and I were in a race to see who could visit the most countries in the world. I had started out way ahead, but because of her work with the UN, she was catching up fast.

The last stage of our vacation was a trip by air to visit Iguazu Falls. I am ashamed to admit that until I contacted the Argentinean Tourist Office, I had never heard of Iguazu Falls; nor had Bruce. The woman I spoke to was adamant that if we were in Buenos Aires and wanted to take a side trip, it was an absolute necessity to visit the falls. It was the wrong time of year to go to the South Pole, so I acquiesced, and she made the reservations.

Now with Buenos Aires and Uruguay under our belts, it was time to see this watery wonder of the world. We had an early flight and traveled back to the airport by taxi. Upon arriving at the domestic terminal, we encountered a familiar problem. The plane was standing in the middle of a row of small planes lined up on the tarmac, each with a flight of a dozen floating stairs. This time, we did not have to say a word. I had owned up to difficulty with stairs at the time I made the reservation. The minute we checked in, an attendant arrived with a wheelchair to escort us through security, around the back of the plane that was standing on the tarmac, doors open and baggage being rapidly stowed by a gang of men, who despite the noise of the idling engine and wearing ear-protectors, were engaged in lively, loud conversation. As they saw us approach, four of the baggage handlers stopped what they were doing and approached us. Before I knew what was happening, two men were in front of me and two behind, and they hoisted me up the steps, seated regally in the wheelchair. They continued their animated conversation the whole time, and since the two distinguishable words were futbol and gol, and this was Argentina, I concluded there must have been a football match the night before, and judging by the smiles on their perspiring faces, their team had won. The men unloaded me at the entrance to the cabin and, in an instant, disappeared. Bruce, grinning broadly, reminded me he had called me an old bag on more than one occasion, and now he had his proof.

After the short flight to Iguazu, I was unloaded by the baggage handlers and taken on a short car ride to the entrance to the falls. A guide met us and told us that a wheelchair and pusher were assigned to the "handicap woman." For an instant, I wanted to object, to say that I could walk, but the guide insisted that it was a long way, the path was wet and slippery, and maybe the señor would like a wheelchair too. The señor declined, with thanks. When the wheelchair arrived, it was unlike any wheelchair I had ever seen. With one large pneumatic tire in front and two behind, it looked more like a wheelbarrow than a wheelchair. Before getting into my chariot, I was enshrouded in a vast cloak of plastic, covered from top to toe. Bruce had one too. I laughed at him and told him how ridiculous he looked. He retorted that he wished he had a mirror so I could see myself. "People sitting in rubber wheelbarrows ought to be careful where they point their sharp tongues," he added.

We heard and felt the falls long before we saw them. The roar of falling water made conversation impossible. Enveloped in moisture denser than fog but lighter than rain, we were grateful for our plastic cloaks. After a steep climb—or in my case, roll—we rounded a bend and saw a vast semicircle of tumbling water throwing off clouds of spray and rainbows everywhere. It was breathtaking! The spray became a summer shower, and the rocks became more and more slippery as we got closer. Bruce, at one point, joked that he wished he had a wheelbarrow to ride in too. I was not entirely sure he was joking.

We stayed and stared for as long as our pusher would allow us, but eventually, he told us that it was time to go back because darkness would come quickly, and the path was too dangerous in the dark. With our last seconds at the falls, we drank in the natural magnificence, and Bruce reminded me of a quote from Eleanor Roosevelt, who, upon seeing Iguazu for the first time, had gasped, "Oh, my poor Niagara!"

Back at the hotel, we decided to take it easy, have a quiet dinner, and head for bed, having had enough excitement for one day. We made no plans for the following day, knowing that we had to be at the airport by 3:00 p.m. We hung the room service card on the door, having checked every box except for the scrambled eggs, and were asleep before ten o'clock.

The next morning, Bruce opened up the curtains in our room, and we were thrilled to see a pair of toucans perched, in their unlikely black, white, and orange splendor, on the balcony railing, surveying the jungle beneath and deciding what they would eat for breakfast.

Once we arrived home, I had to steel myself for the last few days of work. On my last day, there was a retirement party. It was a desultory affair, attended by my body but not my spirit. I felt as welcome as snow in harvest as I shook hands, hugged, accepted and doled out platitudes, ate a piece of the obligatory retirement cake, thanked everyone for my gift, and wondered how quickly I could make my escape. Many of the good wishes were genuine, I knew, but there was a boatload of phoniness too. My real retirement party took take place at a different time, in a different place, and it was a blast!

As I walked down the concrete slope to my car for the last time, my overwhelming sentiment was relief. The cries of, "We must have lunch or dinner," rang in my ears. Most would never materialize, and that would be just fine.

BIBLIOGRAPHY: CHAPTER 10

Burns, T. G. Mr. & Mrs. *Mason City Globe Gazette* (3/18/60). Page 5. Accessed July 13, 2018. https://www.newspapers.com/newspage/7475595/

Hitchens, Christopher. "Topic of Cancer." Vanity Fair (August 2010). Accessed July 13, 2018. https://www.vanityfair.com/culture/2010/09/hitchens-201009

CHAPTER 11

Astereognosis, Alexia, Anosognosia, and Other Excuses

RELIEVED OF THE PRESSURE OF GOING TO WORK EVERY DAY, I FELT A pressing need to invest time and effort in trying to understand, in more depth, what had happened to me. In my professional life, both as a therapist and as a consultant, I had always wanted to know as much as possible about issues confronting me. My natural curiosity had lain dormant for almost four years following the stroke. No doubt being immersed in research projects with extremely bright researchers had stimulated a revival of more analytical thinking and pushed me to start looking for answers to riddles that continued to plague me.

Participation in research studies exposed me, for the first time as a stroke survivor, to large numbers of other survivors. I became acutely aware of similarities and differences in how people were affected physically and, even more strikingly, the many variations in how they were affected psychologically, perceptually, and emotionally.

As I observed my fellow participants, I saw that each had one arm or the other either hanging limply from the shoulder or held stiffly with twin right- angles at elbow and wrist and a leg either encased in a brace or swinging in an arc from a hip as they walked. I saw stroke faces—mouth and eye drooping at the corner, to greater or lesser degree; the lopsided smile; the mask of drama, quick to flip from comedy to tragedy. But what didn't I see?

What do people not see when they look at me? All that lies beneath—the brain-cell specific losses that affect every sense, which altered my personality and took away the ability to read, to recall, and to dream. None of that is visible, yet it is a very big part of stroke. With the passage of time, I became much more aware of my limitations, having denied them all, initially, but I still didn't know enough to really understand the cause-and-effect relationship between the area of the brain that was damaged and the lasting deficits. Enough curiosity had been stimulated in my little gray cells to make me want to learn as much as I could.

It had taken most of the four poststroke years to recover some, but not all, of my former energy level. I found that I was often awake very early in the morning with nowhere to go and enough energy to get up and go to my computer. Sarah was in Sudan, serving with the UN, and I found that this quiet, undisturbed time worked well for keeping up with emails to her. I wrote to her first and then turned my attention to learning what I could about my brain in its current compromised condition.

Obviously, I am not a neuroscientist or any kind of expert in the workings of the brain, but I knew enough to respect it as an instrument more complex and sophisticated than anything man has come close to replicating. It is a kilogram of wet darkness, capable of conjuring great love, light, and beauty but also capable of great betrayal. Each minute particle of brain tissue has a specific function. Those particles, woven together, create a virtual fabric, the pattern of which is so intricate, so colorful, and so rich that it encompasses every element, sense, movement, and feeling in the universe. Once disrupted, the patterns have a seemingly unending ability to reinvent and re-create themselves, sometimes in pleasing alternatives, sometimes not.

I read the operative report that had cyber-migrated through e-mail from Professor Aziz to Bruce and forwarded to me, after I insisted on seeing it, and saw the scan taken later that showed a large, black hole in my head. The report mentioned the cerebral cortex, swelling, coma, and uncertain prognosis. Approximately one-third of a cup of soft-clotted blood had been removed from the right parietal lobe of my brain. That gave me a place to launch my exegesis. While I still struggled with reading books, I had learned that Google gave me access to sight bites that were mostly easily digestible.

I pecked "right parietal lobe" into the subject line and learned that the parietal lobe of the brain is situated above the occipital lobe and behind the frontal lobe. In lay terms, it is above and a little behind the ear. The name derives from the Latin name for the bone that covers that part of the brain, the *parries*, or wall. My Latin teacher's prophecy that Latin would be one of the most useful things we would learn was borne out once again.

The main function of the parietal lobes is to integrate sensory information from other parts of the brain and from the body to form a single perception. This is known as cognition, or the ability to recognize objects or stimuli. The secondary function is to construct a spatial coordinate system to represent the world around us. The parietal lobes are involved in vision, hand/eye coordination, and movements of the arm. The parietal lobes are the home of the sensory cortex, the outer gray matter that allows us to feel touch, temperature, and vibration. The left and right parietal lobes perform different functions, so damage to the right parietal lobe would produce different results from damage to the left. My damage was to the right parietal lobe, and from what I learned, my issues were fairly typical.

The main symptoms of damage in that area of the brain, I read, included homonymous quadrantopsia, an elaborate way of saying that vision in the lower quarter of the visual field on the opposite side to the brain injury is lost. This is not damage to the eye itself but disturbance in the brain's ability to interpret what the eye sees. This is not a problem that could be solved by glasses or contact lenses.

Another common feature of damage to the parietal lobe is spatial dysperception, or difficulty interpreting visual information in our surroundings, such as the length, depth, and size of objects. Another is loss of hand/eye coordination or difficulty bringing one's hand to a spot where one is aiming (this is particularly evident when one is trying to pick up an object— for example, a fork full of food—and bring it to one's elusive mouth). Inability to visually scan surroundings, words on a page, or visual stimuli in the peripheral field of vision can also result from damage to the brain's parietal lobe.

Now with the benefit of hindsight, I understood so much better my relationship with my altered world in those early weeks and months after the stroke. The reason the wheelchair and I had so much trouble getting along was not that the wheelchair was defective. The frequent collisions were entirely due to pilot error. I was flying blind! I began to comprehend my dependence on my ears instead of my eyes for quenching my thirst for words. I had been a rapid reader before, trained to scan chunks of a page and extract meaning all at once. That talent was gone. I could now read only one word at a time and might sometimes have to read it several times to be sure I had it right. Things were not necessarily where my eyes said they were. A humbling realization that I had been wrong about the scrambled eggs scrolled across the bottom of my screen of awareness. I only thought I had put an X next to the "toast" box, but my faulty navigational system had directed my hand to the "scrambled eggs" box. Oh, bloody, cheating, lying eyes—why could you not have chosen something—anything—else?

Sensory symptoms included the inability to experience sensations such as touch, temperature, and vibration, as well as disturbances in sensory comprehension. I was always cold, not because the temperature in the room or outside was low but because my ability to interpret the feeling was impaired. My arm and leg were telling my brain that they were cold, regardless of the actual temperature, because they believed sincerely that they were. Poor misguided limbs—what did they know? *"For they like sheep, have gone astray."*

For just a moment, Handel's *Messiah* and a light-blue and navy high-school uniform surrounded me, chirping in the school choir, to celebrate the town of Grantham's five hundredth anniversary; it disturbed my investigation.

Astereognosis, I read, is the failure to recognize objects by touch in the absence of any other visual or auditory stimulation. This I knew, in theory, from my OT training and hand therapy practice but not from experience. If an object was placed in my right, unaffected hand, and my eyes were covered, I could tell what it was by feeling its shape, texture, weight, temperature, and size. If the same object was placed in my left hand, I could tell nothing about it whatsoever. I would not even know it was there unless I was told, or I cheated by opening my eyes to look.

"Abnormalities of self-perception are a marked feature of strokes affecting the right side of the brain," a brief article noted. Reading this description was the most illuminating so far. It said that people with damage to the non- dominant side of their brains—in my case, the right side—had a tendency to ignore the opposite side of the body. Neural pathways crossed over in the brain stem, causing the left side of the brain to control the right side of the body, and vice versa, a development that occurred a mere half billion years ago. This deficit can be extremely striking and is best exemplified by people who are left with hemiplegia—paralysis of one side of the body—after a stroke that affected both motor and sensory cortices. The writer went on to say that not only do these people ignore the fact that one side of their bodies is completely paralyzed, but they can't even recognize their own body parts on that side of their body. Consequently, they fail to shave or wear lipstick on that side of their face.

I immediately identified with these words and found myself becoming increasingly angry. I felt the heat of blood rushing up my neck into my burning face. My chest tightened, and pulses throbbed in my temple like piston engines. There is no doubt my blood pressure would have measured sky high at that moment.

"How dare you?" I seethed. "Mr. Wikipedia writer, you wearisome wordsmith wimp, how dare you spout these things from your anonymous author pulpit! Yes," I continued, playing to an imagined audience, "and they wear food on their faces, and they only put one arm in the sleeve of their sweaters and then spend twenty minutes trying to move the hand of someone who is sitting next to them. How would you like it if you looked in the mirror and saw your auntie Mary with a Mohawk looking back at you? Don't you dare criticize me until you have walked a mile in a bloody AFO!"

I was too angry to go any further with my research that day. It turned out to be a good thing that I didn't continue because the very next thing that I read when I was ready to forgive the assault on my person and get back to my task, a few days later, was that outbursts of irrational anger can be a feature of damage to this part of the brain.

Another day, another definition: *Hemi-spatial neglect* is a condition, after damage is sustained to one hemisphere of the brain, that produces a deficit in attention to and awareness of one side of space. It is defined by the inability of a person to process and perceive stimuli on one side of the body or environment that is not due to a lack of sensation. So while I may deny having a left arm or leg, the aforementioned limb will still hurt like hell when I bang it into a wall, lose it in the bed, or wash it in scalding hot water. Neglect may also present as a delusional form, where the patient denies ownership of a limb or an entire side of the body. Since this delusion often occurs alone, without the accompaniment of other delusions, it is labeled as a monothematic delusion. *That is a relief! I am delusional but not mad!*

It is important to note that I was doing my research four years after my stroke and at a time when I knew and could describe what my symptoms were. In the early days, my education and training did not make a difference. Occupational therapist or not, I was in as great a state of denial as anyone else. Not only did I not know what I did not know, but I did not know that I did not know what I did not know!

I returned to reading the printed-off pages of my rudimentary research into the functions of the parietal lobe to find the fourth and final entry was the most illuminating, all-encompassing, and ubiquitous category: "Other."

There were no pretentious Greco-Roman titles for the first three bullets: inattentiveness, apathy, and dullness. My blood pressure might have gone up a little, but I was calmer on that day and determined not to take personally what I perceived as criticism.

Fair dues, I thought. I now had enough insight to recognize that all three words could have been accurate descriptors of me at various points in my recovery. As I really drilled down, I concluded that my personal experience was not so simple as to be distilled into three mundane words. If I appeared inattentive, was it because I had to focus on a task that was performed by rote muscle memory or autopilot before? When you walk, normally, do you have to tell yourself tighten, tighten, tighten, and shift the weight? Do you have to look at your foot to know where it is? If you want to pick something up, do you have to figure out first whose hand you are going to use, locate it with your eyes, and implore the fingers on it to open and close? Do you have to keep telling yourself to keep the fingers closed to avoid dropping whatever you are carrying?

Apathy: Am I apathetic if I condition myself not to care or at least show that I care about all the things that I want to do and cannot? Am I apathetic if I say I don't want to go somewhere or do something that I know will consume more energy than I have at my disposal? Am I apathetic if I say, "I don't care" a lot? I say "I don't care" about dancing, riding, cruising around a party and talking to people, or going for a walk. It is not apathy. It is a coping mechanism. Caring would have opened the door of my bunker and let in more pain than I could allow across my emotional threshold. If I let it in, I would have to deal with it.

I had only gone through some of the stages of grief at this point. I had done denial (a double dose, actually; denial resulting from brain injury and denial related to loss), anger, and depression. I had tried bargaining. Oh, how differently I would do things if Archie would just let me wake up and find that this was a bad dream. I would not bottle things up. I would not rush around. My needs would be much simpler. I would savor every step I took and play the piano every single day. I would give thanks after completing every simple activity that required two hands, like blow-drying my hair, peeling an onion, or putting on my necklace or earrings. I was still nowhere near ready for the fifth stage of grieving—acceptance.

Dullness: Can you remain sharp when you have endured blunt force trauma to your head? That does not necessarily mean being hit in the head in the conventional sense, but it is something brain-damage survivors have in common. Each has been hit, one way or another—a bullet, shrapnel, a blood clot, a rock, a tumor, an exploding artery, a surgeon's knife, deprivation of oxygenated blood, a virus or bacterium. Some of the dullness may stem from the insult to the brain itself, but how much comes from the life and identity detritus the insult leaves in its wake?

The next word that made me sit up and pay attention was *anosognosia.* I liked the sound of the word as I read it out loud several times, trying the emphasis on a different syllable each time. *An*osognosia, ano*sog*nosia, anosog*nos*ia, anosogno*sia.* However it's pronounced, anosognosia,

I read, is fairly common following brain lesions, particularly those affecting the parietal areas of the cerebral cortex and, even more particularly, those affecting the nondominant side of the brain; in my case, the right. A person who is disabled appears unaware of his or her condition. It may include unawareness of major disabilities, such as blindness or paralysis. "When associated with stroke, the sufferer seems unable to attend to or even comprehend anything on a certain side of their body, usually the left." So I was not the only one!

I continued reading about anosognosia and learned that it is a condition that people with brain damage share with those suffering from severe mental illness. Oh, how Keith would laugh! All those years ago, he told me I was locked in my room because I was mad. He would seize this piece of information and run with it, as only a tormenting big brother could. Of people committed to mental institutions, a high percentage are diagnosed as suffering from anosognosia. They refuse to take their medication because there is nothing wrong with them, in their own eyes.

Reading on, I wondered if there were any treatments for this condition. The article began by saying that for neurological patients, no long-term treatment exists. But for reasons not quite understood, it said, caloric reflex testing might temporarily ameliorate unawareness of impairment. What, I wondered, was caloric reflex testing? I never encountered that in my training or practice. Did it have something to do with food? Could something be added to a patient's diet to help her become more aware of the missing pieces? Further investigation was called for! I finally found the answer—a caloric reflex test involves squirting ice-cold water into the patient's left ear. It sounded like something that might happen to a prisoner in Guantanamo Bay. "Thanks, but no, thanks!" I decided to forgo the experience, in light of what the rest of that particular article said: "Most cases of anosognosia simply disappear over time."

I learned that lack of awareness of a deficit makes working with therapists difficult. Neurorehabilitation is difficult because anosognosia impairs the patient's desire to seek aid and impairs his or her ability to participate in rehabilitation.

Through the fog of war in my brain—my battle between intellect and emotion; the tension between what I knew, and what I thought I knew; the juxtaposition of clinician and patient residing inside the same skin; the conflict between what I could do and what I thought I could do—a shadowy image started to emerge. It encompassed both my own stroke and my brother Tony's. He did not participate in any form of rehabilitation because he said it was unnecessary. He did not lose the use of his arm or his leg, but his personality changed dramatically. He went from the pithy, pugnacious, sometimes annoying but lovable character who had been so successful in the entertainment industry—despite Mum's constant warnings, when he ditched school to go to the cinema, that he'd never make a living there—to a docile, drowsy shadow of his former self. He lost all initiative, and despite his prior love of adventure travel, he really wanted nothing more than to sit in his chair in front of the television.

I wanted to know more about the nonphysical aspects of stroke, especially anosognosia, and found one article that really grabbed my attention. It was about President Woodrow Wilson, who suffered a right-brain stroke while in France to sign the Treaty of Versailles at the end of World War I. He exhibited no signs of paralysis, but according to his fellow world leaders, his personality changed overnight. He went from being a consummate diplomat, visionary, and conciliatory at the beginning of the peace conference to being angry and vindictive by the end. He went from being shy and withdrawn to being socially outgoing.

A few weeks later, another stroke paralyzed his left side. Despite this now- obvious paralysis, he still claimed nothing was wrong with him and continued in office. President Wilson dismissed his Secretary of State for trying to talk to him about his disability and accused him of trying to usurp power. Wilson went on to try to argue in favor of the United States joining the ill-fated League of Nations, but he couldn't do it, and the League fell apart, setting the stage for World War II a couple of decades later.

Another high-profile person who suffered a right-brain stroke, I read, was Supreme Court Justice William O. Douglas. Despite paralysis of his left side, he denied any form of disability.

He directed an aid to issue a press release stating that his left arm had been injured in a fall. Justice Douglas developed signs of paranoia and other personality changes that caused his fellow justices to convince him, after a year of "not being himself," to step down from the bench.

I started to wonder if there had been issues with my performance at work, of which I was unaware, that had resulted in my being pushed down the slippery slope toward early, unwanted retirement.

Was it possible that I had not been doing my job? Was it possible that I had done things that I should not have been doing? Bruce had remarked that I was more outspoken than I used to be, especially about politics. I had grown up taking every word out of my mouth to look at it before it was uttered to avoid provoking mood changes. I became a natural diplomat. With an expression that remained neutral, I could pick my words as I navigated verbal minefields and avoid showing emotion or allegiance to either side of an argument until I could determine the prevailing wind. Had this ability been lost? This was a rhetorical question. I knew that it had. I knew that I sometimes blurted things out and that words could get away from me in ways I would never have allowed before. Before, if someone I knew pretended not to see me, I would have reciprocated; now, I would call them out. "There's no need to pretend you haven't seen me."

I imagined slights and took offense where none had been intended. I often pictured myself as a piece of lint being flicked off the lapels of people who had once sought me out for my opinion or counsel.

I wondered about political orientation and whether that too is hard-wired into the brain. I could not find out exactly where in the brain this function was controlled, but I could no longer keep quiet about my liberal inclinations. I remembered a funny song in my youth, sung by the team of Michael Flanders and Donald Swann. The song told of two climbing plants, the right- handed morning glory and the left-handed honeysuckle, one of which twined to the right and the other to the left. No matter how hard the gardener tried, he could never get either plant to twine in the opposite direction. It reminded me of Keith and me. We have the same genes, the same environment growing up, yet he twines as resolutely to the right as I twine to the left.

As my uncertainty about my job performance grew, I remembered that I had something in my desk drawer that neither the former President nor the Supreme Court Justice had, though maybe they should have. It was a small pile of performance evaluations that were filled out twice every year from the time I went back to work until I left. I pulled out the most recent one, to see if there was anything there to suggest that I was not doing my job.

I read the review, line by line, three times to be sure I was not missing anything. There was not one single negative comment, many positive ones, and my scores were all fives, the highest rating. Unless the reviewers had perjured themselves, I was performing all aspects of my job very well.

I became increasingly aware of and disturbed by my difficulty with reading. Although it was definitely better, I was still struggling. Most of my reading was still done with my ears, rather than my eyes. Audio books were my salvation. My word-thirst was as powerful as ever, and I needed the soothing chemicals released into my system, much as I imagine a junkie needed a fix.

At home, I was grateful to PBS and its English historical dramas and, increasingly, to HBO, a relatively new addition to my remotely controlled universe, for its series and documentaries. Bruce, never a fan of TV, commented sometimes, as he looked over my shoulder, that I had already seen whatever I was watching at least three times. I could recite the dialogue along with the characters, under my breath, and gain comfort from the familiarity. How could I explain that to him—or to anyone else? I could not explain it to myself, other than that books were my solace in my childhood bunker. We did not have many books because in post-war England, there was a great shortage of paper. The limited supply of children's books we had at home was augmented by the library van that came to the village every other Tuesday. Each child was able to borrow two books. Having read mine within the first few days, there was no alternative but to reread either the borrowed ones or a favorite from the well-thumbed, dog-eared volumes on the living room bookshelves. Far from being bored, I found many books were actually better the second or third time around. Speed-reading was about capturing the essence of the plot and characters and rushing toward the denouement or unraveling, where all would become clear, the villain revealed, and the heroine saved. It was more about the story and less about the writing. I missed a lot of detail. I was often surprised by a character flaw or nuance that I had failed to notice the first time around. Things that had not quite added up and had left me dissatisfied were suddenly crystal clear.

Sometimes at Sapperton, my grandparents' farm, on a summer evening, the only reading material I could find was the *Farmer and Stockbreeder.* There was not much of a plot in that journal, but that didn't stop me from climbing into my perch on the deep, cold, stone kitchen window ledge and devouring it from cover to cover. Prices of grain, outbreaks of foot-and-mouth disease, livestock for sale—not the stuff of childhood adventure, but it quenched my thirst.

Sitting in that window seat, I believed I was invisible. Adult family members sat around the big pine table telling stories—some fact, some fiction masquerading as fact—periodically swatting at moths or flies that were attracted to the flickering paraffin lamp swinging above the table, oblivious to my presence. When asked in later life how I came to be in possession of certain pieces of family information, it was almost always traceable to that window seat.

Late one night, I was at my computer, looking for anything I could find on the subject of reading and where exactly in the brain the required skills reside. I knew that speech and reading are closely related but didn't know exactly how. I also knew that the expressive part of speech—the part that allows you to talk—is located in Broca's area, and that is in the frontal lobe.

Wernicke's area manages the receptive part of speech and allows you to understand what is said to you. It is located in the temporal lobe. What happens in the parietal lobe? I saw a link to a website called Brain-Mind.org and clicked on it. I found an article titled "Dyslexia and Alexia—the Inability to Read." I was excited by this and paused only to laugh at myself and wonder if there was any other middle-aged woman sitting at a computer at the crack of dawn, getting a buzz from such a title. Could the author have any idea that this paper had just made someone's day or night? There it was: an explanation of an aspect of reading of which I was unaware, the phonological aspect. Words are not only seen by the eyes in reading, but they are also spoken aloud within the privacy of one's head.

Reading involves not only Wernicke's and Broca's areas but also the inferior parietal lobe (IPL). The inferior parietal lobe, said the article, becomes highly active during reading.

The IPL matches auditory images to visual images and associates both to form complex concepts, including those necessary for reading and the comprehension of written language. Damage to the IPL can disrupt a person's ability to spell by sound and to engage in phonological processing, such that the patient can no longer hear in her head the sound of the word she is reading, nor can she match the sounds she hears to the visual symbols (words) she sees on the page. Eureka! I could hear and understand words with the ears on the outside of my head but not the ones on the inside. Another fact extracted from this article was that the IPL, along with Wernicke's area and the middle temporal lobe, is linked to Broca's expressive speech area. This explains why some people move their lips when they are reading. As children, we depend upon the phonological process as we learn to read, matching the sound of the word to its visual image through the function of the IPL. With practice, we learn to bypass this process and develop what is called lexical reading, whereby meaning is extracted directly from the visual image of the word. In sustaining damage to the parietal lobe, the patient may be transported back to childhood and need, once more, to practice in order to read perfectly.

I continued reading the paper, my eyes glossing over some of the chapters and my IPL glossing over more, until I found another attention-grabbing headline: "Spatial Alexia." Spatial alexia is associated with lesions of the right hemisphere of the brain. This disorder is due to visual/spatial abnormalities, including my old friends, neglect and inattention. The patient may fail to read the left side of words, sentences, or even the left half of the entire page. I was starting to think it was a good thing that my lobes were not on speaking terms because they could not have understood each other anyway, what with half of everything missing.

I had become aware, both through self-observation and by hearing from multiple external sources, family members, friends and therapists, that there was something wrong with my timekeeping ability. This was not about punctuality. I was never the most punctual person except when absolutely necessary—to catch a plane, deliver a speech, or meet a client. My tardiness stemmed more from the desire to cram a quart of activity into a pint pot of available time, than from disorganization or disregard for the value of other people's time. It was not about the timely recording of time, as in billable hours entered into a companywide system that would allow the client to be billed and the business to stay afloat. The dreaded *carpe diem*—seize the day, not to enjoy it but to make the most of it, to turn it into tiny increments of obscenely costly hourly rates; it haunted me that we consultants were obliged to charge what we did. I was always slow to turn in my hours, not due to inefficiency but out of reluctance to own up to the large sum someone would have to fork over to receive the benefit of my advice.

It was not about that but about having lost all sense of how much time elapsed between events. For months I did not know the difference between a minute, an hour, and a day. I unjustly accused people of leaving me alone for hours and even days. I used to have a reliable internal clock for knowing how long it would take me to do something or get somewhere in the car. That ability was completely gone. I really wanted to understand the mechanism and search for enlightenment from my usual source, Google. I entered key words such as time concept, time lapse, time sensibility, time perception and, eventually, after grinding through several screens of advertisements for stopwatches, atomic clocks, and timekeeping systems, found two entries. The first was titled "Cortical Networks Underlying Mechanisms of Time Perception." It was an article published by the National Institutes of Health, so it must be a reliable source of information. I did not understand most of what was contained in the article due to the highly technical language in which it was written, but I found the one thing I was looking for. It was one sentence, where the authors concluded that their research showed the right hemisphere prefrontal-inferior parietal network was involved in timing. It was all I needed to see. A second article, intended for neuroscientists, was very heavy going for a neophyte but said that brain imaging studies had shown the parietal cortex to be important in human time perception. This study focused on whether disruption in either cerebral cortex would interfere with time perception. Their conclusion was that the right parietal lobe plays an important role in the perception of time. I could not begin to understand the whys and wherefores of how this occurred, but I didn't need to. I just needed to understand the connection between what happened in my head and the quirks left in its wake.

One morning, while I was in the thick of my investigative phase, Bruce awakened full of enthusiasm about the dream he had just had. It was about his childhood. He told me, in minute detail, about being in his house on Eastern Parkway in Brooklyn. His parents, his grandparents, and various other family members were there, having a meal, sitting around the solid wooden table, dressed for a holiday—white tablecloth, best china, silver candlesticks gleaming. He could taste the food they were eating, an eggplant spread followed by chicken in the pot. He was excited by having seen everyone again. He said it was as real as if it had been the day before. He said it must be a product of aging, as if old movies, stored in his head, were replaying of their own accord.

It made me envious and a little sad as I thought about all who had gone before me and how much I would like to see them again, if only in a dream. I would love to have experienced those seconds between being asleep and being awake when I have had a good dream. I missed those brief, warm, fuzzy instants when I didn't know it was a dream, which dissipated and melted away as wakefulness intruded. I have not had a dream since before the seismic shift that divided my life into hemispheres of pre-stroke and post- stroke. I don't know why I don't dream. I asked a couple of my doctors if they could explain. One said it was probably because of taking sleeping pills. The other said everyone dreams and that my problem could be not remembering my dreams. Neither answer was particularly satisfying, but since there were many more important things to worry about than dreams, I had not pursued the subject; but while in an investigative mode, I thought it would be worthwhile to find out more about dreams and where in the brain they reside.

So another early morning, more emails to Sarah, and back to my search. I banged in all the key words I could come up with to do with the brain and dreams. A lot of stuff popped up about the meaning of dreams, an advertisement from a psychic who reunites you with your loved ones who have "crossed over," dream vacations, dream weddings, dream cars, "your dreams come true" dating sites, and finally a simple post. The heading, in red, bold, eighteen-point font shouted at me. "To

Dream or Not to Dream: Do People Have a Choice without the Right Equipment?" It was a blog post. The blogger wrote that dreams seem to play a necessary but unknown function in the way the brain processes information. She quoted a researcher who had written, "Dreams let you consolidate and integrate your experiences, without interference from the outside world and without conflict with other input from real life." Dreaming is like the brain saying, "I'm going home and turning off the phone. Nobody talk to me. I have work to do."

As I read on and learned about various aspects of the act of dreaming, I found the pot of gold at the end of the rainbow, the answer to my simple question, "Who doesn't dream and why not?"

A researcher at Saint Bartholomew's Hospital in London had the answer I sought. He had found that those who have damage to the parietal lobes do not dream. He explained that the parietal lobes have two functional regions, one that deals with sensation and perception and the other with integrating sensory input, mostly visual. The second has to do with the creation of dreams. When damage occurs, the ability to create visual imagery is lost and without the ability to create pictures in the mind, how can one dream? There is evidence of a connection between dopamine release and dreams. That is why you feel so good after a satisfying dream. Patients who lost the ability to dream, in his study, showed evidence of apathy, dullness, lack of spontaneity, and depression. Studies show further evidence of a relationship between dopamine and dreams. I apparently would have to make do with reruns and audiobooks for mine, as nothing I read concluded that there was any treatment for missing dreams. One study mentioned administration of a drug called levodopa to patients during sleep that resulted in vivid, frequent, long dreams but commented only that it appeared not to affect REM sleep and did not advocate any therapeutic or (dare I say) even recreational use of this drug for dream deprivation. Freud's theory on dreams was that they represent the unconscious desires of the dreamer. What of *my* unconscious desires, Dr. Freud? Are they suppressed, sublimated, projected, or transferred, or do they simply cease to exist? Do the trees that fall in my cerebral forest make a sound if my brain is unable to hear them?

With my lack of dreams explained, albeit with no prognostication as to if or when they might return, my next challenge was to tackle the most troublesome of my poststroke challenges: memory. If asked to name my most precious possessions before the stroke, after naming my husband and children and a few other sentient beings, I would have answered, without hesitation, "My memory." From a very early age, I was conscious of having a remarkable memory. I could recreate scenes, events, and conversations word for word, years after they occurred. Some years after my grandmother died, an uncle asked if anyone knew what had happened to the Irish linen press, known as the "mangle," that had stood in the farm kitchen at Sapperton. I piped up that I did. The adults regarded me with skepticism as I told the story of how Granddad had believed the ancient piece of furniture to be valuable. After a dismal harvest, he had decided to sell it. He called the auctioneer to come and give him an estimate of its worth.

The auctioneer, a large man with a ginger handlebar moustache and wearing country gentleman gear—plus-fours, a tweed jacket, shiny brown leather knee boots, and a deerstalker—had arrived amid great excitement and speculation. He admired the piece from afar, remarked upon its style and grace, and then pulled out his magnifying glass to get a closer look. After a few minutes of peering, clucking, and head shaking, while Granddad chewed anxiously on the tips of his mustache, waiting for the verdict, the auctioneer faced him squarely and said, "Mr. Rimington, this is a truly magnificent piece of furniture. It is mahogany, made in Ireland in the eighteenth century, and the workmanship is remarkable." Granddad's face started to relax into the beginnings of a smile but the auctioneer had not finished. "Had the piece been in good condition, it would have been worth a considerable sum. Unfortunately, it is riddled with woodworm, and as such, I'm afraid it is worthless."

No sooner had the auctioneer swung the crank handle to start his ancient car and pulled out of the yard than Granddad started heaving the enormous mangle out of the kitchen and into the farmyard, some distance from the house. Once there, perspiring profusely, he fetched a sledgehammer from a nearby outbuilding, with me as the only audience member, and set about demolishing the mangle with deft, vengeful blows.

As he reduced the once-magnificent treasure to a pile of sticks, cursing the whole time, using vocabulary most unbecoming of his position of church warden, he created a pyre with hay and other pieces of farmyard kindling, doused it with gasoline, took a box of matches from his pocket, struck one, and threw it into the mix. A gleam of satisfaction illuminated the forget-me- not blue eyes shining from his smudgy, smoky countenance as he took my small hand in his and led me back to the kitchen. I was no more than three and a half at the time.

My mother had that same gift. I know that having a good memory can be a blessing. It can also be a curse if used to dredge up past transgressions, real or imaginary, and to get in the way of forward momentum and relationships. My memory was mostly a blessing, allowing me to remember people's faces and names, keep track of complicated transactions, and do really well on fact- based testing, rote memorization, and recitation. It also allowed me to remember the lyrics of every song I ever heard and poems and passages from literature.

Suddenly, it was all gone. I did not lose my memory in the B-movie sense of amnesia, but I found myself trapped in the present. The doors to the past had no key and only seemed to open if activated by some unseen automatic switch. I could answer questions rationally and provide reasonable, accurate answers, but I could not find the keycard that opened the file room of stored data that *must* be in my head.

Now it was time to tackle the science on this ticklish topic. Do the parietal lobes play any part in memory?

As I reentered the kingdom of key words with this new quarry in my sights, there was not much to see. Most sources firmly linked memory to other parts of the brain, but lo and behold, there was one paper titled, "Some Surprising Findings on the Involvement of the Parietal Lobe in Human Memory," by a team at Temple University in Philadelphia. Well, they might have been surprised, but I was not.

Their research confirmed the involvement of the parietal lobe in short-term or working memory and pointed to its involvement in long-term, mnemonic, and autobiographical or episodic memory retrieval. After wading through two lengthy papers, most of which could have been written in Mandarin, for all that I could glean from the page,

I learned that most research on the topic of the parietal lobe and memory has been conducted on primates, particularly macaques. I'm not going to monkey around, but the study showed that there is little documented evidence of memory disturbance in patients with parietal lobe damage. It went on to elaborate that such patients are hardly ever tested for memory deficits because they are subtle and often concealed by perceptual and language deficits or other anosognostic effects of that damage. No one ever asked me if my memory was affected, and I never was tested, but I can say without doubt that there was a profound effect that lasted for several years. There is one place where my memory, recall, and concept of time come together that has not recovered at all. I can recall trips I took and events in which I was involved in minute detail but not when they took place. I constantly have to ask what year a particular event took place. I keep my prescription pills in plastic boxes, marked with the day of the week because I clearly remember taking the pills but could not say whether that was an hour ago, yesterday, or last week.

While I may have misunderstood or misinterpreted material I read, at the conclusion of my investigation, I felt that my chrysalis of rediscovered self was metamorphosing into something or someone that I could live with. I would not be the same person I was, but I could turn this increased knowledge and understanding of what happened to me into a tool that might help others. At some point in the future, I would write a book about it. Perhaps I could help other people find themselves after stroke.

BIBLIOGRAPHY: CHAPTER 11

alexa09. Blog, *To Dream or not to Dream: Do People Have a Choice Without the Right Equipment?* Accessed July 12, 2018. http://serendip.brynmawr.edu/exchange/alexa09/dream-or-not-dream-do- people-have-choice-without-right-equipment

Ardila, Alfredo and Roselli, Monica. "Spatial Alexia." *International Journal of Neuroscience*, July 7, 2009. Accessed July 13, 2018. http://dx.doi.org/10.3109/00207459408985991

BrainMind.org . According to their website, the organization's goal "is cultivating conscientious leadership and investment in the science of brain and mind." Accessed July 12, 2018. https://www.brain-mind.org/

Garrow, David. "The Tragedy of William O. Douglas." *The Nation*, 4/14/03.

Google Books. *The British Farmer and Stockbreeder:1975.* Accessed July 12, https://books.google.com/books/about/British_Farmer_and_Stock_Breeder.h id=-NhPAAAAMAAJ

Olsen, IR and Berryhill, M. "Some Surprising Findings on the Involvement of the Parietal Lobe in Human Memory," February 2009. Accessed July 12, 2018. https://www.ncbi.nlm.nih.gov/pubmed/18848635

Parent, A. and Carpenter, M.B. *Carpenter's Human Neuroanatomy.* London, England. Williams & Wilkins, 1995.

University of Arizona Health Sciences. Health Sciences Library webpage, with a January 23, 2012 update by Joan Schlimgen of the following article, "Woodrow Wilson–Strokes and Denial." Accessed July 13, 2018. http://ahsl.arizona.edu/about/exhibits/presidents/wilson

Wikipedia. "Anosognosia." Accessed July 12, 2018. https://en.wikipedia.org/wiki/Anosognosia

Wikipedia. "Astereognosis." Accessed July 12, 2018. https://en.wikipedia.org/wiki/Astereognosis.

Wikipedia. "Flanders and Swann." Accessed July 12, 2018. https://en.wikipedia.org/wiki/Flanders_and_Swann

Wikipedia. "Hemispatial Neglect." Accessed July 12, 2018. https://en.wikipedia.org/wiki/Hemispatial_neglect

Wikipedia. *Messiah*, composed by George Frideric Handel, with scriptural text compiled by Charles Jennens from the *King James Bible* and the Psalms included with the *Book of Common Prayer*. Accessed July 16,2018. https://en.wikipedia.org/wiki/Messiah_(Handel)

Wikipedia. "Parietal Lobe." Accessed July 12,2018. https://en.wikipedia.org/wiki/Parietal_lobe

CHAPTER 12

A Better Foot Forward

WITHOUT THE ROUTINE OF GOING TO WORK, MY DAYS WERE SOMEWHAT amorphous, shared between obsessive, fevered attempts to reach or exceed 90 percent, physically, and finding a new purpose in my professional life. I felt I had been stuck around 70 percent for too long.

My exercise routine was very vigorous. I was working with Ryan, a fresh- faced, handsome young man who had recently complete his master's degree in nutrition and was filling time while looking for his next career move. Ryan made no concession to my infirmity, once assured that a further stroke as a result of sit-ups, push-ups, and leg presses was a possibility remote enough to be worth the risk. He pushed me to levels of fitness heretofore unimaginable. Our sessions ended with ten minutes of boxing. Ryan was impressed by my ability to bob and weave, throw a right hook, and land a punch every now and again. I explained to him that my father had thought I should learn the same basic skills as my brothers, a very progressive outlook for a man born in 1906. Because of his conviction, I knew how to repair my own shoes, do basic carpentry, and box!

My left ankle continued to be my major physical problem. If I wore the rigid brace, my knee ballooned and was extremely painful. As mentioned, the tape was a good temporary solution, but I could not apply it myself.

I had a course of Botox injections, aimed at reducing the spasticity in both my ankle and wrist. My wrist was noticeably less tight, but there was no sustained improvement in the ankle. Sandy teasingly told me that after all the investment in Botox, she had expected some improvement in my face, but, as sad as she was to burst my bubble, it was the same old face.

On a routine visit to Dr. Eliades, *Captain, my captain*, I tentatively broached the subject of reconstructive surgery. I had brought it up to various doctors in the past but they fobbed me off as, "Not a good candidate," "Too much to lose", or with that universal deterrent to patients' creative suggestions, "Your insurance won't pay for it."

Not Dr. Eliades. He thumbed through my chart thoughtfully, nodding periodically. It was a fat chart, so it took a while. He did not shoot me down in flames immediately, which was a good sign. I allowed myself to feel optimistic, but I was still nervous. I was almost out of options but still not ready to settle.

After what felt like a very long time, he took a deep breath and told me that he had reviewed all the treatments I had received: the brace, the tape, the Botox, the electrical stimulation, the physical therapy, the acupuncture, the Pilates. He didn't say it, but I thought "and the faith healer" (numerous appeals made to Archie had gone unanswered).

"I think," said Dr. Eliades, "that we can honestly tell your insurance company that we have tried every possible conservative, noninvasive technique to stabilize your ankle, including some experimental ones. You have had Botox injections without success, and reconstructive surgery is the treatment of last resort."

Who gets excited at the prospect of surgery? I did! It was all I could do not to throw my arms around his neck and kiss him. He went on to tell me that he would refer me to the best foot and ankle surgeon he knew, Dr. Amy Jo Ptaszek.

I was surprised that the surgeon was a female. From my years of working with orthopedic surgeons, I could think of only one female who had made it through the ranks to become a Fellow of the Royal College of Surgeons. She had done so by dint of being an irresistible force, large, masculine, and single-minded. I was so elated to have the referral that I did not want to go home to call. We stopped at Dr. Ptaszek's office on the way and made the appointment in person.

On the day of the appointment, we arrived uncharacteristically early. Bruce was with me for moral support. I was nervous and apprehensive, counseling myself to keep my hopes high and my expectations low. There was a low- grade churn in my stomach, and my morning oatmeal was humping the back of my throat.

If I had been surprised to learn that the surgeon was a female, I was even more startled when, after a brief discussion with a nurse in a consulting room, there was a tap on the door and in walked a young, blonde, petite, and very attractive young woman. Extending her hand toward me, she introduced herself as Dr. Amy Jo Ptaszek. In a friendly, warm manner, she asked what brought me to see her.

I gave her the history of my ankle, as succinctly as I could. Starting with my childhood weakness, I moved quickly through all that had happened since. "I'm using clinical terminology," I explained, "because I'm an occupational therapist, trained in orthopedics." I did not want her to think I was an uppity patient and desperately wanted her to think that I was a good candidate for the surgery.

I was sitting nervously on a hard, white-paper-covered examining table, aware of the usual accoutrements of consulting rooms—stainless steel pedal- operated sink, x-ray viewing box, wall-mounted paper-towel dispenser— while the doctor examined my ankle thoroughly, through every plane of movement. My left foot, devoid of tape, looked like a tired pinkish-purplish tulip dangling from its stem after too many days in the vase. In looking closely at my exposed leg, I become aware of a sizeable indentation where a muscle should have been. The bulge of the human calf is made up of three muscles: plantaris, gastrocnemius, and soleus. On my leg, the first two were clearly visible, but where soleus should have been there was a crater, more lunar than solar.

Dr. Ptaszek asked me to walk a few brace-less, tapeless steps without my cane, while she observed. Self-consciously, I set off. She saw my ankle turning inward and my hip making its wide-arced swing so I could clear the ground. On the fourth step, I did not swing my leg out far enough and tripped over my foot. I caught myself on a door handle and missed falling by a hair's breadth. Breathing heavily and shaking from the scare of yet another crash, I accepted the arm proffered by a nurse and hobbled back to the examining table.

Dr. Ptaszek asked what my functional goals were and what I hoped that the surgery would do for me. I paused for a minute, wanting to give a compelling answer. It was right there on the tip of my tongue.

"I can circumnavigate the globe on wheels, wings, or waves, but I can't walk around the block or even my own backyard without fear of falling. I would just like to be able to walk safely, without further damage to my knee."

I was given a pair of paper pantaloons to put on and, looking like a gimpy medieval court jester, made my way to the x-ray department. Afterward, back in the examining room, Dr. Ptaszek told me she thought I was a good candidate for a SPLATT procedure. I didn't hear the rest of what she said. Like most patients in the presence of their doctors, I seized the first few words and hung on to them, playing them over and over in my head. *I am a good candidate! I am a good candidate!* With jubilation dancing inside my head and my face an expressionless mask, the rising tide of excitement obliterated any fear or anxiety. We were speaking the language of surgical solution. This I understood. It was why I became a hand therapist, choosing orthopedic specialization over neurology, psychiatry, or pediatrics. The cut- and-dried solution to a problem; the mechanical over the often mystical (to me) approach to rehabilitation; the ability to see and measure where you have been and what you have accomplished.

Bruce asked a few sensible questions about the procedure—what kind of anesthesia would be used, how long I would be in the hospital, and what kind of aftercare I might need. I asked no questions at all. My mind was stuck, fixated on the fact that something was going to be done. My ankle was going to be repaired.

Next, the talk was of scheduling and details of what the surgery would involve. The doctor said that she would perform a "split anterior tibialis tendon transfer" (SPLATT) procedure. In simple terms, she explained that the strong tendon that was pulling unopposed and causing my foot to turn in would be divided, and part of the tendon would be attached to the outside of my ankle to pull the it into a normal, neutral position. Screws would hold the new tendon in place. The Achilles' tendon would be lengthened, having contracted during the five years that I had not been able to bear weight properly on my foot.

I would wear a cast and be confined to a wheelchair until the swelling had subsided, and then I would be able to walk in a large boot for a few weeks until everything healed. After that, I would need to wear a brace for a while, just until I got used to using my new foot; then, if all went well, I should be able to take the brace off permanently.

The ten days between the initial visit and the surgery seemed like an age, but the day came, finally, when I was NPO (*nil per os*—nothing by mouth) after midnight. We set off for the hospital early on a bright May morning. Because of my compromised mobility and inability to use crutches, I would stay in the hospital for a couple of days. Before the surgery, I was prepped and informed. I signed in several places that it was my left ankle that would be operated on and saw a large letter L and downward arrow drawn in black marker on my bright yellow skin. I signed a privacy statement for the umpteenth time and then the consent.

Dr. Ptaszek sat beside Bruce and me and went over everything she would do. Before I signed the consent, she told me that she might add a cadaver tendon graft at the outside of my ankle to fix the old instability, if it appeared desirable. After a momentary pause to wonder how it would feel to have part of a dead stranger permanently incorporated into my body, I agreed, and as the premedication started to take effect, I surrendered myself to the general anesthesia that would insulate me from worry, pain, and knowledge for as long as it took for the surgery to be performed.

The next thing I knew, after what seemed like about three minutes, someone was tapping gently at the side of my face.

"Wake up now," said an unfamiliar voice." Your surgery is all done."

"Can't be," I slurred, my mouth made of cardboard. "I jussht got here."

By the time I was fully alert, I was in a regular hospital bed, my leg swathed in bandages and elevated in front of me, and Bruce and Sandy were sitting beside me. Bruce squeezed my hand and told me that everything had gone well. There were no surprises, and my ankle should be stable.

Sandy grinned and said, "The doctor says you've got a dead dude's tendon in your ankle. Cool!"

I had received a cadaver graft, courtesy of an anonymous donor.

I spent the first few postoperative days at home, with a nurse's aide to take care of me. I couldn't put my foot to the ground, and my balance was too precarious to hop very far. After a week, Bruce took me back to the hospital. Dr. Ptaszek's assistant removed the cast and bandages to reveal a foot that was pale yellow and blue, with a few tiny black stitches here and there. The remarkable thing about this foot, though, was that it was facing in the right direction. My toes were looking straight at me. We had not met each other's gaze in almost five years!

I was not allowed to try to move the foot myself this time, just to look at it. The doctor gently moved my foot through its full range of motion, and then her assistant washed and dried it carefully and applied a fresh cast. Once the cast dried, in a matter of minutes, the technician produced a saw and cut it in half, leaving in place only the back half to support my foot and ankle. What used to be called a back-slab in my orthopedic days was bandaged into place, and then my whole foot and lower leg was strapped into a gigantic boot. The boot, made of gray, rubbery plastic with a thick sole, looked suitable for skiing or doing the moon dance. Once it was in place, the medical assistant hoisted me into an upright position and instructed me to put weight evenly on both feet. Somewhat nervously, I did! Then a physical therapist entered the room, pushing a strange-looking device that was supposed to help me get around at home. I was supposed to kneel on this "scooter" with my left leg bent at the knee, steer with my hands and push with my right leg.

This experiment never got off the ground. My left knee, riddled with osteoarthritis, did not take kindly to being knelt upon. I didn't have two hands with which to steer, and I most likely would go in circles, just like with the walker and the wheelchair. It became clear instantly that neither knee nor hand would cooperate with this form of locomotion, and the scooter was steered out the door by the physical therapist who had brought it, almost as quickly as it came in.

The other two options, crutches or a walker, were also tried and discarded due to poor performance by the patient. In the end, we agreed that for the next month, I would use a wheelchair when necessary to cover long distances, and around the house, I would use my cane or cruise the furniture. The good news about the boot was that it offered me a brief opportunity to wear some of the fancy shoes still leering at me from the confines of my closet. I only needed the right one. The left could stay in hibernation! Once or twice, I even wore a high heel on my right foot.

As a bonus to my euphoria at having come through the surgery so well with minimal pain, the prescribed Vicodin having been discarded after two days due to making me feel worse than the surgery did, Sue, my college roommate and long-time friend, arrived from Pakistan to join her two daughters for good.

Sue and I had not seen each other for almost thirty years, and now here she was, in Chicago, staying with her daughter, Amina, and at loose ends for the moment as she figured out how to build a new life in the United States. Neither of us could have imagined when we met, as eighteen-year-old occupational therapy students in Northampton, England, that we would both someday be living in Chicago, Illinois.

Sue was the ideal companion for my convalescence, helping me flesh out my resurging memory, connecting dots between people, places, events, and particularly dates. We laughed for hours, causing Bruce to ask if we had been hitting the bottle.

Mostly we reminisced about our OT training days. We had met on the first day of college, and outfitted in our starched gray dresses with red collars and cuffs and blue, floor-length, hooded cloaks, side by side with twenty-two other girls, we navigated the sometimes bizarre pathways of our college days. A few sentences were enough to open floodgates in my memory and take me right back into the alternative universe that was an English psychiatric hospital in the early 1960s. I couldn't help comparing the education received by the therapists with whom I now worked, especially those in research at RIC and Northwestern University, with the on-the-job training that we received. We attended classes for part of each day and spent the rest with the patients.

Many of those with whom we worked had been in the hospital for decades and were beyond treatment. We lovingly referred to them as the "chronic schizes." They had suffered from schizophrenia or other psychotic disorders and were in what was referred to as the "burned-out" stage of their disease. Their personalities had been eroded by their disorders and the treatment until all that was left was a curious collection of idiosyncrasies. One man constantly turned somersaults when he became excited. He had been a drummer for one of the famous big bands during the war, and the sound of Glenn Miller could produce as many as fifty somersaults in a row.

Another liked to lick his index finger and touch people or things. He could do that for hours, which would have been fine, except that his innocent licking sometimes produced hostile reactions from the recipient of his attention. A woman, who hailed from an aristocratic family, walked everywhere on her tiptoes with her arms spread out, like the wings of a gigantic bird of prey or dinosaur. Her jaws were in constant masticatory motion, a side-effect of her medication.

I recalled that I was once given the task of taking a group of these patients to a service in the chapel, a fine stone building close to the golf course. With a lone, Spanish male nurse, I lined up my charges in the locked ward, made sure my key was attached to my belt, and started shepherding them toward the door. There were six patients, not one of whom has the slightest connection with reality, all ambulating with one form of bizarre, drug- induced gait or another. As I opened the door, I felt but did not see someone push past me. As the fleeing form passed into view, I recognized him. He was one of the alcoholic patients who had recently been on a major bender and lost his privileges. My nurse companion set off at top speed to intercept him before he reached the gate and temporary, boozy freedom again.

Meanwhile, alone with my charges, who were milling around freely in front of the hospital, I set about the task of corralling my motley crew and steering them in the direction of the chapel. No sheepdog at trials was ever as challenged as I was that morning. Within seconds, two of my charges were on all fours, grazing contentedly on grass, mushrooms, dried leaves, and sticks. I hoped the mushrooms were not poisonous.

One woman ran on tiptoes in large circles, arms akimbo. One stood as still as a statue, staring intently at something amusing but invisible to anyone else and laughing hysterically. I grabbed the hand of one very large woman, who used to be a chorus girl until rendered unemployable by syphilis, the tertiary stages of which now ate at her remaining brain cells. I attached her other hand to that of a man who mumbled and spat and whose neck went into spasm periodically, jerking his head violently to one side. He, in turn, was linked to another woman, young and angry-looking with black eyes that stared, unblinking. She was subject to sudden outbreaks of violence. She was from Jamaica, where it was rumored she had, as a child, killed someone with a pair of scissors. She was a descendant of the first English colonists there, and her mental deficiency was attributed to too much in-breeding, like Rochester's bride from *Jane Eyre* or a character from *The Wide Sargasso Sea*.

With my elaborate, if macabre, line dance in place, I began steering everyone across the grass toward the chapel. We picked up those who had gone ahead of us along the way. The nurse, who had re-incarcerated the wayward patient, joined me as we entered the chapel to the sound of muted and slightly off-key organ music. The organist was a patient too, a promising concert performer in her youth, forty years or so before. She had become pregnant, had delivered the child in a secluded convent, and had given it up for adoption. She then was placed in the mental hospital to spare her family any further embarrassment.

The service was conducted by another patient, resplendent in a black cassock and gleaming white surplice. He was an ordained minister but had been found not guilty by reason of insanity, of molesting several choirboys. He had been locked away in relative luxury to serve out his time. I was starting to relax, as everyone seemed calmed and soothed by the soft music and droning words until, glancing out of the corner of my eye, I saw the former chorus girl quietly tearing pages out of the hymn book, stuffing them whole into her mouth, and swallowing them.

Sue and I reminisced about the years before she left England, originally for America and I for Mauritius, when we had shared a house in London and traveled in Europe as time and funds permitted, and my mind returned often to college.

"Sports Day" was the highlight of the summer term. This event was a masterpiece of comic genius. Patients and students together participated in an Olympic-style array of activities. Running, jumping, and throwing such articles as a javelin didn't really lend themselves to a population immersed in the deep end of mania, paranoia, delusions, or dementia, but they were not entirely omitted. However, serious athletic challenges were reserved for those who were fairly well on the road to recovery, if only temporarily.

For our beloved chronic schizes, there were glorified party games, which they took very seriously. For us students, it was a constant battle to keep the games moving and to keep from bending double with the laughter at the sight of middle-aged, overweight ladies, attired only in bloomers and flimsy shirts, competing in the egg and spoon race. Some stopped halfway to eat the egg, shell and all. A man and woman, an ankle of each tied to an ankle of the other with a colorful scarf, took wild, kicking swings at each other, with the unattached leg when they failed to win the three-legged race. High drama came in the Men's 100 Yard Dash, when two contestants, both in high stages of mania, kept going right past the finish line and headed straight for the main gate, passing the sign that never ceased to amuse me: "Please do not pick up hitch-hikers outside the hospital." A posse of male nurses soon captured and returned them to the fold.

The Ladies 100 Yard Dash showcased a half dozen of the younger female patients doing the "side-effect shuffle." One fell down, sat up, shrugged, lay down again, and fell asleep. Another let out ear-splitting, bone-chilling, blood-curdling wails as she surged toward the finish line.

Our occupational therapy treatment with psychiatric patients in those days had been all about keeping them busy—art, crafts, music, sports—a stereotypical version of a profession that would evolve dramatically in the coming years.

Sue accompanied me on regular visits to Dr. Ptaszek to have the sutures removed and to test the range of motion in my foot and ankle and the stability of the ankle joint. Each time the report was good; progress was on schedule or better than expected. This was a tiny tissue transplant in the grand scheme of things but one that would make a great difference in my life.

At the time of the surgery, I had recalled that the very last stroke patient I'd seen before leaving England was the late Sir Peter Medawar, who had received the Nobel Prize for biology and was widely considered to be the father of tissue transplantation. A physician friend had asked me to meet with Sir Peter, who was a patient of hers, to see if I could help him with assistive devices so he could continue with his research.

What irony that I, the OT who didn't like to treat stroke patients, should have had the honor of working with this physical and intellectual giant of a man after he had lost the use of one of his hands due to a stroke and then find myself similarly afflicted, a direct beneficiary of his work.

Between visits to the doctor, I clumped around, boot on one foot, and a Ferragamo or Chanel on the other. Once liberated from the gray boot, I had to wear the AFO again, just temporarily while attending physical therapy, to learn to use my newly constructed foot and ankle. I was thrilled to find that my new foot fit into a regular shoe, as long as it was completely flat and held in place by straps, zippers, or Velcro. I was delighted to find a very-much- marked-down pair of Prada Mary Janes on the sale rack at Saks. I would never again wear heels, so I removed the last ones from my closet, boxed them up, and donated them to Goodwill.

At my penultimate session, the PT noticed that my knee was very swollen, and he suggested I go back to the orthopedic surgeon, Dr. Beigler, to have it examined. Once again, the knee joint was full of fluid, and he used a large needle to fill a sizeable jar. . The ankle was not the only joint on my left side that had been problematic. I had had three surgeries on my left knee also. Stroke finds you where you live, often not in a perfect physical or mental state. It shows no mercy to preexisting conditions; on the contrary, it goes out of its way to aggravate them.

Dr. Beigler, very impressed by the results of the surgery, suggested that I ask Dr. Ptaszek's permission to go without the brace that, he believed, was putting undue pressure on my knee. Permission was granted quickly, and with the pressure removed from my knee and my foot encased in a firm-fitting but very ordinary shoe, I could walk more comfortably than I had in years. I mentioned to the doctor that we were planning to take a trip to Vienna to meet my brother, Keith and his partner, June. The doctor cleared me to travel and prescribed more physical therapy, this time for my knee.

Right before Halloween, with our tickets already booked for Austria, I went back to Dr. Ptaszek for the final postoperative visit and was released with the caveat that further surgery might be required if my toes showed signs of clawing as the tendons continued to heal.

That very night, while attempting to place the bowl of Halloween candy on the hall table, I slipped on the hardwood floor and landed with a thud and a sickening, deep, *crumping* sound on my left side.

Sandy and her husband rushed anxiously over to where I lay, stunned, to help me get up. I had knocked every drop of breath out of my lungs, hit my head, and banged my shoulder, but my one thought was for my newly reconstructed foot and ankle. As soon as I was upright, I looked down in dread and was greatly relieved to see that my foot was still pointing in the right direction. My knee was all right too, and there was no visible sign of injury. In shock, breathing heavily, and shaking, I sat on the kitchen chair that Sandy dragged to the hall and drank a cup of hot, sweet tea. Bruce came up from his basement office, looking worried, and asked if he should call an ambulance.

"Absolutely not!" I insisted. "I haven't broken anything, and we'll be there all night, waiting to be told that they can't do anything for me. I have one more PT appointment for my knee before we go away. I'll mention the fall to the PT, and he'll check me out."

My real fear was that if I had done something serious, the trip to Austria would be off. That night and for the following few days, I hurt all over but could not trace the pain to any particular body part. Bruises started to appear on my left side—one on my left hip bloomed in glorious shades of burgundy, indigo, and black. I did mention the fall to the therapist, who examined my leg through my clothes and noted that, as I was able to bear weight, do my exercises, and walk just about as well as before, I most likely just bruised myself.

"Since you are going on vacation," he said, "let's see how you are when you get back. If you are not better, we'll send you to the doctor to get an x- ray. You should take a wheelchair with you," he advised. "You don't want to mess up your new ankle."

Oh, here we go again with the wretched wheelchair!

In mid-November, we took off for Salzburg, where we were to spend a week before going on by train to meet Keith and June in Vienna. I did not walk much on the trip, using every excuse—cobblestone streets, tramlines, unfamiliar terrain—to illustrate that it was better if I rode in the chair so I wouldn't slow everyone down. There was so much to see and do, and we had such limited time, I was loath to admit that my left hip was causing me a lot of trouble. Once or twice, I almost fainted from pain as a well-meaning tour van driver insisted that he could help me climb the steep step into his van. I thought I felt the grind of bone on bone as he pushed my leg from behind. Just as with everything else on my left side, feedback from the pain nerve endings is imprecise. The pain was acute, but I was not able to pinpoint its exact origin.

The highlight of Vienna, for me, came on Sunday morning as we watched the fabulous Lipizzaner stallions perform their breathtaking routines. As a former very basic-level student of dressage, I was so honored to watch these elegant horse-and-rider teams perform the boldest yet delicate movements, so perfectly in tune with each other and the music that they appeared as one creature. I was banned from getting back in the saddle myself but experienced vicariously the almost spiritual thrill that emanates from moments of perfect harmony between horse and rider.

The day after our return to Chicago, I called to make another appointment with Dr. Beigler. I saw him a week later when he examined me and ordered x-rays.

Once he had read them, he gave me a long, quizzical look and said, "You are either one very tough bird or completely crazy, but you have a fracture of the neck of your femur."

Bruce, who had driven me to the appointment, responded, "She's tough *and* crazy!" But he couldn't disguise his concern.

"Had you come to me on the day of the fall," the doctor said, "I would have operated immediately, but since you have walked on the leg for more than a month, and it is starting to heal with just a modest amount of displacement, you have a choice. I can do the surgery to replace the joint now, or you can continue to walk on it and hope for the best."

I opted for hoping for the best, though the doctor warned me that the head of the femur might become necrotic, and then there would be no choice but to operate.

Dr. Beigler said he would see me every other week and x-ray the hip frequently until he was sure that the bone had healed satisfactorily. He told me that the hip would have to be replaced at some point in the future and perhaps my knee too. It would be hip first, then knee. I was not so far removed from rehab as to have forgotten the screams from the knee- replacement patients, and I promised myself that I would do everything I could to avoid either one. I had been warned that one more bad fall was all that separated me from replacement surgery, so I knew that I had to be extremely careful.

My hip fracture eventually healed, leaving my left leg about three quarters of an inch shorter than the right, but my precious foot surgery held up, despite everything.

As Dr. Ptaszek had warned me, I did need another procedure to straighten my toes and spent another six weeks wearing the boot, this time with pins protruding from several toes and a large screw permanently inserted in my big toe.

By the time my hip was strong enough to allow me to venture out, we were in the depths of Chicago winter, and fear of falling kept me close to base. While homebound, a couple of unexpected things happened to relieve the monotony. First, I received a call from a former colleague, asking if I would do some pro bono consulting for a civic nonprofit organization in Chicago. I readily accepted. That invitation was quickly followed by another one from a former colleague in a senior position at a company that was a competitor of the one I had recently left. We had worked together a lot, and at first, I was enthusiastic about working with him but it did not take long for me to realize that I had no interest in going back to the kind of work I had done before. I was no longer the person who had lived in that high-risk, high-reward world. I could not go back to hand therapy; two useful hands were required for that. Still, I could do something useful. I began a period of deep soul-searching, asking Archie on a nightly basis to point me in the right direction.

I was serving on the boards of directors of two nonprofits by this time and on the advisory board of a five-year research study at the Rehabilitation Institute of Chicago, but it was not enough to fill my days. Sandy was married and working, and Sarah was still in Sudan. Bruce, fully occupied with his practice, was busier than ever.

Sue came for the weekend frequently, and we relived many of our youthful adventures—our trips to Spain; the horse-drawn caravan trip around the south of Ireland with Maggie; the train trip to Denmark; and especially the three of us being bridesmaids at Alison and John's wedding.

The very end of each day was set aside for thanking Archie for the gift of living people—doctors and therapists—and particularly two dead men, Sir Peter and the anonymous donor who together helped me to put a better foot forward.

BIBLIOGRAPHY: CHAPTER 12

Illinois Bone and Joint Institute. CV of David Beigler, MD. Accessed July 12, 2018. http://www.ibji.com/physicians/beigler-david-md

North Shore University Health Care System. Patient website, with biography of Amy Jo Ptaszek, M.D. Accessed July 12, 2018. https://www.northshore.org/apps/findadoctor/physicians/amy-jo-ptaszek

Wikipedia. Biography of Sir Peter Medawar. Accessed July 12, 2018. https://en.wikipedia.org/wiki/Peter_Medawar

CHAPTER 13

Circles

IT TOOK SIX YEARS AFTER THE STROKE FOR MY MEMORY TO GET BACK TO *almost* normal. While I still experienced momentary word-finding problems and short-term lapses, my long-term memory and connection to my past were accessible. I could recall, freely and accurately, pretty much everything that had happened in my life, up to and including the stroke. I could also recall in detail most things that had happened since the stroke but not when they happened. As each day closed, it dropped into a pool of time gone by, where events were clearly marked but their place in time was not. To know precisely when something had happened or when I had gone somewhere, I needed tangible reminders, such as calendars, prompts from others, and my growing pile of calendars and notebooks.

I had gained enough understanding of what had happened in my brain to make sense of why I behaved in certain ways and especially why I had been so resistant to therapy, but now I found myself confronted with a new set of challenges, caused not by the stroke but by the hip fracture. Deathly afraid of another fall, I ventured out only when I had to. I became more comfortable walking backward, not physically but mentally, preferring to relive my former, active, able-bodied life in my mind, rather than grappling with the constraints of the current one. I still struggled to accept the permanence of my remaining impairments, particularly with my hand and eye.

To the casual observer, my hand looked normal, except for the fact that my wrist lapsed into begging-paw position any time I was not looking directly at it and consciously pulling it back. My fingers could perform almost any motion. They could open, close, spread apart, and make a fist. I kept them supple through passive stretching and range-of-motion exercises, but they could not do anything useful. If I put something in my hand, one of two things happened: If it was too heavy, my wrist bent forward, my fingers splayed, and whatever I was carrying fell to the floor; if the object was small, I could not feel it, would forget about it, then would spend an inordinate amount of time looking for it.

On a routine visit to the eye doctor, I passed the visual acuity test easily. The only glasses I needed were magnifiers that I could purchase at the drugstore. Then he decided it would be a good idea for me to come back and have a peripheral vision test—and another nightmare began. On the appointed day, I checked in and waited to see the technician. Eventually, she appeared, petite and officious, carrying a clipboard. She was wearing too much makeup for my taste, and her hair was a shade of blonde never found in nature's palate. In a strong, guttural Eastern European accent, she ordered me to follow her down a long hallway. Her very high heels—at least four inches—made a distinctive, metallic pecking sound as she scurried ahead of me.

"Faster," she barked. "I have many patients today."

"I'm going as fast as I can," I mumbled.

"Why? What is wrong with you?"

"I had a stroke and—"

"Why did you not bring nurse?"

"I don't have a nurse—"

She did not wait for my answer before nudging me through the open door of a cavernous, dimly lit room. There was a large chair in the middle of the room, with a sizeable step in front of it.

"Sit. Sit. Get in chair," she commanded.

I started sizing up the situation, wondering how I was going to manage it. The arms of the chair were raised upward for ease of access, and I could not see anything to hold on to. The technician, seeing my hesitation, stepped behind me and informed me that she would push me.

"That won't help," I whispered miserably. "I need something to hold on to."

"Thats why you need nurse," she snapped.

I was starting to feel like my nine-year-old self, confronting the class bully. Tears pricked my eyelids but I was determined not to give her the satisfaction of making me cry. I could not summon the strength to go through the whole stroke explanation routine, and she was patently uninterested in anything I had to say anyway.

Gritting my teeth, I hugged the back of the chair and launched myself sideways. On a wing and a silent prayer, I landed far enough on the chair to avoid falling off again and then inched my way across the vinyl covering of the seat until I judged I was as close to the center as I was going to get. Without further discourse, she enclosed my head in a giant trap to stop it from moving.

"Do exactly what I tell you, when I tell you," she commanded, as if I had a choice.

She started by testing my right eye. Aside from feeling acutely uncomfortable and nauseated by the restraint, I did a reasonable job, I thought, of telling her when I could see flashing lights. Abruptly, she moved to my left side and leaned in to tighten the clamp around my head. She started the flashing-light routine again. At first in a normal voice and then progressively louder, she said, "Tell me when you see light. Say you see light."

I did not see any light and reflexively tried to turn my head so I *could* see light.

"Do not move head!" she bellowed and tightened the clamp one more notch. She continued to yell at me and made loud, disgusted clucking noises and exclamations about how poorly I was doing on the test.

I, meanwhile, was about to pass out from acute claustrophobia. I couldn't breathe. I felt as if she were sitting on my chest. There was a fearsome crick in my neck, and I wanted to yank my head out and leave. I didn't give a tinker's cuss about her be-knighted peripheral vision test. I tried to explain that I had a problem with my eye because of damage to my brain. "I was taught to turn my head to compensate for loss of a portion of my field of vision—"

She brushed my attempted explanation aside. "Pay attention to lights." When the ordeal was finally over, and she released my head, I was like a limp, damp rag, draped across the infernal chair. I slid weakly to my feet and made a grab for my purse and cane. She told me to sit again, this time indicating a plain pink, plastic-bottomed chair with metal legs. She grabbed the printout of my results and perused it, sighing, shaking her head, and grunting. Then she said authoritatively, "Not drive."

"I beg your pardon?" I began.

She cut me off, gold-ringed fingers pointing menacingly toward my face and too many gold bangles clinking around her wrist. "You not drive. You not safe. You not see good."

"But I drove here …"

By then she had clucked, tutted, and teetered her way out of the room, clipboard tucked under her arm, shaking her head. I gathered my belongings and headed for the nearest exit. I did not stop at the desk to check out. I did not make eye contact with anyone. I stopped at the water cooler to take a long draft of water and headed for the closest bench outside the hospital, where I collapsed in the shade offered by the four-story concrete building.

I foraged in my purse, found the valet parking ticket, and turned it over in my hand until my hand was black from the ink-stamp marking the time I had surrendered my car. I did not know what to do.

Was I less capable of driving than when I'd driven here a few hours before? I had been driving without incident for several years. I had passed the disabled driving test. I had been taught to turn my head to compensate for my missing slice of vision. It was probably much worse then. But the nagging voice of risk-management training in my head kept repeating, "If you get in the car now, after this person has said you can't drive, and something bad happens, how will you defend your decision? How will you live with yourself if you hurt someone else?"

I thought of calling Bruce, but I knew he had a day packed solid with patients. Anyhow, he could not drive two cars home.

It took a while for rational thinking to reassert itself, but the reality that my car was not going to drive itself home and that nothing had happened to make me more of a hazard on the road than I was on the way here overcame my anxiety. I gave the attendant my ticket, and once installed in the driver's seat, I took off to drive home as cautiously as a sixteen-year-old on a driver's test. I turned my head in an exaggerated motion to be sure that I did not overlook anything. I also gave a verbal running commentary on everything I encountered, just as I had during my lessons at RIC.

I wanted to work again, but my faith had been shattered, not only in my ability to work but to get myself around independently. My confidence in myself was at an all-time low. I asked Archie on a nightly basis to give me direction, to help me find something useful to do with my life. I tried to throw open the doors of my mind as wide as possible to let myself *feel* rather than *think* about what possibilities there might be for making a silk purse out of this sow's ear. I pondered the fact that I had had two careers already and wondered if a third was feasible in my current state.

My first career, in occupational therapy, had been about patient care and had afforded me the international currency necessary to live and work in other countries. By exposing me to amazing mentors, truly great people, it had shown me the difference between greatness and hubris. It had eventually led me to meeting Bruce in Thailand. It had been a good fit with raising small children, allowing me to work regular hours close to home.

My second career, in management consulting, was the direct result of going back to school or, in my case, attending a university for the first time and obtaining a master's degree in public health, focused on occupational health and human resource management. That career had taken me into an exhilarating and exhausting world, where my patients were not people but corporations. I never for a moment thought they were the same thing, but I became hooked on the glamour of the work and lifestyle. In that world, there was an abundance of hubris, and greatness was extremely scarce. Much more remunerative than my initial career, the second allowed us to educate the girls, show them the world, indulge their passions, and generally enjoy a more affluent lifestyle than we would have otherwise.

I saw that each career had fit my needs and abilities at a certain period in my life. Might it then be possible that I could find something that would fit my current capability? Could my skills and experience meet a need somewhere and allow me to feel useful again?

I was slowly redefining my criteria for what ought to take up space in my life, and there was no room for the hubris, the almighty billable hour, and the constant pressure to sell oneself that is an unavoidable part of being a consultant. I wanted to do something that made me feel, even in my depleted state, that I could make a useful contribution. I was looking for a bull whose horns I could grab, if only with one hand. If I circled back to the nonprofit sector, might I find my bull there?

Desperate as I was to execute a grand plan, there were still days when I despised my own timidity. I was never a timid person before; in fact, I had relished taking risks. I had used several of my nine feline lives already, but now I was finding every excuse possible not to go out. When I had to go out alone, I walked like a very old person, shuffling, leaning heavily on my cane. I grabbed onto trees, lampposts, traffic lights, fences, anything solid that would support me when I didn't trust my balance. I developed a morbid fear of the wind, not that it would blow me away but that it would blow me over. That had already happened.

One particularly blustery morning on my way to get my hair cut, I was blasted by a huge gust of wind as I rounded a corner. Caught off balance, I teetered and flailed in a vain attempt to regain my equilibrium. A young man walking in the opposite direction leaped forward, arms outstretched, to catch me. Before we could steady ourselves, a second mighty gust assaulted us, and the damp, leafy sidewalk claimed us both. We landed, a spaghetti bowl of arms and legs, close to the entrance to the salon, in full view of a row of patrons observing us through the large picture window.

While neither of us was hurt beyond scratches, bruises, and pride, it took a while to remove the thorns and dead leaves from our clothing. I was upset, both by the fall and by the spectacle that I had unwittingly created. A couple of employees rushed out to help me. Though I tried to laugh it off, I was mortified by attracting so much unwanted attention and knew I could never go to that salon again.

The list of places that I could not go and things that I could not do seemed to be getting longer rather than shorter. I craved anonymity, to be able to go about my business, to blend in, and not to be the "old hemi." I did not want this wretched stroke to turn me into the crazy woman in the hospital mirror, someone so feeble I would lose all respect for her, but it was getting very close to doing just that. I also craved spontaneity, to be able to go somewhere without the constant worry of what obstacles I might run into—wind, ice, steps. I hated having to ask about accessibility before making a plan or accepting an invitation. I was familiar with work-arounds from my consulting career but resentful that my whole life had become a work-around.

If the darkest hour is truly just before the dawn, Archie was about to turn on the lights. I was invited to serve on the board of directors of a nonprofit organization, the United Nations Association of Greater Chicago, whose mission is to promote better understanding of the work of the United Nations, locally. Another part of my life was coming full circle.

This invitation came after a chance encounter with the president of the board, an immigration attorney, at a business women's luncheon to which I had been invited by a friend. I almost did not attend on the grounds that it was too far, too cold, too hard to park, and innumerable other excuses. Once I heard about the organization, it seemed like a good fit for me. Bruce and I had met while working for the World Health Organization, and Sarah was working for the United Nations. I felt a surge of enthusiasm for reconnecting with a part of my life that seemed far removed from my current situation.

I was asked to serve on the advisory board of a national stroke research project, after being a subject in research projects at RIC. This brought me into contact with high-functioning stroke survivors, among them two other women with whom I sat at meetings in Chicago and Washington. Together, we became known as the "Mount Rushmore" of the advisory board. The brilliant researchers with whom we interacted were studying issues around returning to work after a stroke. This was a timely topic for me and one for which both of my careers had prepared me.

A third event, seemingly coincidental, shifted me into high gear and propelled me from zero to sixty miles an hour with more purpose than I would have thought possible a few short weeks before. I received a phone call from Amazon.

A representative informed me that a book I had written about managing work-related injuries a few years before was out of print, and she wondered if I had thought of writing a second edition. Pre-stroke, I had indeed thought of writing a second edition and had found a publisher. I had been so busy at that time that the rewrite had been consigned to life's back burner. Post-stroke, a couple of years before,

I had resurrected the project, done quite a lot of work on it and sent what I had done to the publisher. It was rejected. It was apparently a pile of gibberish.

Now the representative was saying that if I were interested, Amazon would be pleased to help me publish a new edition of the book. My initial reaction was to think I couldn't do that, but maybe I could. At least I could try. I began reaching out to potential contributors and found a gratifying amount of enthusiasm for the idea.

Reflecting on what these projects were, I saw a pattern of circles, of closing loops. Involvement with the United Nations group would bring me back to my love of internationalism and history with WHO. The research advisory board would allow me to put my perspective of being both an occupational therapist and a stroke patient to constructive use and hopefully help make the path smoother for others. The book would test whether my addled brain and overworked hand were up to the task of combining my love of writing with my desire to improve how sick and injured people were treated in the workplace.

Serving on the board of UNA–USA brought me in contact with the executive director of a refugee resettlement agency, who asked if I might be willing to interview for a seat on their board of directors. I knew nothing at all about resettlement but had a lifelong interest in refugees, traceable to growing up in post-war England. I played the role of a Hungarian refugee in the school play in 1956, my first year at Kesteven and Grantham Girls' School.

The agency was located in the Uptown neighborhood of Chicago, the location of Bruce's and my first home together. As if that were not coincidence enough, Bruce's oral surgery and political offices had been located in the same bank building that housed the refugee resettlement agency.

With all these new opportunities swirling, Sarah, who was working in Sudan, told us on one of her regular Sunday phone calls that she had met someone special, most likely "the one." We had one overseas trip to make before I could concentrate on my new commitments.

Meeting our future son-in-law, a Palestinian whose family resided in Jordan, meant traveling to Amman. We always knew Sarah was unlikely to marry the boy next door, so we were not surprised by this turn of events.

There was no longer any argument about taking a wheelchair, but the one I had was battle-scarred and wonky from being thrown in the holds of planes and trunks of cars so many times. I was content to use the ones provided at the airport, but Bruce hated waiting around for it, so we invested in yet another new, lightweight one to take on the trip. He was as pleased as a cat with two tails as he piled the hand luggage on top of me as we got out of the car at the airport. The seat of this chair was made of very thin plastic stretched across a metal frame with no upholstery, and the skinny, solid tires absorbed nothing at all. As Bruce stuck his knee in the back of the chair to navigate a bump, he succeeded only in pushing me forward in the chair so that I dumped everything stacked on my lap in a heap on the floor in front of us. More than once, in the airport, on a moving sidewalk, where I had no business being with a wheelchair, we had to chase our fleeing belongings. I made a mental note to work on improving my walking when we returned so I could be done with the chair forever.

After spending a week in Cairo by ourselves, we took the short flight to Amman. Within minutes of our arrival at the hotel that Sarah had picked out for us, she and "the one," Firas, joined us. I wished that I could have met him before, but he would never know me as I used to be. That thought stung but only for a moment. We spotted them crossing the lobby, walking together easily, hand in hand. My eyes lit on her first. She looked well, relaxed, and happy. Then I looked at him, my son-in-law-to-be—tall, head and shoulders above her five-foot-four frame, with dark brown hair and a light complexion. He hung back a little, warm brown eyes illuminating his handsome face as we hugged Sarah. Then, smiling broadly, in perfect, only slightly accented English, he welcomed us to Amman. He was dressed in light-colored chinos and a crisp short-sleeved shirt, and he looked comfortable not only in his clothing but also in his skin. The banter between him and Sarah was easy and animated as they brought us up-to-date with what was happening in Sudan, their work with the UN, and their extensive circle of friends. We sat in the bar and ordered drinks only after Firas assured us that not only would he not be offended but would join us. It did not take long for me to see that he had indeed walked into Sarah's life and heart in much the same way her father had walked into mine.

Sarah had planned an itinerary that included trips to Petra and the Dead Sea, two places easily reached by car from Amman. Arriving at the outskirts of Petra, I took one look at the rough cobbled streets, loose boulders, and steep slopes and immediately announced that there was no way I could walk on such rough terrain. Using the wheelchair was out of the question; the axles would have snapped in minutes.

"Find a place to park me. You three go."

I barely had finished the sentence before Firas etched a permanent place in my heart by saying, with a smile, "No, we are not going to let you miss this. It is one of the great wonders of the world. We will find a way to get you around."

Before I could protest, I was led toward a rickety wooden-wheeled cart, Bruce holding one arm and Firas the other, each kicking rocks out of the way, to create the smoothest path possible. Sarah, with her skill in horsemanship, had managed to maneuver back and forth until the cart was next to what appeared to be a rudimentary stone mounting block. Firas and Bruce positioned flat stones to create steps and stood one on either side to support me, as I climbed up and squeezed myself into the front seat beside Ahmed, a Bedouin guide, whose scrawny, old white horse, he told me, was named Michael Jackson. Sarah climbed into the back under a fringed canopy, while the men set off on foot.

Ahmed had very few teeth, and his powerful body odor matched that of his equine pal, Michael Jackson. Scrunched up next to him as I was, there was no escape. I turned around periodically, on the pretext of saying something to Sarah to take a deep breath of fresh air. Still, he charmed us as we knocked, bobbled, and squeaked along the steep, rocky path. At one point, he picked up speed as we went down the hill past the Treasury, and my teeth started to rattle in my head. Ahmed flashed me a jack-o'-lantern grin and said, "Bedouin massage; no extra charge."

Deep inside the ancient city, we came across a gaggle of scruffy, scraggly vendors, who had set up an impromptu bazaar, selling everything from soft drinks to carpets. Firas identified them as Bedouins, although they were all wearing tired, Western clothing. I decided to buy a string of chalcedony beads, and Firas started the bargaining process in Arabic. He indicated that the seller was willing to drop the price from the original sixty dollars to twenty-five.

"Forget it," I snapped. "It's twenty dollars or nothing!"

Firas looked at me with new respect as the merchant quietly wrapped the beads in a scrap of old newspaper with one hand as he snatched the proffered twenty-dollar bill with the other. My time in Mauritius and India had served me well. Heck, I would even barter at Macy's.

After leaving the majesty of Petra's ruins, our next stop was a splendid hotel on the beach at the Dead Sea—again, Sarah's choice. Everyone was eager for me to experience the health benefits of the famed black, salty mud. It sounded good, but my occupational therapist instincts warned me there might be problems. I could visualize getting into the sea and floating but not how I might get out again, there being no hoists, handrails, or other such luxuries in sight. The staff kept trying to encourage me to give it a go, telling me proudly that the last person of note to use this particular spa was Vladimir Putin. I was quite content to sit in a chair and daub whatever parts of me showed, while my companions cavorted and floated, and we all looked at the Israeli coast on the other side of the Dead Sea. Would that Bruce possessed my resolve or would heed my advice, but not so! Common sense might have dictated that frolicking in Dead Sea salt was not the smartest choice for someone who, due to a severe case of traveler's diarrhea, had a badly inflamed backside, but he would not listen. His blood-curdling screams as he kicked up his feet and surrendered his rear end to a couch-like wave will haunt me to my dying day.

As our time in Jordan wound down, Bruce and I agreed that Firas would be a welcome addition to our family. We both had warm feelings about Sarah's returning to Sudan with a partner for the first time.

After returning from Amman, I found my calendar devoid of appointments outside the house except for quarterly board meetings and twice-weekly sessions with an athletic trainer, which had been penciled in before we went away. I was still committed to reaching 90 percent—might even have been around 80 percent already—but the reality that my arm and leg were never going to recover fully was finally becoming apparent.

In evaluating my own musculature, I was struck forcibly by how very precise the residual damage was. Just like the soleus was missing from my calf, the supinator was missing from my forearm. I knew where it should be because I could still visualize Sir Herbert's writing on my arm. The muscle was gone, and without it, I lost 60 percent of my ability to supinate, or turn my wrist palm up. I couldn't see my shoulder blade region, but I knew there was muscle wasting there because my shirts had developed a tendency to slide off my shoulder. The only reason I knew about the gluteal muscle going was that my nearest and dearest were forever coming up behind me and hitching up the left side of my pants. If muscles had wasted to such an extent, they definitely would not come back. Ninety percent might be overly optimistic, but still, obsessing about the wrong things, I reluctantly revised the estimate downward. I might have to settle for eighty five percent.

I spent most days working on my textbook, usually with one dog at my feet, another one on my lap, and Chloe, my cat, sitting behind the computer monitor, periodically taking a swipe at my typing hand. Bill, now back in Chicago, came to the house once a week to help with the typing and formatting, and we went for lunch at one of a few restaurants in our neighborhood. We made friends with the proprietor of one, Ramon, who always escorted us to what he called our special table. When I arrived with Bruce one day, Ramon asked me where my husband was, causing great amusement as I explained that this actually was my husband and the other man was my boyfriend!

Sarah brought Firas home in June to introduce him to her friends and extended family. In an old-fashioned, chivalrous gesture, he asked Bruce for her hand in marriage. After considering many romantic alternatives while he and Sarah took a long bike ride together, Firas proposed in front of the pond at home. The wedding was set for June of the following year.

They would both still be working in Sudan, so they would need help with logistics. Despite my shortcomings at Sandy's wedding, Sarah asked me to help with the preparations, although this time, we would definitely use a professional wedding planner.

Sarah would fly home from Khartoum at Christmas to pick out her dress and make as many arrangements as possible. I would be her surrogate until they both arrived two weeks before the wedding. About thirty of their friends would fly from Khartoum for the wedding. Add that number to our New York and English families, as well as Sarah's friends from school, college, and horseback riding, and it was to be a sizeable crowd. With memories of Sandy's wedding still fresh in our minds, we had the wild-card factor to consider and speculated on the possibility of folks showing up who hadn't been invited.

My jobs included finding both an American and an Arabic caterer who would work together to provide a feast suitable for all tastes. Because of the diverse religious backgrounds of the wedding party and guests, certain food items were taboo. There could be no pork products on the menu and no shellfish either. The bride was a vegetarian, the groom, a carnivore, as long as the meat did not come from a pig, and some of the guests were vegan, so it was not an easy task.

I found a likely team, but the relationship between them was uneasy from the start. Neither wanted to play second fiddle to the other. After the tasting and a little more than a week before the wedding, they had a massive fight, and each pronounced that he would rather roast in his version of hell than work with the other. I had no choice but to fire them both.

Finding one caterer a week before a wedding would be tough but finding two was nearly impossible. The wedding planner found an American caterer who was able to step in, and Bruce and I threw ourselves on the mercy of the proprietor of a Lebanese restaurant close to home who agreed to help, as long as we promised to name our firstborn son Joseph, after him. Given that we were unlikely, at our age, to have a son, we readily agreed. Imagine his delight a year later when Sandy did name her firstborn son Joseph. Our friend, the restaurateur, has always assumed the naming was in his honor, and we have done nothing to disillusion him. Two days before the wedding, disaster struck again when torrential rain flooded the backyard, rendering it unusable for the reception.

Our stellar wedding planner was able to avert disaster by locating a venue that had been closed for renovation and had not yet started taking bookings. She also found a fleet of buses to transport everyone there after the ceremony.

On the wedding day, the sun shone, and everything went off as smoothly as if we had planned it that way. The overseas guests arrived without a hitch, except for the best man, who didn't get his visa in time to travel. Firas had wisely lined up a couple of "understudies" and used both of them. One, he said, could not be trusted to keep track of the rings, and the other could not be trusted to make a politically correct speech. By the time I got my wedding finery on, I was tired but pleased to have been an active member of the disaster recovery team.

As I stepped out of the front door to take my place at the front of the tent, Keith came over to give me his arm.

"Wow, you look nice in that get-up," he said, referring to my pink lace ensemble. "You look just like Maggie Thatcher." I think he meant that as a compliment.

The ceremony was short, simple, and breathtakingly beautiful, as Mikhail and Margot, the swans, performed their water ballet on cue, and wild birds, butterflies, and dragonflies mingled with flowers in every shade of pink to provide the pastoral backdrop to the string quartet playing for the garden wedding that Sarah had dreamed of since she was a little girl. A lone monarch butterfly that we all took to be Nonny's shape-shifting presence fluttered in and out of the tent the entire time.

At the end of the ceremony, the judge made a simple announcement that buses were waiting to transport guests to the reception. Bruce and I were planning to go on one of the buses, but when we reached the end of driveway, I realized the step into the bus was too high and, as usual, I could not get my foot off the ground. Instead, we piled into the single white stretch limo that was waiting to transport the wedding party, along with the bride, groom, four bridesmaids, two best men, two ushers, and three flower girls. It was a tight squeeze, but we made it!

The guests at the wedding were from more than twenty different countries, and it was a joy to watch them all dancing and celebrating without the slightest idea of the torrential rain and dueling caterers that had led up to the day. I might have tried a slow shuffle with Bruce, but I couldn't actually get to him. The revelers, in need of a hook to pull people in to one of their corybantic dances, requisitioned my cane. I was marooned at my table for much of the evening but pleasantly occupied, watching the antics on the floor, chatting with people who stopped by, and giving free rein to my own reflections.

Looking at the assembled crowd, I saw not only Sarah's friends and family but a living tableau of my own life. My surviving brother was there, along with my two widowed sisters-in-law and cousins, representing my English family. Sue and Alison, two of my best friends from college, were there. Pam and Anthony flew in from London for a long weekend. Pam, a friend since Stanmore days, and her husband, Anthony, live in London, and ever since I moved to America, they have opened their home to us whenever we needed a place to stay. As Sarah's godparents, they had attended her christening and celebratory tea party at Sapperton Manor, many years before. Uncle Arthur and the General both silver-haired, ramrod straight, brimming with kindness, and beaming with happiness had pulled off a perfect day.

My friend Carole was there, having once again flown all the way from Mauritius. I was at both of Carole and Zulfi's wedding ceremonies, the Christian and the Muslim. Mary, Gillian, and I, still close friends from our time in the Government Flats in Mauritius, had travelled by train to Carole's hometown in the north of England to attend the church service and traditional wedding reception. We had then piled into cars and were driven at high speed back to London to attend the Nikah and an extravagant traditional feast at a restaurant in Knightsbridge.

At one point I caught sight of Sandy, radiant in her green bridesmaid dress, administering artificial respiration to a large, stuffed Homer Simpson that Firas won for Sarah at a fair a couple of days before. Homer, a guest at the wedding, had come apart at the seams. Sarah, meanwhile, was belly-dancing like a professional, coins jingling, hips gyrating, alongside her usually very staid and proper new mother-in-law. My eyes veered off to a corner of the room where I caught a glimpse of Jonny and Anna dancing with their three small children. In a blink, I saw my former self behind the wheel of that rented Mercedes, driving into Oxford, and walking into the chapel. I smelled the candles and flowers and heard the gentle organ music on the day that marked the end of life as I knew it. It was a heart-stopping reminder of how far we had all come since their wedding in 2002.

CHAPTER 14

Acceptance

I am not what happened to me, I am what I choose to become.
—Carl Jung

ACCEPTANCE IS WHAT HAPPENS WHEN YOU ARE DONE WITH DENYING that you have a problem, done with the anger because it was nobody's fault, done with the bargaining because nothing you can say or do is going to change the outcome, over the depression, and are ready to make the best of what you still have. This started to happen for me shortly after the wedding party dispersed and when Sarah and Firas returned to Sudan. I began to feel that a new chapter in my life was beginning. I was no longer tilting at windmills against my foe, the stroke, but gradually was accepting the reality of my situation. I was never going to recover fully, never going to be who I used to be, but that mattered to me less than it had before.

I was still keenly aware of my underemployed status and decided it was time to do something about it. I had just finished the new edition of the book, and it was with the publisher when Bruce mentioned that the receptionist at the office had quit. I asked Leon and Lana, our good friends and owners of the practice, if I could have the job on a voluntary basis, figuring it would be a good way to ease myself out of the house and into a routine of going to work again. It was not the kind of work I aspired to, but it would be a form of self-administered occupational therapy, or "work hardening." It was also a lesson in humility. I might have been a big shot once but not anymore.

Two days a week, for most of the next year, I drove myself to the office, where only low-income, badly neglected patients, who had waited for months for an appointment, were treated. I answered the phone and dealt with angry patients, explaining that they had waited so long for an appointment because Dr. Douglas was the only oral surgeon in our suburban county who saw public-aid patients. I talked to frustrated pharmacists and reassured them that I was sure that the doctor most certainly had not ordered eleven refills of narcotic pain medicine, and that, yes, I would ask him to write out the word "one" in the future.

I found that my infirmity actually worked to my advantage when confronted by hostile patients and that something about the appearance of a middle-aged woman with only one good hand, a cane, and a vestige of an English accent managed to diffuse some potentially nasty situations.

My dental receptionist days came to an end when a consulting project for one of the organizations for which I served as a board director unexpectedly morphed into a part-time position, thereby launching my third career.

The refugee resettlement agency, RefugeeOne, was in need of human resource management, a skill I had honed in both of my earlier careers. My new senior colleagues included former refugees who had survived unbelievable adversity themselves. They were from Iran, Bosnia, Eritrea, Ukraine, and South Africa. While about one-third of staff members were American-born, others were from Sudan, Afghanistan, Iraq, Somalia, Congo, and Burma. The contrast between this workplace and the corporate one I'd left behind both amazed and amused me as I compared the lack of diversity in my old work world with this environment, where white males were an endangered species. Between them, the employees spoke over thirty languages. Their faces wove a tapestry worthy of the centerfold in *National Geographic* magazine.

The work was very challenging, as there was never enough money to go around. Refugees arrived from the most troubled parts of the world, including Iraq, Darfur, Sudan, Congo, Afghanistan, Bhutan, Somalia, and Burma (the refugees never used the name imposed on their country, Myanmar), and now, Syria.

I used to travel the world to meet people from different countries, but now I sat in my office and watched the world flow past my door, the colors of the rainbow rippling through their worn but striking national dress. Mirrored in their faces were a thousand years of conflict, age-old feuds, failed foreign policies, and man's inhumanity to man. Impressed by the dignity of their bearing and the fatigue and disorientation mingled with cautious optimism etched in their proud faces, I marveled at the strength and courage that carried them this far and hoped that this land could be their land, just as it had become mine.

RefugeeOne case managers greeted new arrivals at O'Hare, the same airport that I arrived at as a new immigrant and later rushed through several times a week on my way to and from consulting projects. For half the year, our clients arrived in bitterly cold temperatures without adequate clothing, just as I did, except that I possessed the means to buy a warm coat; they did not. I had the promise of a good job at the Rehabilitation Institute of Chicago to expedite the immigration process for me; they had to wait and accept whatever menial job was offered to them. What few possessions the refugees had were crammed into cheap suitcases. Sometimes entire families arrived; sometimes a single mother or father with children, the other parent having perished in war, or died in childbirth or from disease or malnutrition along the way. Some of the women were mothers because they were raped, a common weapon of war. Some of the children were handicapped. Some of the older refugees were simply worn out after years of trauma and deprivation, walking thousands of miles and living in refugee camps.

Sometimes a single person arrived, alone in the United States with no one but our agency to depend on for help. I know what it feels like to be alone in this country, but there the comparison ends. Except there is one more experience they will have with which I can identify. In 1997, I stood in the federal building down town, and after one of the most moving experiences of my life, the naturalization ceremony, stood with my hand on my heart and tears in my eyes and pledged allegiance to the United States of America. It took me more than twenty years after I became eligible for citizenship to get around to it. My reluctance to become a citizen had nothing to do with negative feelings about the United States. It was about foreswearing allegiance to any other flag than the Union Jack. At my core, I am and always will be English. Becoming a citizen meant admitting that the dream that someday I would return to live in England was not likely to become a reality. In truth, it had become less and less likely with every passing year because England was no longer the country that I had left, and I was no longer was the person who left her. My England became accessible only through novels, movies, and PBS television series. The old me had been chipped away by years of different pronunciation, different vocabulary and different rules. What knew I of no white shoes after Labor Day?

For my parents' sake, as well as my own, it had been more comfortable to think of the move as temporary. Ironically, it was Mum who set me straight. On her last visit to Chicago, she was in the middle of reflecting on how she was one of very few people who had been alive for two of Halley's Comet's visits, when she paused abruptly, looked me straight in the eye, and said, "Are you ever going to become an American citizen?"

Blind-sided and wrong-footed by her question, I paused to consider the range of reactions that my answer might unleash. If I said I was, how might that go over? Would there be tears and recriminations? Would I be a traitor? She stunned me with her next statement: "It's not right that you don't vote."

I recalled how seriously she and my father took their civic responsibilities and how my brothers and I joked that they got themselves gussied up to go to the polling station every time there was an election, only to cancel each other out. Mum was a staunch Tory, and Dad leaned quite far to the left. After she returned home, I applied, took the test, and demonstrated that I could repeat, "The stars and stripes are red, white, and blue" after the immigration official had read it to me three times, swore allegiance to the flag, and proudly became a citizen.

I count the years I have been working at RefugeeOne by the number of spiral-bound calendars in my drawer. There are seven already completed, and I am in the middle of the eighth. I never know how much longer I will be there, but I will treasure this opportunity to be useful for as long as I can.

My disability is so insignificant at this stage, relative to the suffering most of our clients have endured, that it is not an issue. It takes a village to get me to work and back—Bruce or Sandy puts on my left earring, occasionally asking if is strictly necessary for me to wear them. I respond that only when all else fails will I be willing to lower my standards. I got dressed up to go to work at my corporate job all those years, and I will not disrespect our refugee clients by doing less now. I need help with the left earring because not only can I not find the hole, but I cannot find the ear either. I have to pass inspection before leaving the house to ensure that the left side of my shirt is tucked into my pants. I often overlook that part because I am still not aware of anything on that side of my body, back or front.

One of the security guards at the office building, Malek, helps me to cross the street from the parking lot when Windy City winds howl. Another guard, Gus, helps me get back. Arm in arm, we thread our way through snow and slush, around potholes that somehow evade the city's fixing crew, or, in summer, dodge puddles or patches of molten tar. A third guard, Geraldo, makes sure I get into the elevator with the correct button pushed. My progress from the elevator to my office is punctuated by smiles, nods, and broken-English versions of good morning. I do not avoid people, and they do not avoid me. When I attend meetings, a colleague stops by my office to carry my pen and papers, so they are not scattered on the floor if I forget to tell my fingers to remain closed around them.

I still get out of the car at least a couple of times a week with my arm inside the seat belt and experience the momentary panic of being tied down. Reversing the car out of the garage is my first big challenge of the day, and the dings and paint scratches on the side of my car testify to the fact that the blind spot in my left eye has not gone away. That said, driving has become one of my greatest pleasures because behind the wheel, I feel like my old self. I no longer dream of a chauffeur, except for parking, which I detest as much as I ever did, but I relish the independence afforded me by my own set of wheels. I am frustrated that when we travel, it is often impossible for me to drive because the two small adaptations that I require—a spinner knob and a turn signal extension—are seldom available from rental car companies. Who would have guessed that turn signal levers come in so many shapes and sizes that there is no universal extension handle available? I worked with engineering students to come up with a design, and a freshman class came up with an excellent prototype, but the upperclassmen dropped the ball, so it never materialized. I have waited at rental car desks for hours for adaptations to be installed, only to find that the car had been adapted so that it could be driven with both hands and no feet but not with one hand and one foot.

The faulty eye still makes it impossible for me to read a spreadsheet because the lines I see have a sharp bend in them. It also causes me to make typographical errors and hit the letter A instead of the caps lock. There is no point in proofreading my own work because I cannot see the errors. Microsoft Word catches major mistakes but not if they are in proper names or numbers.

I often get soaked to the skin by sudden rain showers because even as an OT, I have not figured out how to manage an umbrella and a cane with the same hand. My best solution, to date, is to make sure that all of my coats have hoods because it is a logistical nightmare to try to hold onto a hat and a cane in the Chicago wind.

The stroke eliminated the twenty-year age difference between Bruce and me, making me older than him in some ways. I was supposed to be pushing him around in a wheelchair at this stage of our lives. He is, after all, a nonagenarian. Instead, when distances are too far or require speeds in excess of my customary poke, he pushes me. Bruce drives his car like a New York cab driver and pushes the wheelchair in much the same way. He assumes the expression of righteous preoccupation common to those caring for the sick and pushes way too fast, runs red lights, mounts curbs, and scatters pedestrians. I, meanwhile, sit white-knuckled, steadfastly avoiding eye contact with people we almost plow down, just praying that I make it to our destination in one piece.

We cope with dueling disabilities. Bruce is extremely hard of hearing, and my voice, as a result of the stroke and perpetual allergies for which I cannot take medication for fear of raising my blood pressure, is foggy, weak, and quiet. This makes for some interesting miscommunication. At a distance, he cannot tell the difference between yes and no. Consequently, I end up with miscellaneous unwanted drinks, snacks, and grocery items and am deprived of things I really need when we go shopping. When we lose sight of each other in a public place, Bruce calls my name loudly, making me cringe. I respond as best I can, knowing that he will not hear me. He keeps on yelling my name until he sees me, by which time we have usually attracted a crowd of curious onlookers.

"Why do you keep yelling my name when you know you won't hear my response?" I ask.

"Because then you know where I am and can track me down," he responds with a beatific smile.

Our interchanges are often hilarious. As we were getting ready to go away for a weekend recently, I asked, "Can you get my suitcase?"

"Put your up foot on the bed," Bruce ordered.

"Why in the world would I do that?" I asked, puzzled.

"So I can tie your shoelace," he grumped. "You know I don't like bending down."

We have tested both the "in sickness and in health" part of our marriage vows and the "for richer and for poorer" clause, but the one that really stands out the most is "for better and for worse." In the early post-stroke days, there was a lot more worse than better, particularly from me to him, as we dealt with the strains that illness and disability place on any relationship. I have to admit to sometimes resenting that he has enjoyed so many years of healthy, fit, old age that I will never have, though I never for a minute wish that he had had the stroke instead of me. Bruce, for a long time, mourned the loss of his capable, independent, dance-of-life partner. I was so obsessed with the belief that if I pushed myself hard enough, I could recapture *her* that I often shut him out. Bruce always wants to be helpful, but we sometimes struggle with the concept of *what* help means. My definition of help is that he does exactly what I ask him to do and only when I ask him. His definition of help is sometimes tinged with overtones of "father knows best," such as when he assumes he knows what I need and refuses to listen to my request for something different, using the excuse that he can't hear what I am saying.

I have lost count of the number of one-handed gadgets "as seen on TV" that he has ordered for me that I have consigned to the garbage after successfully demonstrating that even he, with two good hands, cannot open a can, slice a tomato, or peel a grape with that particular device. By far the most useful and versatile device in my kitchen remains the garbage disposal unit. Not only will it support a bottle of wine, so I can use the corkscrew one-handed, but it also holds cans of soup and jars of pasta sauce so that I can open them one-handed too.

We no longer go to the theater or movies because Bruce constantly would ask, "What did he say?" and would make me miss the next few lines as I tried to explain—and we both would lose the thread of the plot. We sometimes incurred the wrath of people around us. On one notable occasion, there was almost a fistfight. Bruce was using the hearing device provided by the movie theater to amplify the sound. It did not fit very well, and the only sound it amplified was that of a man sitting next to him, chomping on a supersized carton of popcorn. Repeated requests to eat more quietly, following pointed, ignored shushing requests, led only to louder and louder chomping, until our entire polarized row became involved on one side or the other. The movie became incidental to cries of, "For God's sake, shut up," and "It's a free country; let the guy eat his goddam popcorn."

We now wait for movies to be available at home, where, with the miracle of closed captions, we can watch together without incident. We discovered opera. The libretto scrolling above the proscenium arch allows us both to follow along and, to our delight, the Shakespeare Theater now has plays that are open captioned. Bruce received a cochlear implant and that has helped his hearing a lot, especially if there is a loop for him to access. More often, the cochlear is used for me to relay dialogue through a hand-held microphone directly into Bruce's ear. This allows him to participate in conversations with family and friends at home or in a quiet restaurant. We have learned to request a booth in a quiet corner, away from the kitchen and any source of music for maximum effect. In a noisy environment or if our companions have heavy accents, it can become a stressful nightmare. With the microphone in my hand, I am unable to eat or drink. I still react to stress by talking. What I say may not make a lot of sense and may be too loud, but it is a coping mechanism.

We used to be avid antique collectors, specializing in buttonhooks. We started collecting them on our honeymoon and built a collection of well over a thousand from all over the world. We had borrowed the idea of collecting buttonhooks—because of their close identification with occupational therapy—from an English OT friend. Her rationale for collecting them, aside from their relevance to the profession, had been that they were small, affordable, easy to carry, and easy to display. Collectors of antique furniture often run out of both money and space before satisfying their appetites.

In our post-stroke phase, we discovered that antique stores are not renowned for their accessibility. I had failed to notice, in my rushing-about days, how many stores were accessible only by climbing steps and that most had no handrails to grab. I had not paid attention to the fact that crowded shelves, placed too close together, are deathtraps for wobbly people with canes. After spending too many hours parked on a bench or in the car outside an antique market, I decided my collecting days were over. The realization that our children had no interest in inheriting anything we had collected gave Bruce pause to reconsider whether our passion for collecting could be satisfied by other means. We settled on collecting visits to national parks and presidential libraries. Both are beautiful, historic, and, by law, accessible. We have built an impressive collection of both, and the best part is that we can't bring them home with us, they don't take up any house room, and everyone gets to inherit them, as long as we elect the right presidents.

Bruce has a habit of leaving water running in the kitchen or bathroom. It does not bother him because he cannot hear it. Whether or not it bothers my ears, it bothers my bladder, and I, still in thrall to my Pavlovian training, need to pee on command. I often have to do my best imitation of a run to the bathroom, even if I had been in a deep sleep.

I never regained the ability to dream, but Bruce dreams as vividly as ever. I tried to get him to roll onto his side one night, after his soaring, snoring symphony had penetrated my thin wall of oblivion. As I poked, prodded, and pushed to get him off his back, a fist flew out from the under the covers and delivered a right hook to my nose.

"Get your face out of my car window!" he snarled.

When Bruce had applied ice to my nose, and my eyes had stopped tearing, he apologetically explained that he was in the middle of an attempted car- jacking in Brooklyn when I woke him up.

We continue to travel as often as possible and have added an impressive list of countries to our long list. We have been on quite a few cruises and visited so many Caribbean Islands that they have long since blurred together, both in terms of topography and timing of when we went there. I am still ahead of Sarah in our country-count competition but only by blatantly cheating, counting every tiny island as a separate sovereign nation. We went to Turkey with Keith, and after watching an authentic Whirling Dervish perform for more than an hour, I astounded myself and my companions by walking unaided down three flights of stairs that had no handrail. This performance, in contrast to the tourist version we had seen in Cairo, demonstrated the Sufi Muslim fusion of the mind, the heart, and the body with God through movement. I wish I could have bottled the mesmeric confidence that resulted from surrendering myself to that rhythmic beat and brought it home with me.

I am now comfortable with reading again, due to the arrival in my life of an iPad, a gift from Sarah. Not only does this tiny device do away with the need to carry an extra bag full of books for a trip, but it can be managed easily with one hand, and the pages don't keep flapping, causing me to lose my place.

We gave up trying to dance but amuse ourselves by watching those we have styled as members of the "Arthur Murray Alumni Association" as they twirl and dip in our place. The slow waltz from participant to spectator is a feature of post-stroke life that it is not without its rewards. At social occasions, instead of flitting around with a drink, having quick, superficial interchanges with many people, I sit and enjoy a meaningful conversation with one or two. Sometimes this approach backfires, and we find ourselves trapped at the kids' table or the one reserved for the misfits and eccentrics who don't belong anywhere else.

Instead of feeling compelled to enter every store in the mall, I sit on a bench outside and watch people rushing by, observing and judging details about them that I would surely have missed when I was one of them. The infinite variety in the ways that people walk, the unbelievable damage that women inflict on their feet by cramming them into ludicrous shoes, the way mothers yank on the arms of their small children, the collisions—those that happen and the near misses—caused by people looking at their phones rather than where they are going provide free entertainment. Once in a while, I am reminded of my days at the psychiatric hospital where I trained when I catch sight of someone walking along alone, flinging his arms around, laughing loudly, having a spirited conversation with an unseen person on speakerphone, oblivious to how ridiculous he looks.

Bruce and I are in many ways, a typical couple, who have been married for more than forty years, a mix of compassion born of passion, friendship, bickering, shared interests, patience, impatience, and great love. There is one big difference: together with Sandy, whose five-year marriage ended shortly after their son was born, we are raising a small boy.

The daily presence of our grandson, Joey, makes it hard to be preoccupied with either age or infirmity because he has a zero-tolerance policy for either. Now seven, tall for his age, with dark brown curls when he hasn't given himself a crew cut with the kitchen scissors, and shining blue-green eyes that belie his Hispanic origins, Joey is a merry, loving presence in our lives. He expects us to be ready to read stories, play ball and hide-and–seek, and engage in endless tickle-fests at any time. I attend parent-teacher conferences when Sandy has to work, provide the second pair of ears at doctor's appointments, and shop online for boys clothing to keep pace with his nonstop growth. Grandpa has a constant companion for running errands, going for haircuts, and on secret missions to the Golden Arches. Joey, already a talented mimic, does a passable imitation of both of us. For "Deedee," the name he gave me when he first started to talk, he grabs a stick, an umbrella, or anything long and thin, bends his left elbow to a right angle and taps along. For Grandpa, he pulls on his earlobe and says, "I didn't hear you!"

The arrival of Sarah and Firas's son, Adam, added another precious dimension to our lives, so trips back and forth between New York, where they now live and Chicago are part of our regular routine. We relish the growing relationships between our three grandsons.

Sean, born a few months after my stroke is now a teenager, adept at teaching Joey how to catch frogs at the pond. Facetime visits on Sunday mornings, when Joey and Adam make faces at each other or when they practice their version of yoga, fill the house and our hearts with their joyful giggles.

We take a vacation each year with the family, usually to our beloved Mexico. The combination of grandparents' idiosyncrasies and the energy and mischief of small boys has left some devastation in our wake. In one notable week, I stumbled, steadied myself with the curtain, and pulled the whole expanse of mottled brocade, metal rail and all, off the wall. Adam, one year old at the time, pulled himself up to standing by holding on to a picture frame above our bed. Imagine his surprised delight and his mother's horror as the frame came apart in his hands and scattered wooden frame parts and ragged canvas all over the bed and floor.

Grandpa's pièce de résistance came when he, wanting a surreptitious midnight snack, had the brilliant idea of hard-boiling an egg in the microwave. We were all blasted into wakefulness, prepared for fight or flight, by a loud explosion as the door was blown off the microwave and tiny particles of egg and shell flew all over the kitchen floor and walls. Who knew one measly egg could do so much damage? By the time we left at the end of the week, the apartment looked as if it had been trashed by B1lack Sabbath.

As much as I was devastated by the loss of my former way of life, I began to make sense of what had happened and accept that my new life, in fact, is a more authentic depiction of the real me. It seems that Archie had needed to give me a hefty clout on the head to get my attention. I found myself on a healthier track, where my priorities were clearer and where the work I was doing, while limited in scope, brought me a level of satisfaction that I originally experienced as a newly minted occupational therapist but seldom found in my twenty years in the much more remunerative corporate world. On reflection, I am proud to admit that I am much more suited to an environment that emphasizes feeding need rather than greed. The new version of me is able to recognize the importance of shedding negativity and of dropping people and activities that were a drain on my fragile hold on positivity.

When I first returned to work, a colleague from San Francisco told me that she had cried when she heard about my stroke because she knew what was ahead of me and what it would take to get my life back. A year ago, I received a call that had the same effect on me. It was the wife of a friend, letting me know that her husband had a massive stroke. I broke down in tears on hearing the news.

"Can you come and see him?" asked Margaret, George's wife. "He knows you know what he is going through."

When I saw George, it was a heart-breaking sight. His stroke had affected the left side of his brain. He was aphasic, unable to speak except for gibberish, and without the use of his right hand. He is a builder by profession. After I had visited a few times, we figured out how to communicate. He has expressive aphasia but understands everything that he hears. Margaret asked if I would be willing to work with him, to follow through on the exercises prescribed by his therapists.

"He won't take orders from me," she said, tears welling in her eyes. "He gets very angry and pushes me away. He will listen to you because you understand. You were an OT, and you are a stroke survivor too."

One morning each week, I go to George's house, and on Saturday mornings, he comes to mine, the house he and I lovingly renovated over the past decade and a half. We tour some of the rooms where he added windows or completed other major renovations. I can feel him exhale with pleasure as we discuss various aspects of the work.

I use the word "discuss," but I articulate both sides of the conversation. I ask him a question and then offer answers until I get the right one, and he says loudly one of the few words he can say: "Yes!"

When this happens, the broad grin on his face tells me I am communicating with George, the real person, the skilled builder, the person he was and desperately wants to be again. He is not a patient; he is not a stroke survivor; he is certainly not an "old hemi"—he is George.

All I do for him in the way of therapy, since I no longer have a license to practice, is deep-tissue massage on those muscles in his shoulder and back that I know are loaded with painful trigger points, so that his muscles relax, and we can move his arm and hand through a full range of motion. Most important, I make him laugh.

In our sessions, he has to use words; gibberish is not accepted. Gradually, his speech therapy is working, and he can say more and more words. He has a very long road ahead of him and some obstacles to overcome that are even bigger than mine. I could always communicate. I did not suffer the cruelty of aphasia. I had the use of my right hand. I worked mainly with my head, not with my hands. That is all irrelevant. This is not about me. My job is to encourage George, to reinforce what his therapists tell him to do, and to give him and Margaret hope. If I can do that, they have given me a great gift—the gift of making my stroke experience and my occupational therapy background directly useful to someone else.

I approached my stroke as an enemy to be fought and conquered. It did not work out that way. It took me many years to accept that I wasn't going to achieve the 90 percent of pre-stroke function that I said I would settle for, much less the 100 percent that I really wanted, but what matters is that I became 100 percent of who I am now.

BIBLIOGRAPHY: CHAPTER 14

Goodreads. Website entry, quote from C.G. Jung: "I am not what happened to me, I am what I choose to become." Accessed July 13, 2018. https://www.goodreads.com/quotes/50795-i-am-not-what-happened-to-me-i-am-what

AFTERWORD: 2018

ALMOST FROM THE TIME IT HAPPENED, FAMILY, FRIENDS AND MEMBERS of my therapeutic community encouraged me to write a memoir about my stroke journey. They said it might be cathartic for me. They also said that sharing my dual perspective of being both an occupational therapist and a stroke patient could be helpful to others going through a similar experience, as well as their families and care providers. When the idea of a book was first raised, I could neither read nor write normally. These were facts I kept concealed from those around me and denied even to myself.

It took almost ten years of therapy, some professional and some self- administered, to be strong enough mentally and physically to tackle writing the book. It took five years more years, attending two workshops at the University of Iowa Summer Writing Festival, completing a second edition of a textbook written ten years earlier, dozens of notebooks crammed with recaptured memories and internet research findings, three discarded versions, the help of a writing coach, and several skilled readers to complete the manuscript. I read as many memoirs about stroke and brain damage as I could lay my hands on—or rather, my ears on, as most were audiobooks.

There were many times I considered shredding my effort. I asked myself if my writing could possibly match up to the skill of those who have gone before me. At my most discouraged moments, I often looked back at comments written by my classmates in Iowa, praising my efforts and encouraging me to persevere.

Their words, together with my desire to share what I had learned as a patient but never fully understood as a therapist, kept me going.

Stroke and brain damage survivors may have similar characteristics—a useless arm; a flailing, brace-encased leg; and a droopy smile, but they are not a monolithic group. They come from different age groups, different races, different walks of life, and different socio-economic groups. Under the cloak of seemingly similar handicaps beats the heart of the person they used to be. I desperately wanted to be identified and respected as the person I was and had to come to terms with the fact that I was a different version of that person. The eventual realization that much of my strange post-stroke behavior was related to the precise location of the damage to my brain and beyond my conscious control was an enormous relief to me and enlightening to those close to me. The fact that I had worked with stroke patients as an occupational therapist ought to have been helpful, but two factors got in the way. First, I had intensely disliked working with those patients, finding them slow, frustrating, and annoying; and second, I was so convinced that there was nothing wrong with me that I failed to take advantage of much of the therapy that was offered, especially during my months of in-patient rehabilitation, when I wanted to do nothing more than sleep. I put my personal Humpty Dumpty together again by creating a framework from elements that defined my identity before the stroke—family, work, travel, exercise, and learning to color within the lines of my new reality. It was not until I was stimulated by exposure to research therapists to investigate and understand the causes of my own limitations that my training in occupational therapy became useful.

A story should have a beginning, a middle, and an end. My story has a beginning and a middle, but how it ends still remains to be seen. I am, however, profoundly grateful to have had all these years and will, hopefully, continue moving forward with optimism, enjoying a rich and rewarding life for as many more as I am given.

I said I wanted ninety percent of my pre-stroke capability, but what I really wanted was a hundred percent. I did not get what I wanted, but being forced to reevaluate what was important to me and following a different path gave me so much more.

ACKNOWLEDGMENTS

THIS BOOK CAME INTO EXISTENCE BECAUSE OF THE INSPIRATION, support, professional writing expertise, technical assistance, publishing expertise, and love given to me by many people.

For inspiration, I thank the stroke survivors I have known as family members, patients, and friends and those I came to know as a patient myself. I also thank the physicians, nurses, therapists, and athletic trainers who helped me put Humpty Dumpty together again.

I thank the research staff at the Rehabilitation Institute of Chicago and Northwestern University Feinberg School of Medicine, Department of Physical Therapy and Movement Science, for allowing me to be a guinea pig and lab rat and to learn more about the science of neurological rehabilitation than I could have dreamed of as an occupational therapy student and practitioner.

I thank the staff and clients of RefugeeOne under the tireless leadership of Melineh Kano for allowing me to observe the grace of the human spirit under extreme pressure and to be useful at a time when I felt anything but.

For support, I thank my readers, Dr. Amina Chaudhri, Dr. Bruce Douglas, Dr. Lourdes Torres, Linda Illes, and Margaret Stepien. Their keen insight and detailed feedback helped me focus on what was relevant, interesting, and useful to the reader, rather than just what was entertaining and cathartic for me to write. I also thank my friends Susan Chaudhri and Lana Razdolsky for just being there.

For professional assistance with my writing, I owe a huge debt of gratitude to two people: Sarah Saffian and Tom Hartman. Sarah was my instructor two years in a row at the University of Iowa, Summer Writing Festival, and had the patience and fortitude to stay with me as a coach for a few years afterward. Sarah taught me that writing a memoir is like carving a sculpture out of stone. She played the role of skilled artisan to my apprentice, as I chipped away pieces of stone—sometimes too little and sometimes too much—and eventually smoothed out most of the rough edges. Sarah's advice to show as well as tell my story was a constant reminder to include details that would enhance the reader experience.

Tom, a good friend as well as a talented creative writer, is one of the funniest people I know. Tom encouraged me to retain humor in my storytelling and to distill paragraphs for maximum impact, removing words or phrases that added nothing to the narrative. His color-coded edits—red for delete, yellow for rework, and green for retain—were invaluable. Tom believed in my story and its value to others and kept me going on those occasions when I was tempted to head for the shredder.

For technological support, — I thank Bill Mastric, Paddy Coyle and Nancy Qutub. As a technological dinosaur, I need a full-time help desk. My friend and colleague, Bill Mastric came to my rescue, as he has for the past twenty years, and faithfully produced multiple iterations of this manuscript. Paddy Coyle was instrumental in incorporating edits from multiple sources and safeguarding the structural integrity of the manuscript. Nancy Qutub, a dear friend, came to my rescue at the tail end of the process, bringing her expertise in editing and style.

For publishing expertise, -— I thank my team at Archway Publishing from Simon and Schuster, especially Virginia Morell, Gwen Ash and the editorial crew for helping this dream become a reality.

For love and helping me get over losing who I was and embracing who I am now, I thank my husband, Bruce who was and is always, there for me, even at my most unlovable; my daughters, Sarah and Sandy; my stepson, Cliff; my sons-in-law, Firas and Larry, daughter-in-law, Martha, and all the grands who play an active role in my life—Austyn, Krystle, Chris, Melissa, Sean and especially Joey and Adam. I thank the four living generations of my English and American family, especially Keith and Sheila, for keeping me in their sights, bridging the Atlantic as often as they can, and being there for every important milestone. Finally, I thank my friends too many to name and too scary to list, for fear of missing someone, for the love, the laughs, and the encouragement.

ENDNOTES

1 Pinterest. Attributed to Shannen Heartzs. Accessed July 16, 2018. www.pinterest.com/pin/189291990565078709

2 Jane Austen, *Pride and Prejudice* (London: T. Egerton, 1813), 1.

3 Percy Dreamer and Ralph Vaughan Williams, eds., *The English Hymnal* (Oxford: Oxford University Press, 1906), 714.

4 Percy Dreamer and Ralph Vaughan Williams, eds., *The English Hymnal* (Oxford: Oxford University Press, 1906), 714.

5 N.E. Herlevich, "Reflecting on old Olympus' Towering Tops," Journal of Ophthalmic Nursing Technology, 9(6), (Nov-Dec 1990): 245–6. Abstract accessible online July 11, 2018. https://www.ncbi.nlm.nih.gov/pubmed/?term=Herlevich+NE%5BAuthor%5D

6 John Keats, "Ode to a Nightingale," Bartleby website, accessed July 16, 2018, https://www.bartleby.com/101/624.html

7 Goodreads entry for Robert Frost, accessed July 10, 2018. https://www.goodreads.com/quotes/5609- if-we-couldn-t-laugh-we-would-all-go-insaned

8 Wikipedia. Entry for Alfred Denis Godley's "The Motor Bus," first published in 1914. Accessed July 12, 2018. https://en.wikipedia.org/wiki/The_Motor_Bus

Made in United States
Troutdale, OR
04/30/2024

19530208R00181